Ref
658

UNDERSTANDING BUSINESS: PROCESSES

D0491533

This book – *Understanding Business: Processes* – is one of a series of four readers which constitute the main teaching texts of the Open University course *Understanding Business Behaviour* (B200). The other titles are: *Understanding Business: Environments* edited by Michael Lucas; *Understanding Business: Markets* edited by Vivek Suneja; and *Understanding Business: Organisations* edited by Graeme Salaman.

This course is one of three core courses which are compulsory elements in the Open University's BA in Business Studies. In addition to the compulsory courses, students who are working toward this degree also study courses which include topics such as Economics, Organisational Change, Design and Innovation and Quantitative Methods.

The approach of *Understanding Business Behaviour* (B200) as an introductory course in Business Studies is innovative. The traditional approach employed by courses in this area is to offer introductions to the key social science disciplines: sociology, economics, law, etc. This course uses another approach: it focuses not on disciplines but on key elements of the business world: environments, markets, processes and organisations. This still allows for the discussion of relevant social science theory and research but organises this material not by the logic of academic structures and disciplines but by the logic of business applications and relevance.

As with all Open University courses, students are not only supplied with teaching texts; they also receive comprehensive guidance on how to study and work through these texts. In the case of B200, this guidance is contained in four Study Guides which are supplied to students separately. These guides explain the choice of readings, identify key points and guide the students' work and understanding. A core feature of the guides is an explicit focus on the identification, development, deployment and testing of a series of business graduate skills. These include study skills, cognitive skills of analysis and assessment, IT, and numeracy.

Each student is allocated a local tutor and is encouraged to participate in a strategically integrated set of tutorials which are held throughout the course.

Details of this and other Open University courses can be obtained from the Course Reservations Centre, PO Box 724, The Open University, Milton Keynes, MK7 6ZS, United Kingdom; tel: +44 (0) 1908 653231; e-mail: ces-gen@open.ac.uk

Alternatively, you may visit the Open University website at http://www.open.ac.uk where you can learn about the wide range of courses and packs offered at all levels by The Open University.

For information about the purchase of Open University course components, contact Open University Worldwide Ltd, The Berrill Building, Walton Hall, Milton Keynes, MK7 6AA, United Kingdom: tel.+44 (0) 1908 858785; fax: +44 (0) 1908 858787; e-mail: ouwenq@open.ac.uk; website: http://www.ouw.co.uk.

Withdrawn

Accession Number   T039027

Class Number   658 Ref

SERIES INTRODUCTION

It is hardly necessary to justify the study of business, or to over-emphasise the importance of a knowledge and understanding of business organisations and their functions, or of the environments of business. The world of business is the world in which we live and work, every aspect of which may well be on the verge of fundamental change as a result of the Internet and converging communications technologies. It affects us as consumers, workers, voters, citizens, whether of nations, unions of nations or of the world. We have to understand it. We have to understand how organisations work and their core processes. This involves an understanding of their impact on employees and consumers; how markets work (and don't work); the role and nature of business environments and how these impact on business organisations (or vice versa).

This book is one in a series of four readers which bring together classic and seminal materials, many of them summaries and reviews, which are designed to achieve the teaching objectives of the Open University course *Understanding Business Behaviour* (B200) – a core course in the Open University's BA in Business Studies. The volumes are organised in an innovative way around four key areas of the world of business: environments, markets, processes and organisations.

The volumes have been designed to supply a selection of key introductory materials in each of these areas of business applications and, with the use of appropriate study guidance, to allow the identification, development, deployment and practice of a range of skills required from Business Studies courses in general. Therefore, while they constitute the core teaching resources of this Open University course, they would also make admirable selections for any course concerned with these areas. They are not intended to be cutting edge or fashionable. They are designed as a resource for anyone seeking an understanding of the nature and development of the world of business.

Each of these volumes has been edited by an individual member of the course team. But in a very real sense they are collective products of the course team as a whole. That is why all the members of the course team deserve recognition and acknowledgement for their contribution to the course and to these collections. The course team consisted of:

David Barnes, Hannah Brunt, Rob Clifton, Mike Conboy, Martin Dowling, Gill Gowans, Carol Howells, Jacky Holloway, Bob Kelly, Mike Lucas, Alison Macmillan, Chris Marshall, Jane Matthews, Konrad Mau, Terry Morris, John O'Dwyer, John Olney, Anthea Rogers, Judy Rumbelow, Graeme Salaman, Dawn Storer, Jane Sturges, Vivek Suneja, Tricia Tierney, Richard Whipp.

Two other members of the team deserve special mention for their enormous contribution to the course as a whole and to the work of managing the course team and the processes involved in assembling and organising these collections: Chris Bollom and Georgina Marsh. To them, many thanks.

UNDERSTANDING BUSINESS: PROCESSES

Edited by
DAVID BARNES
at The Open University

In association with

LONDON AND NEW YORK

First published 2001
by Routledge
11 New Fetter Lane, London EC4P 4EE

Simultaneously published in the USA and Canada
by Routledge
29 West 35th Street, New York, NY 10001

Routledge is an imprint of the Taylor & Francis Group

© 2001 Compilation, original and edited material, The Open University.
All rights reserved.

Typeset in Plantin and Rockwell by
Keystroke,
Jacaranda Lodge,
Wolverhampton
Printed and bound in Great Britain by
Bell & Bain Ltd, Glasgow

All rights reserved. No part of this book may be reprinted or reproduced or utilised in any
form or by any electronic, mechanical, or other means, now known or hereafter invented,
including photocopying and recording, or in any information storage or retrieval system,
without permission in writing from the publishers.

British Library Cataloguing in Publication Data
A catalogue record for this book is available from the British Library

Library of Congress Cataloging in Publication Data
A catalog record for this book has been applied for

ISBN 0–415–23861–7 (hbk)
ISBN 0–415–23862–5 (pbk)

CONTENTS

FIGURES

TABLES

ACKNOWLEDGEMENTS

The author and publishers would like to thank the following for granting permission to reproduce material in this work:

Gower Publishing Limited, for extract from John Gattorna, *The Gower Handbook of Logistics and Distribution Management*. Copyright © Gower Publishing Company, 1990.

HarperCollins Publishers, for extract from Michael Hammer, *Beyond Reengineering*. Copyright © 1996 by Michael Hammer. Reprinted by permission of HarperCollins Publishers Inc.

International Thomson Publishing, for extracts from P.J.H. Baily, *Purchasing and Supply Management*, published by Chapman and Hall; extract from *International Journal of Production Research* 17(2), 1979. Copyright © Taylor & Francis Ltd; figure from G.C. Stevens, 'Integrating the Supply Chain' in *International Journal of Physical Distribution and Materials Management* 19(8), 1989.

Kogan Page, for extract from Colin Coulson-Thomas (ed.), *Business Process Reengineering*. Copyright © Colin Coulson-Thomas, 1994, 1996.

Letts Educational, for extract from G.A. Cole, *Management Theory and Practice*, 5th edition, 1996. Copyright © G.A. Cole, 1996.

McGraw Hill, for figures from D.J. Bowersox, D.J. Closs and O.K. Helferich, *Logistical Management*, 3rd edition, published by Macmillan, 1986 and K. Ohmae, *Mind of the Strategist*, published by Penguin Books, 1983.

MCB University Press Ltd, for extract from *International Journal of Quality and Reliability Management* 4(4) and *International Journal of Operations and Production Management* 14(12).

Oxford University Press, for extract from John Kay, *Foundations of Corporate Success*. Published by Oxford University Press, 1993. Copyright © John Kay, 1993.

Pearson Education, for extract from Martin Christopher, *Logistics and Supply Chain Management*. Published by Pitman Publishing, 1992, 1993. Copyright © Martin Christopher, 1992.

Prentice-Hall Inc. for J.H. Heizer and B. Render, *Production and Operations Management*, 3rd edition, published by Prentice-Hall, 1988. Adapted by permission of Prentice-Hall Inc., Upper Saddle River, NJ.

Simon & Schuster, for extract from Michael E. Porter, *Competitive Advantage*. Published by The Free Press, a division of Macmillan Inc., 1985. Copyright © 1985 by Michael E. Porter.

Every effort has been made to contact copyright holders for their permission to reprint material in this book. The publishers would be grateful to hear from any copyright holder who is not here acknowledged and will undertake to rectify and errors or omissions in future editions of this book.

INTRODUCTION

Our aim in assembling this collection of readings is to offer an understanding of business behaviour by considering what business organisations do. The result of the activities of organisations can often be observed, and in many cases experienced, in the form of the goods and services that they produce. However what goes on within the producing organisation is often hidden from the outside world. Our aim is to shed some light on organisational activities and thereby facilitate a better understanding of their behaviour. Making any sort of sense of business behaviour requires an understanding of what organisations do. Indeed, what an organisation does provides one way of defining what an organisation is. As Stafford Beer puts it 'A company *is* what it does'.

Our consideration of organisations in terms of their activities is underpinned by the application of systems theory. This considers organisations to be complex assemblies of interrelated sets of activities in which inputs are converted into outputs. This approach enables the behaviour of the organisation to be studied in a multi-dimensional way by considering the interactions between its people, technology and structures, and between the organisation and its environment. Within this systems perspective, an organisation's activities are seen as a series of business processes in which resources are used to produce goods and/or services for customers. All the chapters in this book take this process view of organisations. There are of course other ways of thinking about organisations, some of which are considered in the other books in this series.

The readings, each presented as one of sixteen chapters, are complied into five sections:

In section 1 the two chapters introduce the transformation model from systems theory. All business activities whether they involve the processing of customers, materials or information, can be described using this model. Such business processes require resources of people, materials, information, finance, energy and so on to produce outputs of either physical goods or intangible services or, more likely, a combination of both. Any business organisation can be conceived as a number of interrelated business processes.

In section 2 all three chapters stress the importance of processes in achieving organisational success. This will depend on the extent to which business activities add value whilst minimising costs. The extent to which an organisation is able to achieve added value and compete successfully is likely to be closely related to its ability to manage its business processes to best effect.

In section 3 the three chapters describe some of the business processes which process customers. The process of acquiring customers through marketing activity is examined. A framework for considering how an organisation processes its customers in a service delivery system is introduced. Processes aimed at retaining customers for the long term through relationship marketing are also discussed.

In section 4 the four chapters describe business processes in which organisations process materials. Purchasing is described as the process of acquiring materials, manufacturing as the process that changes the state of materials and logistics as the process that moves material to the organisation's customers. The special process of reverse logistics, in which the organisation takes back materials from its customers because of some fault in the goods or in order to dispose of unwanted material in an environmentally safe manner is also considered.

In section 5 the four chapters examine the way in which firms organise themselves in order to undertake their business activities. The advantages of adopting a process orientation for the management of organisational activity is discussed, and compared with the problems associated with the management of traditionally (i.e. functionally) structured organisations. The concept of reorganising businesses based on their business processes, known as Business Process Re-engineering, is introduced and critiqued.

The readings are drawn from a number of sources. They range from chapters within basic introductory business studies texts, through extracts from more challenging books, to articles from well-known academic business journals. We hope you will find these interesting and challenging.

SECTION 1: BUSINESS PROCESSES

INTRODUCTION

This section introduces the transformation model that underpins all of the chapters in the book. The transformation model is part of a broader framework of ideas about organisations, which derive from systems theory. It views any activity in an organisation as a process in which inputs of resources are converted into outputs of goods and/or services for customers. Business activities might involve processing customers, materials or information. The resources required for these activities might include people, materials, information, finance, energy and so on. As such any organisation can be characterised as a series of business processes that utilise resources in an attempt to achieve the desired outputs.

In chapter 1, Cole introduces the concept of an organisation as a system. He points out that unlike a mechanical system or a computer system, business organisations are social systems and hence open systems. An open system is characterised by its interdependence on its environment. For most business organisations the most important aspect of its environment is the market for its outputs, the goods and/or services it produces. No organisation is likely to be successful unless it provides its customers with the products they need, and yet in many markets customer demand is increasingly volatile and unpredictable. So it is vital to be able to respond to changes in the environment. This is likely to require changes to its business processes. This might mean changing inputs or perhaps making changes to the conversion process itself. The chapter points out that like any system, an organisation can be divided into a number of sub-systems. Business organisations might typically have subsystems concerned with acquiring and retaining customers, with the manufacture of products, with the obtaining of financial resources and so on. These will often correspond to the various functional departments of the organisation, Sales and Marketing, Production, Finance and so on, and the interrelationship between these subsystems is likely to be important to organisational effectiveness. However, the construction of boundaries between the various subsystems of an organisation is a matter of choice. Unlike a physical or biological system, the structure of a social system is not predetermined.

Chapter 2, by Slack *et al.*continues to use systems concepts to view an organisation as an interrelated set of activities that enable inputs to be converted to outputs. This chapter is the opening chapter of a best selling textbook on Operations Management, which is a subject that has always made extensive use of systems theory. Operations Management is the academic discipline devoted to the study of those organisational activities that produce the goods and services required by its customers. Consequently the chapter is particularly concerned with those business processes taking place within the operations function of an organisation. The relationship between the operations function and the other main business functions is examined, together with the interaction of the operating system with its environment. The transformation model is used to extend our understanding of the range of activities likely to be undertaken in various business organisations by introducing the concept of macro- and micro-operations. Macro-operations are best thought of as those activities that are directly concerned with the production of the goods and/or services the organisation supplies to its customers. Micro-operations are all the activities that go on within the organisation which contribute directly or indirectly to a macro-operation. The chapter points out that we can usefully think of the micro-operations as a series of business processes which collectively contribute (or at least should do) to meeting customer needs. The relationships between these business processes can be complex.

We would however caution that the transformation process model and the systems concepts that underpin it are, like all models, simplifications of reality. The systems approach to organisational analysis is based on certain assumptions, including assumptions that:

- An organisation is a unitary entity, with each separate subsystem, element and individual member of the organisation committed to the organisation's goals and purposes.
- All members of the organisation are driven only by the needs and priorities of the organisation as a whole, which are entirely clear and understood.
- The information on which decisions are made is clear, unambiguous, objective and freely available throughout the organisation.

These assumptions are open to challenge. As such relying entirely on a systems view of organisations can lead to oversimplifications that may fail to adequately reflect the complexities of organisational reality. Taking a process perspective can be helpful in gaining a better understanding of business behaviour, but it can only provide a partial understanding of organisations.

1

ORGANISATIONS AS SYSTEMS*

Gerard Cole

INTRODUCTION

This chapter defines the characteristics of open social systems and summarises the current theoretical position as a prelude to a discussion of the ideas of several outstanding theorists who have contributed to the growing understanding of organisations as systems.

DEFINITIONS AND CHARACTERISTICS

Put at its simplest, a system is a collection of interrelated parts which form some whole. Typical systems are the solar system, the human body, communication networks and social systems. Systems may be 'closed' or 'open'. Closed systems are those, which, for all practical purposes, are completely self-supporting, and thus do not interact with their environment. An example would be an astronaut's life-support pack. Open systems are those which *do* interact with their environment, on which they rely for obtaining essential inputs and for the discharge of their system outputs. Social systems (e.g. organisations) are always open systems, as are biological systems and information systems. A basic model of an open system can be shown diagrammatically as in Figure 1.1.

The three major characteristics of open systems are as follows:

- they receive inputs or energy from their environment
- they convert these inputs into outputs
- they discharge their outputs into their environment.

In relation to an organisation, the inputs include people, materials, information and finance. These inputs are organised and activated so as to convert human skills and raw materials into products, services and other outputs which are discharged into the environment, as shown in Figure 1.2.

A key feature of open systems is their interdependence on the environment, which may be relatively stable or relatively uncertain at a particular point in time. This feature is of considerable importance to business enterprises which need to adapt to the changing fortunes of the market place if they are to flourish. A classification of environments is given later in the chapter.

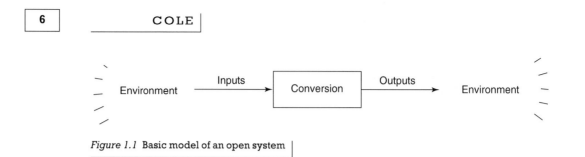

Figure 1.1 Basic model of an open system

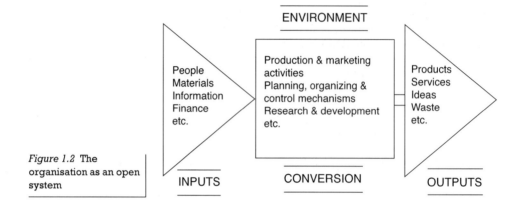

Figure 1.2 The organisation as an open system

Most systems can be divided into sub-systems. For example, the human body – a total system – encloses a number of major sub-systems, such as the central nervous system and the cardio-vascular system, to name but two. Organisations have their sub-systems as well, e.g. production, marketing and accounting sub-systems. The boundaries between sub-systems are called interfaces. These are the sensitive internal boundaries contained within the total system, and they will be referred to again shortly. In the meantime it is important to consider a few points about system boundaries. An organisation's boundaries are defined as much by corporate strategy as by actual fact. This is not so for all systems. In physical or biological systems, the boundaries are there to be seen, and there is no problem distinguishing one motor vehicle, or one human being, from another, for example. In such systems it is also easy to identify boundaries between the total system and its sub-systems. For example, the gearbox of a motor vehicle is a clearly recognisable sub-unit of the whole vehicle. In the same way the cardiovascular system in the human body is a recognisable sub-system of the whole body. These boundaries are matters of fact. For organisations the issue is not quite so straightforward.

The point is the boundaries of an organisation are not visible, for the boundaries of a social system are based on *relationships* and not on things. Thus while certain factual elements, such as physical location, do have some impact on an organisation's boundaries, it is the results of management decisions, i.e. *choices*, that really determine where the organisation ends and the environment begins. Similarly, while the physical presence of machinery for example, may partly determine some of the internal boundaries of the organisation, it is ultimately a matter of corporate, or departmental, strategy which decides where the production system begins and where it ends.

In any organisation, some employees work consistently at the *external* boundary. These are the people who have to deal with the inputs and the outputs to the system, e.g. those responsible for raising capital, purchasing from suppliers, identifying customer requirements etc and those responsible for sales, distribution etc. Other employees work consistently on *internal* boundaries, i.e. at the interfaces between the various sub-systems of the organisation. These people may be responsible for the provision of services to others in the organisation, e.g. management accountants, personnel officers, office service managers etc. They may be responsible for integrating activities, e.g. managers and supervisors. In fact, it is becoming increasingly recognised that *'boundary management'* is of vital importance to the effectiveness of those in managerial and supervisory roles. Boundary management in this context means establishing and maintaining effective relationships with colleagues working in neighbouring sub-systems.

Whilst organisations are open social systems, taken as a whole, their sub-systems may be either open or closed. Production sub-systems and accounting sub-systems tend to be closed systems, i.e. they are relatively self-contained and are affected in ways which are usually predictable. Marketing and R&D (research and development) activities tend, on the other hand, to work best in open systems, i.e. where they can be aware of, and adapt to key influences in the external environment. In the main, closed systems are required for stability and consistency, whereas open systems are required for unstable and uncertain conditions. Closed systems are designed for efficiency, open systems for survival. The early Classical theorists were expounding a closed systems approach. Developments in Human Relations, by contrast, were biased towards open systems. The modern consensus appears to be that both types are necessary for the maintenance and growth of successful organisations.

One of the most useful attempts to summarise the complexities of organisations as open systems has been that of the two American academics, Katz and Kahn (1966).[1] They identified the common characteristics of such open systems as follows:

- Importation of energy and stimulation, e.g. people and material.
- Throughput or conversion, e.g. the processing of materials and organising of work activities.
- Output, e.g. of products or services.
- Cyclic nature, e.g. the returns from marketing the output enable further inputs to be made to complete the cycle of production.
- Negative entropy. Entropy is the natural process by which all things tend to break down or die. Developing negative entropy means importing more energy etc than is required for output, and then storing it to enable survival in difficult times, e.g. firms building up their reserves.
- Feedback. Negative feedback, in particular, enables the system to correct deviations. Organisations tend to develop their own thermostats!
- Steady state. This refers to the balance to be maintained between inputs flowing in from the external environment and the corresponding outputs returning to it. An organisation in steady state is not static, but in a dynamic form of equilibrium.
- Differentiation; e.g. the tendency to greater specialisation of functions and multiplicity of roles.
- Equifinality. This word was coined by an early systems theorist, L. von Bertalanffy, in 1940. It means that open systems do not have to achieve their goals in one particular way. Similar ends can be achieved by different paths and from a different starting point.

The Katz and Kahn summary utilises a number of specialised systems terms (e.g. negative entropy and equifinality) which are beyond the scope of a general text. What is important to grasp at this stage is that the input–conversion–output model, as shown in Figure 1.2, now needs to be expanded to take in the key factors of feedback and steady state. The result of including feedback from output to input is to produce a so-called *'closed loop'* system. A closed loop system is basically a self-regulating system, such as a thermostat in a heating

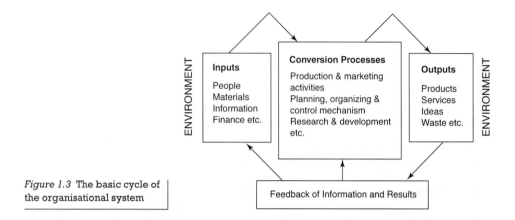

Figure 1.3 The basic cycle of the organisational system

system or, to take a business example, a budgetary control system in a departmental operating plan. In each case, information fed back to the input side of the system enables corrective changes to be made to keep the system on course, i.e. in a steady state. The revised model of the organisation as an open system can now be drawn as in Figure 1.3.

The revised model shows the consequences of the outputs as information and results. The information can take many forms, e.g. sales volumes, new orders, market share, customer complaints etc, and can be applied to control the inputs and conversion processes, as appropriate. The results are the revenues and profits which are fed back into the organisation to provide further inputs, and so ensure the survival and growth of the system. An adaptive system, such as the one described above, is sometimes referred to as a 'cybernetic' system. The term *'cybernetics'* in this context means the study of control and communication in the animal and the machine. Cybernetics was made famous by Norbert Wiener in the late 1940s, but is still very much a developing science. The essence of a cybernetic system is self-regulation on the basis of feedback information to disclose a shortfall in performance against standards and to indicate corrective action.

DEVELOPMENT IN SYSTEMS THEORIES

The dominant theories of organisations prior to the 1960s were (1) the classical/traditional school, who saw organisational design as a rational structure, or mechanism, which could be imposed on people, and (2) the human relations, or social psychological school, who saw organisations primarily in terms of the needs of the individuals in them. The theorists of human relations set out to humanise the workplace, and this they did, but at the expense of studying the organisation as a whole. They did not address themselves sufficiently to several major problems that can arise in practically every organisation, for example the problem of dealing with the tensions between the requirements for structure and the needs of people. Questions of conflict tended to be dealt with in terms of avoiding it by attention to motivation and leadership. A further difficulty in the human relations approach was its emphasis on the practical application of ideas rather than on the conceptual development of organisational theory. This is not to deny the usefulness, to practising managers in particular, of the propositions of human relations, but it suggests the need to look elsewhere for a fuller explanation of behaviour in organisations.

This is where we have to turn to theorists who see organisations as complex social systems, responsive to a number of interdependent and important variables. The key variables that are of greatest interest to those adopting a systems approach to organisations are as follows:

- People – as individuals and in groups
- Technology – in terms of the technical requirements of work
- Organisation structures
- Environment – the external conditions affecting the organisation

Whereas earlier theorists looked at individual variables in isolation, the theorists of systems study the relationship between two or more of them. Initially, the Tavistock researchers, for example, looked at the relationships between people and technology, and between structure and environment. Later studies, such as those of Pugh and colleagues, have developed a more comprehensive and multi-dimensional approach, utilising all the above variables. The principal developments in systems theories of organisation design are discussed in the following paragraphs.

The researches, so far, have indicated that there is no one best way of designing organisations to meet their current objectives. On the contrary, the evidence seems to suggest that the variables are so volatile that only a 'contingency' approach can prove practicable. This suggests that organisations can only be made viable when steps are taken to adapt them to a particular set of prevailing conditions. Naturally this approach appeals more to theorists than practising managers, who must feel daunted by the need to be eternally adaptive. Nevertheless, it offers the best prospect to date of achieving the optimum organisation design. [. . .] [We will now] describe some of the earlier contributions to systems theory as applied to organisations, commencing with the Tavistock researchers.

THE TAVISTOCK GROUP

The Tavistock Institute of Human Relations in London has been engaged in various forms of social research for over fifty years. Despite its title, the Institute has made its reputation for its contribution to *systems* theory. In particular, Trist and Bamforth introduced the concept of 'socio-technical' systems (1951)[2] and A.K. Rice and F.E. Emery promoted several important ideas relating to open-systems theory and types of environment.

The Trist and Bamforth studies into changes in the method of extracting coal in British pits took place in the 1940s. The researchers were interested in the effects of mechanisation on the social and work organisation at the coal-face. Before mechanisation, the coal had been extracted by small, closely knit teams working as autonomous groups. They worked at their own pace, often isolated in the dark from other groups. Bonds established within groups became important outside work as well as during the shift. Conflicts between competing groups were frequent and sometimes violent, but were always contained. This was the system which operated before the coal-cutters and mechanical conveyors were introduced. It was called the *shortwall method*.

The mechanised coal-face was completely different. It consisted of a long wall which required not small groups, but groups of between forty and fifty men plus their supervisors. These men could be spread out over 200 yards, and they worked in a three shift system. The new system, known as the *long-wall method*, was essentially a mass-production system based on a high degree of job specialisation. Under the former shortwall method, each team had provided all the skills required, but in the longwall arrangement the basic operations were separated between the shifts. So, for example, if the first shift cut the coal from the face, the second shift shovelled it into the conveyor, and the third shift advanced the coal-face along the seam. Even within each shift, there was a high degree of task specialisation.

The social consequences of the new method, arising from the breakdown of the previously closely-integrated social structure were: increased haggling over pay, inter-shift competition for the best jobs, the seeking of scape-goats in other shifts, and a noticeable increase in absenteeism. The results of the radical change in working methods and the miners' adverse response to them, led Trist and Bamforth to the conclusion that effective work was a function of the *inter*dependence of technology (equipment, physical layout and task requirements) and social needs (especially relationships within groups). It was not sufficient to regard the working environment as *either* a technical system *or* a social system. It was a combination of the two: a *socio-technical system*.

Eventually a so-called *'composite longwall method'* was developed which enabled the needs of the social system to be met, whilst at the same time utilising the benefits of the new mechanised equipment (the technical system). Tasks and working arrangements were altered so that the basic operations could be carried out by any one shift, and so that tasks within each group were allocated by the members. Payment was changed so as to incorporate a group bonus. The outcome of the composite methods was increased productivity, reduced absenteeism and a lower accident rate.

Alongside the coal-mining studies mentioned above, the reputation of the Tavistock group was also assured by A.K. Rice's (1958)[3] studies into the calico mills at Ahmedabad, India. In his book Rice elaborated on key aspects of systems theory as applied to organisations, two of which are selected for inclusion here: his concept of systems, and his views on work design.

Rice saw any industrial system (e.g. a firm) as an open system, importing various items from its environment, converting them into goods, services and waste materials, and then exporting them into the environment. Within the total system of the firm, he suggested, there existed two main systems: an operating system and a managing system. The operating system deals with the import, conversion and export of the product or service, while the managing system deals with the control, decision-making and communication aspects of the total system. Each system can have one or more sub-systems, which is why it is necessary to develop the managing system, so as to coordinate the interaction of all the systems and sub-systems.

Rice's view of systems can be compared usefully with those of Handy (1993),[4] writing some years later. Handy describes and comments on, not only the operating system but also the *adaptive, maintenance and information systems* in activating the various parts of the total organisation. It is these last three which come closest to making up the managing system formulated by Rice. On balance, the more modern analysis is the clearer of the two in helping to establish the prime focal points of the managing system.

The studies at Ahmedabad produced, among other things, some interesting conclusions about the design of work. These can be summarised as follows:

- Effective performance of a primary task is an important source of satisfaction at all levels of work.
- The capacity for voluntary cooperation is more extensive than is often expected.
- There is great benefit in allowing individuals to complete a whole task.
- Work groups of eight seem to have the best chance of success for achieving group tasks.
- There is a clear relationship between work effectiveness and social relations.
- Where group autonomy has been established, unnecessary interference by supervisors will be counter-productive.

The above findings have been incorporated into current ideas on the design and redesign of work, so as to meet social and psychological needs of employees as well as the requirements of changing technology. They also share much common ground with Herzberg's ideas of motivation and job enrichment.

The final example of the work of the Tavistock Group relates to another key factor in systems theory – the nature of the environment. Emery and Trist (1965)[5] were the first to produce a classification of environments. They described four types of environment as follows:

1 *Placid, randomised* This represents a relatively unchanging and homogeneous environment, whose demands are randomly distributed.
2 *Placid, clustered* This environment too, is relatively unchanging, but its threats and
rewards are clustered. So, for example, in a monopoly situation an organisation's failure
or success depends on its continued hold over the market.
3 *Disturbed, reactive* In this environment there is competition between organisations, and
this may include hindering tactics.
4 *Turbulent field* This describes a dynamic and rapidly changing environment, in which
organisations must adapt frequently in order to survive.

Emery and Trist were particularly interested in the last type, the turbulent field. This is
an area where existing formal, or bureaucratised, structures are ill-suited to deal with their
environment. According to the writers, more and more environments are becoming
turbulent, and yet organisation structures are not becoming correspondingly flexible. This
important point is referred to in the [. . .] 'mechanistic-organic structures' concept
introduced by Burns and Stalker (1961).[6]

The field of management and organisation theory has been poorly served, in general, by
British writers and theorists. The outstanding exception to this situation has been the work
of the Tavistock Group, whose contribution to our understanding of organisations as open
social systems has been fundamental and worldwide.

KATZ AND KAHN

Reference was made to these two researchers earlier. Their view of organisations has had a
considerable influence on the development of systems approaches to organisation theory.
Katz and Kahn saw social structures as essentially contrived systems, where the forces that
hold them together are psychological rather than biological. Social systems are seen to be
more variable than biological systems and are more difficult to study because they have no
easily recognisable boundaries. They have a structure, but it is *a structure of events* rather than
of physical parts. Nevertheless Katz and Kahn set out to describe their view of social systems
and their related sub-systems. They followed similar lines to Rice in advocating an open
system approach, in which they identified five sub-systems at work in organisations.

The five sub-systems they identified can be summarised as follows:

1 *Production or Technical sub-systems* These are concerned with the accomplishment of
the basic tasks of the organisation (production of goods, provision of services etc).
2 *Supportive sub-systems* These are the systems which procure the inputs and dispose of
the outputs of the production sub-system. They also maintain the relationship between
the organisation as a whole and the external environment.
3 *Maintenance sub-systems* These are concerned with the relative stability or predictability
of the organisation. They provide for the roles, the rules and the rewards applicable to
those who work in the organisation.
4 *Adaptive sub-systems* The first three systems above serve the organisation as it is. The
adaptive sub-systems by comparison are concerned with what the organisation might
become. They deal with issues of change in the environment, e.g. as in marketing, and
research and development.
5 *Managerial sub-systems* These comprise the controlling and coordinating activities of the
total system. They deal with the coordination of substructures, the resolution of conflict,
and the coordination of external requirements with the organisation's resources. An
important managerial sub-system is the authority structure which describes the way the
managerial system is organised for the purposes of decision-making and decision-taking.

Other key features of social organisations, according to Katz and Kahn, are roles, norms and values. Roles differentiate one position from another, and require a standardised form of behaviour. The network of roles constitutes the formal structure of the organisation, and the formalised role system. Roles limit the effects of the incumbent's personality on performance in the position. This idea is very much in line with Weber's view of the rational, and impersonal, conduct of an office. In fact, Katz and Kahn describe bureaucratic structures as the clearest examples of their definition of social organisation.

While roles help to differentiate the activities of the organisation, norms and values help to integrate behaviour. Norms, or standards of behaviour, are closely associated with roles, because they specify role behaviour in terms of expected standards. For example, an office manager would be expected to conform to certain norms relating to dress, time-keeping and honesty, to name but three responsibilities. Values are more generally held beliefs; they represent the ideology of the organisation – 'its culture' [. . .] Loyalty to the organisation is an example of a value.

Katz and Kahn have provided us with a useful way of looking at organisations as systems. Their descriptions of the major sub-systems of organisation, together with the pattern of roles which are inextricably linked with them, represent an important step forward in understanding the complexities of the nature of organisations.

NOTE

* This chapter has been adapted from, Cole, G.A. (1996), 'Organisations as Systems', *Management Theory and Practice (5th edition)*, ch. 9, London, Letts Educational.

REFERENCES

1. Katz, D. and Kahn, R.L. (1966), *The Social Psychology of Organisations*, Wiley.
2. Trist, E.L. and Bamforth, K. (1951), 'Some Social and Psychological Consequences of the Longwall Method of Coal-getting', *Human Relations*, Vol. 4. No. 1.
3. Rice, A.K. (1958), *Productivity and Social Organisation*, Tavistock.
4. Handy, C. (1993), *Understanding Organisations (3rd edition)*, Penguin.
5. Emery, F.E. and Trist, E.L. (1965), 'The Causal Texture of Organisational Environments', in *Human Relations*, Vol. 18, No. 1.
6. Burns, T. and Stalker, G.M. (1961), *The Management of Innovation*, Tavistock.

2

EFFECTIVE OPERATIONS MANAGEMENT*

Nigel Slack, Stuart Chambers, Christine Harland, Alan Harrison and Robert Johnston

Operations management is, above all else, a practical subject which deals with real issues. So let us start our examination of the subject with a practical example of an organization which is known for the originality of its operations.

IKEA

IKEA is a furniture retailer with a difference. With around 100 giant stores operating in over 15 countries world-wide it has managed to develop its own special way of selling furniture. IKEA customers typically spend between one-and-a-half and two hours in the store – far longer than in rival furniture retailers. An important reason for this is the way it organizes its stores – all of which are the same in most important respects all around the world. The design and philosophy of its store operations go back to the original business which was started in southern Sweden by Ingvar Kamprad in the 1950s. At that time Mr Kamprad was successfully selling furniture, through a catalogue operation. In response to customer requests to be able to see some of his furniture, he built a showroom in Stockholm, not in the centre of the city where land was expensive, but on the outskirts of town. Instead of buying expensive display stands, he simply set the furniture out more or less as it would be in a domestic setting. Also, instead of moving the furniture from the warehouse to the showroom area, he asked customers to pick the furniture up themselves from the warehouse. This 'anti-service' approach to service, as it has been described, is the foundation of IKEA's stores today.

IKEA's furniture is 'value for money' with a wide range of choice. It is usually designed to be stored and sold as a 'flat pack' but is capable of easy assembly by the customer. The stores are all designed around the same self-service concept – that finding the store, parking, moving through the store itself, and ordering and picking up goods should be simple, smooth and problem-free. At the entrance to each store are large notice-boards which proclaim

IKEA's philosophy and provide advice to shoppers who have not used the store before. Catalogues are also available at this point showing illustrations, dimensions and the available range of the store's products. Perhaps most significantly for shoppers with young children, there is also a supervised children's play area, a small cinema, a parent and baby room and toilets. Parents can leave their children in the supervised play area for a limited period of time. Each child is attired in a yellow, numbered top while he or she is in this area and parents are recalled via the loudspeaker system if the child has any problems. Customers may also borrow pushchairs to keep their children with them as they move round the store.

Some parts of the showroom are set out in 'room settings' while others show, for example, all beds together, so that customers can make comparisons. Customers are not approached by staff offering help or advice. The IKEA philosophy is not to 'hassle' customers in this way but rather to let them make up their minds in their own time. If a customer does want advice, there are information points around the showroom where staff, in their bright red uniforms, can help and guide customers, provide measuring rules, paper for sketching and so on. Every piece of furniture carries a ticket which indicates its dimensions, price, materials used, country of origin and the other colours in which it is available. It also has a code number which indicates the location in the warehouse from where it can be collected. The tickets on larger items ask customers to go to the information desks for assistance. After viewing the showroom, customers pass into the 'free-service' area where smaller items are displayed on shelves. These can be picked directly off the display shelves by customers and put into yellow shoulder bags or trolleys. Customers then pass through the self-service warehouse where they can pick up the items they viewed in the showroom. Finally, the customers pay at the check-outs, each of which is constructed with a ramped conveyor belt which moves the customer's purchases up to the check-out staff member and along to the exit area. At the exit area there are information and service points, and often a 'Swedish Shop' with Swedish food-stuffs. A large loading area allows customers to bring their cars from the car park and load their purchases. Any customers who have bought more than their car will carry can rent or buy a roof rack.

Nor is IKEA's innovative approach to its business confined only to the physical layout and design of its stores; it also extends to its management style and philosophy. All employees in the store wear either red or grey sweatshirts which distinguish customer-contact and non-contact staff.

[. . .]

So why is IKEA able to survive and succeed? It certainly keeps a very tight control of its costs, and it also understands its market and how it can serve the needs of its customers. Furthermore, the products it designs and sells must be regarded by its customers as representing outstanding value for money. At least as important as all these, however, is the way it organizes the delivery of its services within its stores. This is the responsibility of the company's operations management. The staff in the store, the staff who liaise with suppliers, the staff who store and transport goods to the stores and the staff who design, plan, control and constantly improve the way things are done, the buildings, the computers and check-outs, the warehouses and the transportation system – all are engaged in *operations management*. IKEA owes its success, in no small measure, to the effectiveness of its operations management, who provide:

- a smooth customer flow;
- a clean, well-designed environment;
- sufficient goods to satisfy demand;
- sufficient staff to serve customers and stock the warehouse;

- an appropriate quality of service;
- a continuous stream of ideas to improve its, already impressive, operations performance.

Without these, the company, no matter how well it marketed and financed its activities, would not be the success it is.

Now is the point to establish some definitions.

- The *operations function* of the organization is the arrangement of resources which is devoted to the production of its goods and services. Every organization has an operations function because every organization produces some type of goods and/or services. However, not all types of organization will necessarily call the operations function by this name [. . .].
  Note that we also use the shorter terms 'the operation' or 'operations' and, at times, the 'operations system' interchangeably with the 'operations function'.
- *Operations managers* are the staff of the organization who have particular responsibility for managing some, or all, of the resources which comprise the operations function. Again in some organizations the operations manager could be called by some other name. For example, he or she might be called the 'fleet manager' in a distribution company, or the 'administrative manager' in a hospital, or the 'store manager' in a supermarket.
- *Operations management* is the term which is used for the activities, decisions and responsibilities of operations managers.

As we have seen in the case of IKEA, if the operations function is to be effective it must use its resources efficiently and produce goods and services in a way that satisfies its customers. In addition, it must be creative, innovative and energetic in introducing novel and improved ways of producing goods and services [. . .]. If the operation can do these things it will provide the organization with the means to survive in the long term because it gives the organization a competitive advantage over its commercial rivals. An alternative way of putting this in a not-for-profit organization is that an effective operation gives the means to fulfil the organization's long-term strategic goals.
  [. . .]

OPERATIONS IN THE ORGANIZATION

The operations function is central to the organization because it produces the goods and services which are its reason for existing, but it is neither the only, nor necessarily the most important, function. All organizations have other functions with their own part to play. Yet organizations do differ in the way they define their functional areas and the boundaries between them. Here we divide the organization into three other *major functions*:

- the marketing function
- the accounting and finance function
- the product/service development function

and *support functions*, which supply and support the operations function, including:

- the human resources function
- the purchasing function
- the engineering/technical function.

Table 2.1 shows the activities of these functions for a sample of operations.

Table 2.1 The activities of functions in some organizations

Typical functional activities	Church	Fast food chain	University	Furniture manufacturer
Marketing	Call on newcomers Proselytize	Advertise on TV Devise promotional materials	Develop brochures Mail out brochures Attend shows	Advertise in magazines Determine pricing policy Sell to stores
Accounting and finance	Count contributions Manage appeals Pay rents Pay bills	Pay suppliers Collect takings Pay staff	Pay faculty and support staff Monitor expenditure Collect fees	Pay staff Pay suppliers Prepare budgets Manage cash
Product/service development	Search for meaning of existence Retranslate scriptures	Design hamburgers, pizzas, etc. Design decor for restaurants	Develop new courses Design research programmes	Design new furniture Co-ordinate with fashionable colours
Operations	Conduct weddings Conduct funerals Conduct services Save souls	Make burgers, pizzas, etc. Serve customers Clear away Maintain equipment	Communicate knowledge Conduct research Administer courses	Make components Assemble furniture
Personnel	Train priests Appraise priestly performance	Train staff Devise remuneration schemes	Train staff Manage contracts Appraise performance	Recruit staff Train staff
Purchasing	Buy consumables Develop vestment supplies	Buy foodstuff Buy plates, cartons, napkins, etc.	Buy equipment Buy consumables	Buy raw materials, wood, etc. Buy fabric
Engineering/technical	Maintain church buildings, etc.	Develop or purchase equipment, ovens, etc. Install equipment, ovens, etc.	Purchase audiovisual equipment Maintain equipment and facilities	Develop or purchase woodworking machines Maintain machines

Source: Adapted from Heizer and Render[2]

It is important to stress, however, that functional names, boundaries and responsibilities vary between organizations – a complication which is particularly true of the operations function. This leads to some confusion over where the boundaries of the operations function should be. For example, a narrow definition of the operations function's boundaries would exclude all activities shared with any other functions. At the other extreme, a very broad definition of operations would include all activities which had any connection with the production of goods and services – in practice every activity with the exception of the core marketing/selling and accounting/finance activities. Figure 2.1 illustrates how the functional boundary of operations management would differ with narrow and broad definitions.

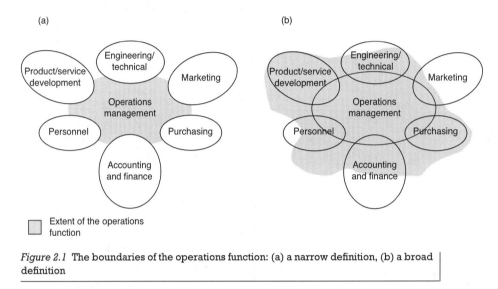

Figure 2.1 The boundaries of the operations function: (a) a narrow definition, (b) a broad definition

THE TRANSFORMATION PROCESS MODEL

All operations produce goods or services or a mixture of the two, and they do this by a *process of transformation*. By transformation we mean that they use their *resources* to change the state or condition of something to produce *outputs*. Figure 2.2 shows this general *transformation model* which is used to describe the nature of operations. Put simply, or to be transformed themselves, into outputs of goods and services.

All operations conform to this general input–transformation–output model. For example, hospitals have inputs of doctors, nurses and other medical staff, administrators, cleaning staff, beds, medical equipment, pharmaceuticals, blood, dressings, and so on. Their purpose is to transform sick patients into healthy patients. The outputs from the operation are treated patients, medical test results, medical research and 'best practice' medical procedures. Table 2.2 shows that one can describe a wide range of operations in this way. However, there are differences between different operations. If you stand far enough away from, say, a hospital or a motor vehicle plant, they might look the same. Each is likely to be a large building into which staff enter and deliveries take place. But move closer and clear differences do start to emerge. For a start, one is a manufacturing operation producing largely physical goods, and one is a service operation which produces changes in the physiological condition, feelings and behaviour of patients. The nature of the processes which each building contains will also be different. The motor vehicle plant contains metal cutting and forming machinery and assembly processes, whereas the hospital contains diagnostic,

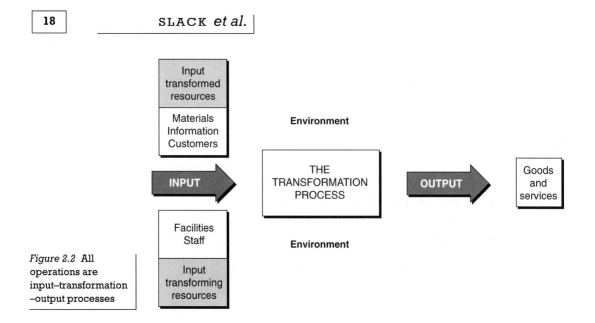

Figure 2.2 All operations are input–transformation –output processes

Table 2.2 Some operations described in terms of input–transformation–output processes

Operation	Input resources	Transformation process	Outputs
Airline	Aircraft Pilots and aircrew Groundcrew Passengers and freight	Move passengers and freight around the world	Transported passengers and freight
Department store	Goods for sale Staff sales Computerized registers Customers	Display goods Give sales advice Sell goods	Customers and goods assembled together
Dentist	Dental surgeons Dental equipment Nurses Patients	Check and treat teeth Give preventative advice	Patients with healthy teeth and gums
Zoo	Zoo keepers Animals Simulated environments Customers	Display animals Educate customers Breed animals	Entertained customers Informed customers Non-extinct species
Printer	Printers and designers Printing presses Paper, ink, etc.	Design Print Bind	Designed and printed material
Police	Police officers Computer systems Information Public (law-abiding and criminals)	Prevent crime Solve crime Apprehend criminals	Lawful society Public with feeling of security
Frozen food manufacturer	Fresh food Operators Food-processing equipment Freezers	Food preparation Freeze	Frozen food

care and therapeutic processes. Perhaps the most important difference between the two operations, however, is the nature of their inputs. Both have 'staff' and 'facilities' as inputs to the operation but they act upon very different things. The motor vehicle plant uses its staff and facilities to *transform steel, plastic, cloth, tyres and other materials*. They make them into vehicles which are eventually delivered to customers. The staff and technology in the hospital, on the other hand, *transform the customers themselves*. The patients form part of the input to the operation – it is they who are being 'processed'. This has important implications for how the operation needs to be managed.

Inputs to the transformation process

The inputs to an operation can be conveniently classified as either:
- *transformed resources* – the resources that are treated, transformed or converted in some way; or
- *transforming resources* – the resources that act upon the transformed resources.

Transformed resources

The transformed resources which operations take in are usually a mixture of:

- materials;
- information; and
- customers.

Often one of these is dominant in an operation. For example, a bank devotes part of its energies to producing printed statements of accounts for its customers. In doing so, it is processing materials and acting as a printer, but no one would claim that a bank and a printer are the same type of operation. The bank also processes customers. It gives them advice regarding their financial affairs, cashes their cheques, deposits their cash, and has direct contact with them. However, most of the bank's activities are concerned with processing information about its customers' financial affairs. As customers, we may be unhappy with badly printed statements and we may be more unhappy if we are not treated appropriately in the bank. If the bank makes errors in our financial transactions, however, we suffer in a far more fundamental way. This is not to say that materials processing or customer processing is unimportant to the bank. On the contrary, it must be good at these things to keep its customers happy. Error-free, fast and efficient *information processing*, though, is the central objective of the bank.

It is the same with other types of operation. Take, for example, a company which manufactures the high-speed machinery used for packaging food products. Some of the company's operation will be devoted to processing the technical requirements of its customers. The operation will also need to 'process' the customers by visiting their factories, by bringing the customers to the factory to see the progress being made on the equipment, by working with the customers during its installation and finally, by educating the customers in the use of the equipment. Yet although the operation will process both information and people, its main task is *materials processing* to make the equipment itself.

Finally, a hospital will process information in the form of patients' medical records. It will also devote some of its resources to processing materials, for example in the way it produces meals for patients. The main operations task of a hospital, however, is to process customers in a way which satisfies its patients, maximizes their health care and minimizes its costs. It is predominantly a *customer processing* operation.

Table 2.3 gives examples of operations with their dominant transformed resources.

Table 2.3 Dominant transformed materials of various operations

Predominantly materials processors	Predominantly information processors	Predominantly customer processors
All manufacturing operations	Accountants	Hairdressers
Mining and extraction companies	Bank headquarters	Hotels
Retail operations	Market research company	Hospitals
Warehouses	Financial analysts	Mass rapid transports
Postal services	News service	Theatres
Container shipping line	University research unit	Theme parks
Trucking companies	Archives	Dentists
	Telecoms company	

Transforming resources

There are two types which form the 'building blocks' of all operations:

- *facilities* – the buildings, equipment, plant and process technology of the operation;
- *staff* – those who operate, maintain, plan and manage the operation. (Note we use the term 'staff' to describe all the people in the operation, at any level.)

Of course the exact nature of both facilities and staff will differ between operations. To a five-star hotel, its facilities consist mainly of buildings, furniture and fittings. To a nuclear-powered aircraft carrier, its facilities are the nuclear generator, turbines, and sophisticated electronic detection equipment. One operation has relatively 'low-technology' facilities and one 'high-technology' facilities, but both are important to the operation concerned. A five-star hotel would be just as ineffective with worn and broken furniture as an aircraft carrier would be with inoperative electronics.

The nature of staff will also differ between operations. The majority of staff employed in a factory assembling domestic refrigerators do not need a particularly high level of technical skill. In contrast, the majority of staff employed by an accounting company are likely to be highly skilled in their own particular 'technical' skill (accounting). Although the extent and nature of the skills needed by staff will vary, however, they all have a contribution to make to the effectiveness of their operation. An assembly worker who consistently misassembles refrigerators will dissatisfy customers and increase costs just as surely as an accountant who cannot add up. Table 2.4 shows the transforming resources to be found in some operations.

The transformation process

The purpose of the transformation process in operations is closely connected with the nature of its transformed input resources.

Materials processing

Operations which process materials could do so to transform their *physical properties* (such as physical shape, or composition or characteristics). Most manufacturing operations are like this. Other operations which process materials do so to change their *location* (parcel delivery companies, for example). Some, like retail operations, do so to change the *possession* or ownership of the materials. Finally, some materials-processing operations do so primarily to *store* or *accommodate* them, such as a warehouse.

Table 2.4 The facilities and staff transforming resources of three operations

	Ferry company	*Paper manufacturer*	*Radio station*

Types of facilities	Ships
	On-board navigation
	  equipment
	Dry docks
	Materials-handling
	  equipment
	On-shore buildings
	Computerized reservation
	  systems
	Warehouses
		Pulp-making vats
		Paper-making machines
		Reeling equipment
		Slitting equipment
		Packing machinery
		Steam-generating boilers
		Warehouses
			Broadcasting
			  equipment
			Studios and
			  studio equipment
			Transmitters
			Outside broadcast
			  vehicles

Types of staff	Sailors Engineers Catering staff On-board shop assistants Cleaners Maintenance staff Ticketing staff	Operators Chemists and chemical engineers Process plant engineers	Disc jockeys Announcers Technicians

Information processing

Operations which process information could do so to transform their *informational properties* (that is the purpose or form of the information); accountants do this. Some change the *possession* of the information, for example market research companies. Some *store* or *accommodate* the information, for example archives and libraries. Finally, some operations change the *location* of the information, such as telecommunication companies.

Customer processing

Operations which process customers might also transform them in a variety of ways. Some change their *physical properties* in a similar way to materials processors: for example, hairdressers or even cosmetic surgeons. Some customer-processing operations *store* (or more politely) *accommodate* them: hotels, for example. Airlines, mass rapid transport systems and bus companies transform the *location* of their customers. Some are concerned with transforming the *physiological state* of their customers, such as hospitals. Finally, some customer-processing operations are concerned with transforming the *psychological state* of their customers, for example most entertainment services such as music, theatre, television, radio and theme parks. Table 2.5 summarizes these various types of transformation processes.

Outputs from the transformation process

The outputs from (and purpose of) the transformation process are goods and services, which are generally seen as being different, for several reasons.

Tangibility

Goods are usually *tangible*: for example you can physically touch a television set or a newspaper. Services are usually *intangible*. You cannot touch consultancy advice or a haircut (although you can often see or feel the results of these services).

Table 2.5 Different types of transformation processes

	Physical properties	Informational properties	Possession	Location	Storage/ Accommodation	Physiological state	Psychological state
Materials processors	All manufacturing operations Mining and extraction		Retail operations	Postal services Freight distribution Port operations	Warehouses		
Information processors		Bank HQs Accountants Architects	Financial analysts Market research companies Universities Consultants News services	Telecoms company	Library Archives		
Customer processors	Hairdressers Plastic surgeons			Public transport Taxis	Hotels	Hospitals Other health care	Education Psychoanalysts Theatres Theme parks

Storability

Partly because of tangibility, goods can also be *stored*, at least for the short time after their production. Services, on the other hand, are usually *non-storable*: for the example, the service of 'accommodation in an hotel room for tonight' will perish if it is not sold before tonight – accommodation in the same room tomorrow is a different output from the service.

Transportability

Another consequence of tangibility is the ability to *transport* goods. Automobiles, machine tools and video cameras can all be moved. However, if services are intangible, they are *untransportable*. Health services, for example, cannot be exported as such (though the means of producing health services can).

Simultaneity

The other main distinction between goods and services concerns the timing of their production. Goods are nearly always *produced prior* to the customer receiving (or even seeing) them. For example, the CD you just bought was produced well before you bought it. Services, however, are often *produced simultaneously* with their consumption. The service which the shop provided in selling you the CD happened at the same time as you 'consumed' the service by buying it.

Customer contact

The implication of this is that customers have a *low contact* level with the operations which produce goods. Although you probably will have bought and consumed bread for most of your life, you have probably never seen the inside of a bakery. Whereas in services, because they are produced and consumed simultaneously, they must have *high contact* between the customer and the operation.

Quality

Finally, because generally customers do not see the production of goods, they will judge the quality of the operation which produced them on the evidence of the goods themselves. Even if we disagree as to the quality of our new personal computer, we can measure its capabilities in a reasonably objective manner. But in services the customer judges not only the outcome of the service, but also the aspects of the way in which it was produced. For example, in purchasing a new pair of shoes you might be perfectly satisfied that the shoes were in stock and that you were promptly served. Yet if the shop assistant was discourteous, you would not consider the service to be of a high quality. Other customers, on the other hand, might be less sensitive than you in judging the service.

Most operations produce both goods and services

Some operations produce just goods and some produce just services, but most operations produce a mixture of the two. Figure 2.3 shows a number of operations positioned in a spectrum from 'pure' goods producers to 'pure' service producers. Crude oil producers are concerned almost exclusively with the product which comes from their oil wells. Other 'commodity-like' goods producers, such as aluminium smelters for example, are again largely concerned with the production of products. However, they might also produce some

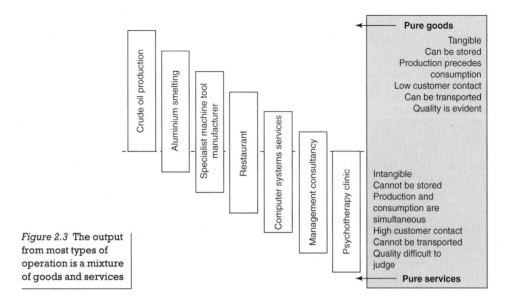

Figure 2.3 The output from most types of operation is a mixture of goods and services

services such as technical advice. Services produced in these circumstances are called *facilitating services*. They are there just to facilitate the sale of the products they support. Machine tool manufacturers are similar insomuch as they too primarily produce goods. To an even greater extent though they also produce facilitating services such as technical advice, applications engineering services and training. The services produced by a restaurant, however, are more than 'facilitating'. They are an essential part of what the customer is paying for. The restaurant is both a manufacturing operation which produces food products and a provider of service in the advice, ambience and service of the food. A computer systems services company will also produce products, for example software products, but primarily it is likely to see itself as providing a service to its customers, with *facilitating goods*. Certainly, a management consultancy, although it produces reports and documents, would see itself as a service provider which uses facilitating goods. Finally, some pure services do not produce products at all. A psychotherapy clinic, for example, provides therapeutic treatment for its customers without any facilitating goods.

The process hierarchy

The transformation process model can also be used within operations. Look inside most operations and they will be made up of several units or departments, which themselves act as smaller versions of the whole operation of which they form a part.

For example, a television programme and video production company has inputs of production, technical and administrative staff, cameras, lighting, sound and recording equipment, studio space, props, video tape, and so on. It transforms these into finished programmes and promotional videos, etc. Within this overall operation, however, there are many smaller operations. For example, there will be, amongst others:

* workshops which manufacture the sets, scenery and props for the productions;
* marketing and sales staff who liaise with potential customers, test out programme ideas and give information and advice to programme makers;
* an engineering maintenance and repair department which cares for, modifies and designs technical equipment;

- production units which organize and shoot the programme and videos;
- the finance and costing department which estimates the likely cost of future projects and controls operational budgets.

The whole television programme and video production operation could be termed a *macro operation*, while its departments could be termed *micro operations* (see Fig. 2.4). These micro operations have inputs, some of which will come from outside the macro operation but many of which will be supplied from other internal micro operations. Each micro operation will also produce outputs of goods and services for the benefit of customers. Again though, some of each micro operation's customers will be other micro operations. This concept of macro and micro operations can be extended further. Within each micro operation there might be sections or groups which also can be considered as operations in their own right. In this way any operations function can be considered as a *hierarchy of operations*.

Internal customer–internal supplier relationships

The terms *internal customer* and *internal supplier* can be used to describe micro operations which take outputs from, and give inputs to, any other micro operations. Thus we could model any operations function as a network of micro operations which are engaged in transforming materials, information, or customers (that is staff) for each other: each micro operation being at the same time both an internal supplier of goods and services and an internal customer for the other micro operation's goods and services.

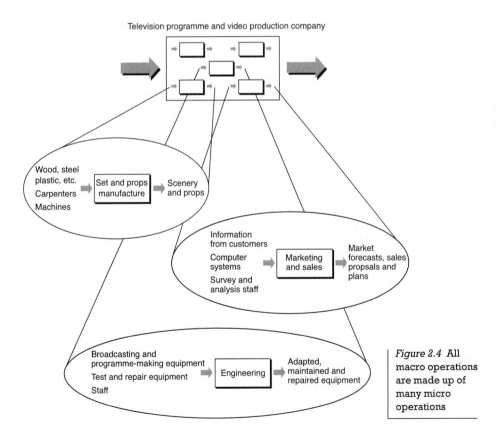

Figure 2.4 All macro operations are made up of many micro operations

We cannot treat *internal* customers and suppliers in exactly the same way as we do *external* customers and suppliers, however. External customers and suppliers usually operate in a free market. If an organization believes that in the long run it can get a better deal by purchasing goods and services from another supplier, it will do so. Similarly, the organization would not expect its customers to purchase its own goods and services unless it could in some way offer a better deal than its competitors. Internal customers and suppliers, however, cannot operate like this. They are not in a 'free market' and they usually cannot look outside either to purchase input resources or to sell their output goods and services (although some organizations are moving this way).

Provided we remember that there are differences between internal and external customers, the concept is a very useful one. First, it provides us with a model to analyse the internal activities of an operation. If the macro operation is not working as it should, we can trace the problem back along the internal network of customers and suppliers. Second, it is a useful reminder to all parts of the operation that, by treating their internal customers with the same degree of care that they exercise on their external customers, the effectiveness of the whole operation can be improved. This idea is one of the foundations of total quality management [. . .]

All parts of the organization are operations

If micro operations act in a similar way to the macro operation, then many of the issues, methods and techniques which we treat in this book have some meaning for each unit, section, group or individual within the organization. For example, the marketing function of an organization can be viewed as a transformation process. It has inputs of market information, staff, computers, and so on. Its staff then transform the information into such outputs as marketing plans, advertising campaigns and sales force organizations. In other words, all functions can be viewed as operations themselves. They are there to provide goods or (more usually) services to the other parts of the organization. Each function will have its 'technical' knowledge. In marketing, this is the expertise in designing and shaping marketing plans; in finance, it is the technical knowledge of financial reporting. Yet each will also have an operations role of producing plans; policies, reports and services.

The implications of this are important. It means that every manager in all parts of an organization is to some extent an operations manager. All managers need to organize their resource inputs effectively so as to produce goods and services. It also means that we must distinguish between two meanings of 'operations':

- *operations as a function,* meaning the part of the organization which produces the goods and services for the organization's external customers;
- *operations as an activity,* meaning any transformation of input resources in order to produce goods and services, for either internal or external customers.

The first meaning of 'operations' is the [one] most commonly used [. . .]. It is always worth remembering the second usage of 'operations', however.

Business processes

Breaking a whole operation down into its constituent micro operations helps to demonstrate that operations management applies to all parts of the organization and helps us to focus on local improvement. But stand back from the macro operation and examine the *connections* between the micro operations. Each micro operation will contribute some part to 'producing' several of the products and services with which the organization attempts to satisfy the needs of its customers. For example, the television programme and video production company, described previously, might satisfy its customers' needs by 'producing' several products and services. Each of these, to different extents, involves the micro operations within the company. So, preparing quotations (estimates of the time and cost involved in potential projects) needs the contributions of the marketing and sales micro operation and the finance and costing micro operation more than the others. Providing technical support (which involves designing systems for, and advising, other media companies) mainly involves the engineering micro operation, but does also need some contribution from the others. Figure 2.5 illustrates the contribution of each micro operation to each product or service. No particular sequence is implied by Figure 2.5. The contributions of each micro operation will not all occur in the same order. In fact the flow of information, materials or customers between micro operations might be complex, involving delays and recycling.

These collections of contributions from each micro operation which fulfil customer needs are called *business processes*. They address the core purposes of the organization and often cut across conventional organizational boundaries. Reorganizing (or 're-engineering') layouts and organizational responsibilities around these business processes is the philosophy behind business process re-engineering (BPR) [. . .].

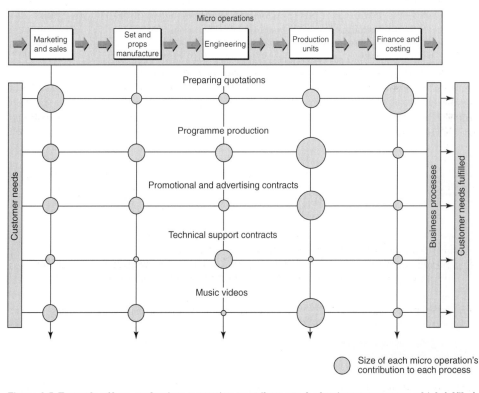

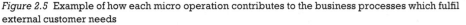

Figure 2.5 Example of how each micro operation contributes to the business processes which fulfil external customer needs

Buffering the operation

The turbulent environment in which most organizations do business means that the operations function is having to adjust continually to changing circumstances. Operations are vulnerable to 'environmental' uncertainty in both supply and demand. A food-processing operation might not be able to predict exactly when some foods will be harvested. In extreme cases, very bad weather might totally disrupt the supply to a factory for weeks. Demand could also be prone to disruption. Unpredictable changes in the weather, a 'health scare' story in the press, and so on, can all introduce turbulence. One way in which operations managers try to minimize 'environmental' disruption is by *buffering* or insulating the operations function from the external environment. It can be done in two ways:

- *physical buffering* – designing an inventory or stock of resources either at the input side of the transformation process, or at the output side;
- *organizational buffering* – allocating the responsibilities of the various functions in the organization so that the operations function is protected from the external environment by other functions.

Physical buffering

One way of protecting the transformation process of the operation against unpredicted fluctuations in the quality or nature of input resources is to build up a store of the resources. Any interruptions to supply will (initially at least) be absorbed by the store (see Fig. 2.6). The operation is storing its input transformed resources before it 'transforms' them. The point here is that operations often do not *need* to store input resources. The reason they do it is that their activities are much more orderly (and therefore usually cheaper) if they can use the 'buffer stocks' to protect themselves.

Similarly, buffering can be applied at the output end of the transformation process. A manufacturer could make its products and put them into a finished goods inventory. Output stocks, however, are not usually relevant to people-processing operations because customers enter the operation as an input. They have usually been processed and the service completed by the time they emerge. Again, operations do not necessarily need to have output stocks;

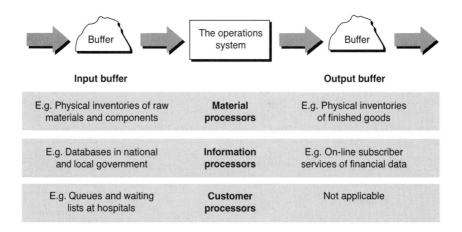

Figure 2.6 Physical buffering can be used to protect the operation against environmental uncertainty

they could react to each customer's request as it was made. Yet if they are able to stock their output, the operation is given much more stability under conditions of demand uncertainty.

Organizational buffering

In many organizations the responsibility for acquiring the inputs to the operation and distributing its outputs to customers is not given to the operations function. For example, the people who staff the operation are recruited and trained by the personnel function; the process technology for the operation is probably selected and commissioned by a technical function; the materials, parts, services and other bought-in resources are acquired through a purchasing function; and the orders from customers which trigger the operation into activity will come through the marketing function. The other functions of the organization are, in effect, forming a barrier or buffer between the uncertainties of the environment and the operations function (see Fig. 2.7).

These relationships have developed partly for stability. Stability is important because it allows the operation to organize itself for maximum efficiency. Organizational buffering, it is also claimed, allows the other functions to specialize in their own particular tasks and leave the operations function to get on with the job of producing goods and services.

The disadvantages of buffering the operation

The whole concept of buffering the operations function is not without its critics, especially in recent years, and partly due to the influence of Japanese operations practice.

A number of objections to buffering can be made:

- The time lag of communicating between the insulating function and the operations function makes change difficult. By the time the insulating function has responded, operations has 'moved on to the next problem'.
- Operations never develops the understanding of the environment (e.g. labour or technological markets) which would help it exploit new developments [. . .].

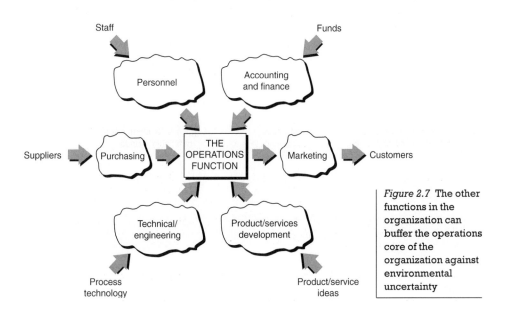

Figure 2.7 The other functions in the organization can buffer the operations core of the organization against environmental uncertainty

- Operations is never required to take responsibility for its actions. There is always another function to blame and unhelpful conflict may arise between functions.
- Physical buffering often involves tolerating large stocks of input or output resources. These are both expensive [. . .] and prevent the operation improving [. . .].
- Physical buffering in customer-processing operations means making the customer wait for service, which in turn could lead to customer dissatisfaction.

For all of these reasons, there has been, in general and in most types of operation, a move towards exposing the operations function to its environment. Operations, in order to cope with this, has needed to develop the necessary flexibility to respond to, and understand, what is really happening with its customers and suppliers.

NOTE

*   This chapter has been adapted from excerpts from, Slack, N., Chambers, S., Harland, C., Harrison, A. and Johnston, R. (1998) *Operations Management* (2nd edn), ch. 1, London, Pitman.

REFERENCES

1   Sources: Thornhill, J. (1992) 'Hard Sell on the High Street', The *Financial Times*, May 16. Horovitz, J. and Jurgens Panak, M. (1992) *Total Customer Satisfaction*, Pitman Publishing. Walley, P. and Hart, K. (1993) IKEA (UK) Ltd, Loughborough University Business School.
2   Heizer, J.H. and Render, B. (1988) *Production and Operations Management* (3rd edn), Allyn and Bacon, p. 5.

SECTION 2: BUSINESS PROCESSES AND ORGANISATIONAL SUCCESS

INTRODUCTION

This section highlights the importance of processes, and the resources they require, to organisational success. In particular it examines their role in an organisation's attempt to achieve competitive advantage. All business activity inevitably adds costs. However, if organisations are to be commercially successful, they need their activities to add value for their customers. Organisations in the private sectors need to add value in order to generate profits for their shareholders and to invest for the future. Although some organisations do not seek profits as such (notably those in the public and voluntary sectors), they still need to offer superior value for money in order to satisfy their various stakeholders. As such, all organisations usually aim to add value through their business processes whilst minimising costs. The extent to which an organisation is able to add value and compete successfully is likely to be closely related to its ability to manage its business processes to best effect.

In chapter 3, Kay poses the question, what is organisational success and how can it be measured? He advocates the use of 'added value' as the best measure of organisational success. Added value is the difference in value between a firm's outputs and inputs. It arises from the firm's activities. He argues that 'adding value is the central purpose of business activity. A commercial organisation which adds no value has no long term rationale for its existence.' This must surely be true for all types of organisations. The way that an organisation manages its business processes is crucial to its success.

In chapter 4, Stalk *et al.* argue that the firm's business processes can be used to achieve competitive advantage if they are viewed as strategic capabilities. These capabilities, which exist within its business processes, are what can set one organisation apart from its competitors. An organisation's capabilities offer the means of achieving superior performance. As such, business processes should be made central to managerial action, and invested in for the long term. As business processes are likely to cut across the existing structural arrangements (of departments, functions, business units etc), they need to be analysed and understood systemically, as decisions taken within one department are likely to have a crucial impact on a process as a whole.

In chapter 5, Porter introduces his influential Value Chain model. This offers a way of examining the activities of an organisation. In particular it provides the means of identifying where value is added and from where an organisation might have a source of competitive advantage. Only by breaking down these activities into discrete elements can one fully understand the organisation strategically, to, as Porter puts it 'understand the behaviour of costs and potential sources of differentiation'. The Value Chain model is in effect a template that offers the means of analysing the activities of any organisation. As such, it offers a way of comparing one organisation with another and of examining linkages between an organisation, its suppliers, channels and buyers. The key message from Porter is that it is essential that organisations have value chains that are appropriate to their purpose and that activities need to add value when viewed through the eyes of their customers.

All three chapters in section 2 stress the importance of the organisation's activities in creating value for the purchasers of its products, its customers. As Porter notes, only those activities that can add value to inputs can create 'a product valuable to its buyers' and thereby generate a margin for the organisation.

3

ADDING VALUE*

John Kay

What is corporate success, and how is it measured? In this chapter I explore the strengths and weaknesses of common performance measures by comparing six British supermarket chains. Some people judge success by size. They look at a firm's sales, its market share, and its value on the stock market. Sometimes performance is assessed by reference to rate of return. This can be measured as return on equity, on investment, or on sales. And sometimes success is measured by growth, reflected in increase in output, movements in earnings per share, or prospectively, the firm's price–earnings ratio.

All of these are aspects of successful performance. But I argue in this chapter that the key measure of corporate success is added value. Added value is the difference between the (comprehensively accounted) value of a firm's output and the (comprehensively accounted) cost of the firm's inputs. In this specific sense, adding value is both the proper motivation of corporate activity and the measure of its achievement.

This chapter defines and develops the objective of added value. It introduces the added value statement and the analysis of the value chain as means of making a quantitative appraisal of a firm's operating activities. This contrasts with the usual financial statements which concentrate, appropriate for their purpose, on returns to investors. [. . .] In the final part of the chapter I use the added value criterion to identify the most successful European companies of the last decade.

Glaxo is not the largest public company in Europe. Depending on the criterion used – turnover, employment, net output – that title goes to Royal Dutch Shell, Europe's largest oil company, to Daimler–Benz, the German engineering conglomerate which owns Mercedes, or to British Telecom. Shell's sales are twenty times those of Glaxo, and Daimler–Benz, with nearly 400,000 employees, has a workforce ten times larger.

The difference in earnings is less marked, but BT's profits are twice those of Glaxo and Shell's twice those of BT. Glaxo's return on capital employed is exceptional – around 40 per cent. But there are many smaller companies which post higher rates of return. And pharmaceutical companies generally show a return on capital which is abnormally high since neither their principal investments (in research and development) nor their principal assets (the value of their drug portfolio) are recorded in their balance sheets.

Glaxo has done well for its shareholders. Money invested in the company in 1980 would have been worth thirty times as much in 1990. But the stock market provides the market's

LIBRARY
BISHOP BURTON COLLEGE
BEVERLEY HU17 8QG

estimate of success. It is not itself the measure of success. You would have done better still to invest your money in Polly Peck over that same period but you would subsequently have learnt that the company's chief executive had been arrested on fraud charges and that your shares were, in fact, worthless. It is unwise to rely on market performance alone as a guide to corporate effectiveness.

So what defines a successful company? Success is intrinsically a relative concept. The best way to understand what it means is to compare the performance of different firms in the same line of business.

BRITISH SUPERMARKETS

Food retailing in Britain is dominated by six chains. The oldest and largest is Sainsbury's. John Sainsbury opened the company's first grocery store in south London over a century ago, and the family tradition and the philosophy of good quality products at competitive prices have remained central to the firm ever since. Conservatively managed, the company came to the stock market only in 1973 and since then has expanded steadily from its loyal, and mostly southern, customer base.

Tesco came into existence as an aggressive discounter and the slogan coined by its colourful founder Jack (eventually to be Lord) Cohen– 'pile 'em high, sell 'em cheap' – still hangs around the company's neck. It is a slogan the company would like to forget because from 1977 the firm executed a bold strategic move. Tesco decided to shift market position and attract a different target customer. It offered higher price, higher quality products more like those of Sainsbury's and put a much greater emphasis on fresh foods and on own label goods. Today Tesco rivals Sainsbury's in both market position and market share.

Both Gateway and Argyll were created by amalgamations between weaker chains. Argyll's most important move was the purchase of the UK operations of the US Safeway corporation, and it has since focused its own shops around Safeway's business concept. Gateway was created by the acquisitive ambitions of Alec Monk, an aggressive chief executive whose star fell as rapidly as it had risen. His sprawling retail conglomerate was taken over in 1989 by a highly leveraged investor consortium, Isosceles, which has not found it easy to rationalize its operations into a profitable business.

Asda emerged from Associated Dairies, which distributed milk and dairy products in the north of England. The company pioneered large out-of-town superstores at a time when these were strongly resisted by established shop-keepers and planning authorities. Thereafter, the company began to lose its way. It diversified unsuccessfully into furniture retailing. It attempted to match Tesco's shift of position but its commitment to the change was signalled less clearly. Asda still has more non-food sales than any of the other stores, and this can be seen in its higher net margins. In 1991 Asda faced serious financial difficulties, embarked on a major fund-raising operation and appointed a new chief executive. With Asda's move up-market, the mantle of 'pile 'em high, sell 'em cheap' fell on Kwik Save, a chain of discount shops selling a limited range of branded goods at low prices from basic stores mostly in secondary locations.

The performance of these companies can be compared in many ways (Table 3.1). Sainsbury's has the largest market share, closely followed by Tesco. The profits of the companies, and their value on the stock market, follow broadly the order of their size. Kwik Save, although the smallest of the chains, is very profitable – its returns on investment and on equity are the highest in the sector. The firm does not do quite so well on either gross or net margin – gross margins are lower in a 'no frills' operation and its net margin is held back by its low-price, high-volume strategy. Asda, with a high proportion of more profitable non-food sales, comes out well here.

Table 3.1 Performance of supermarkets, 1989

	Asda	Gateway	Argyll	Tesco	Sainsbury's	Kwik Save
Size (Ecus m)						
Turnover	3,782	6,308	4,889	6,587	7,902	1,649
Profit	218	286	218	383	515	81
Market capitalization	2,678	2,378	2,319	3,281	4,699	1,184
Return (%)						
Gross margin	*9.3	5.0	5.4	7.3	8.2	6.5
Net margin	6.2	3.5	3.6	3.9	4.4	4.1
ROI	18.9	NA	25.6	22.8	20.5	*40.5
ROE	18.0	17.0	24.0	18.0	21.0	*27.0
Shareholder return (1 year)	−10	3	−2	3	0	*24
Shareholder return (10 years)	45	293	*367	280	326	283
Growth						
Sales Growth (%)	10	−12	8	15	18	*27
EPS growth (%)	14	16	23	17	23	*36
PE ratio	13	14	14	17	18	*23
Efficiency						
Sales/Ecus per square foot	759	NA	1,146	771	*1,323	NA
Stock turnover	13	NA	13	*24	20	19

NA Not available. * Italicized figures show best performer on each measure.
Source: Own calculations on data derived from Micro Extel and company annual reports

Sainsbury's and Tesco show lower returns on investment or equity than either Kwik Save or Argyll. Yet this is more a warning that these are unreliable indicators than a comment on the performance of the companies. Supermarkets have usually sold goods for cash at the checkout before they have paid their suppliers, and working capital for all these companies is actually negative. Little is needed in the way of fixed assets, beyond shop fittings and delivery vehicles, since the stores themselves may be leased. Kwik Save's return on capital is very high because there is very little capital employed in the Kwik Save business.

Sainsbury's and Tesco – the chains which have dominated the sector for many years – have chosen to reinvest heavily in building their own superstores. This would be a foolish thing for them to have done if they could have earned returns as high as those of Argyll and Kwik Save by developing the business in some other way. But they could not. The return on capital is simply a ratio of two numbers, not a guide to what you will earn by investing more in the business, and Tesco and Sainsbury's have been using their capital as effectively as they can. It is worth their while to invest in stores so long as they can earn more from building stores than the 10 per cent or so return on capital they would have got from the bank. It mostly is worth their while, because the Sainsbury's or Tesco name adds value to a site (which a Kwik Save logo does not) and the stores needed for a Tesco or Sainsbury's style of operation are relatively specialist in nature. Ownership is a means by which Sainsbury's and Tesco can retain the whole of the added value their activities create. This reinvestment has the effect of driving down their return on capital but it makes them, taken as a whole, more profitable businesses not less.

What of return to shareholders? In 1989 only Kwik Save did well. This is not because the other businesses were doing badly but because the stock market (correctly) anticipated a recession which would favour Kwik Save's trading approach and damage the sales of other retailers. On a ten-year timescale, the outstanding performers are Argyll (which was a tiny company at the beginning of the decade) and Sainsbury's.

Kwik Save is the fastest growing of the chains – no surprise there, since it is also the smallest. Kwik Save also shows the most rapid growth in earnings per share. The price–earnings ratio is a measure of market analysts' evaluation of the quality of the company's earnings and their expectations of their security and growth. This measure divides the sector clearly into three groups. Kwik Save is on its own, with the highest PE ratio. Sainsbury's and Tesco each have similar ratings. Argyll, Asda, and Gateway have much lower market evaluations.

All these are financial measures of performance. What of the technical efficiency of these firms? Sainsbury's sells more goods per square foot than anyone else. Sainsbury's and Tesco turn over their stock most rapidly, but so they should, given their emphasis on fresh produce. In this light, Kwik Save, which relies heavily on packaged goods, comes out particularly well. All these measures tell us something about these companies. None, in itself, gives a complete picture.

THE ADDED VALUE STATEMENT

What underpins the success of firms such as Glaxo, Sainsbury's, or Kwik Save is their ability to add value to the inputs they use. Table 3.2 sets this out for Glaxo. In 1990 the company bought materials worth 1,528m Ecus. Its wage and salary bill was 901m Ecus and the cost of the capital which the company used – premises, factories, machinery, and equipment – was 437m Ecus. The resulting product was sold for 3,985m Ecus, 1,120m Ecus more than it cost.

That figure of 1,120m Ecus is a measure of the added value which Glaxo created. It is the difference between the market value of its output and the cost of its inputs. It is a measure of the loss which would result, to national income and to the international economy, if Glaxo were to be broken up and the resources it uses deployed in other firms. Adding value, in this sense, is the central purpose of business activity. A commercial organization which adds no value – whose output is worth no more than the value of its inputs in alternative uses – has no long-term rationale for its existence.

This assessment of added value is one which accounts comprehensively for the inputs which Glaxo used. It includes not only the depreciation of its capital assets but also provides for a reasonable return on the capital invested in them.[1] So added value is less than the *operating* profit of the firm – the difference between the value of output and the value of material and labour inputs (but not capital inputs). It is also less than the net output of the firm – the difference between the value of its sales and the cost of its inputs of materials (but not its inputs of labour or capital).

The strength of Glaxo's competitive advantage can be measured by looking at the ratio of added value to the firm's gross or net output. Each unit of Glaxo's sales costs

Table 3.2 Added value statement: Glaxo, 1990

Relationships	Financial Flow	Value (m Ecus)
Customers	Revenues	3,985
Labour	Wages and salaries	901
Investors	Capital costs	437
Suppliers	Materials	1,528
	Added value	1,120

Source: Glaxo plc annual report and accounts

only 0.72 units to produce. Glaxo's net output is the 2,457m Ecus difference between the cost of the materials it bought and the value of the output it sold. It achieved this with only 1,338 m Ecus of labour and capital, representing a cost of 0.54 Ecus per Ecu of net output.

Figure 3.1 looks at the UK supermarket industry the same way. The added value created by the industry as a whole is small at just over 1 per cent of gross output because some individual chains, like Asda and Gateway, are struggling, and partly because five-sixths of the output of the industry is accounted for by the cost of supplies. This is hardly surprising for self-service retailers [. . .] A comparison of added value and net output brings out the performance differences more clearly and this is done in Figure 3.2.

There are two clearly outstanding performers in the sector – Sainsbury's and Kwik Save. The width of the sections in Figure 3.2 reflects the size of the company. Sainsbury's adds most value overall, Kwik Save the most per unit of input. Each Ecu of Asda's output costs it 1.01 Ecus. Each Ecu of Kwik Save's, 0.82 Ecus. In a contestable market, characterized by rivalry and easy entry and exit, a firm with no competitive advantage will sell a unit of inputs for precisely one unit. So these ratios measure the strength of Kwik Save's competitive advantage. As Kwik Save grows – Figure 3.3 – it is likely, perhaps inevitable, that it will move into markets or market segments where its competitive advantage is less strong. But so long as it has some competitive advantage, the added value created by the business as a whole will continue to increase. For a more mature business – like Sainsbury's – overall competitive advantage is less but added value greater.

Glaxo's competitive advantage is stronger than that of any supermarket. By this criterion, Kwik Save's added value is 18 Ecus for each 100 Ecus of output, Glaxo's 46 Ecus per hundred. That results from the different market conditions the latter company faces. In its principal market – that for anti-ulcerant drugs – its main competitors are Tagamet and a more recent therapy with a different pharmacological approach, Losec, manufactured by the Swedish company Astra. But Zantac is widely thought to be superior to Tagamet. Losec must compete with Zantac's established record and reputation with doctors and their patients. The market is not very sensitive to price. Sufferers will readily pay a premium for

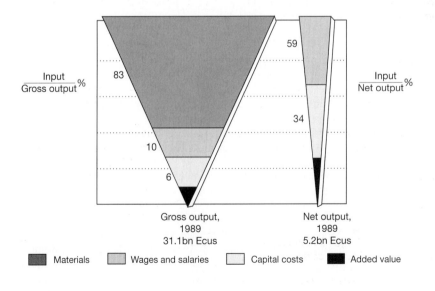

Figure 3.1 Value chains for UK supermarket sector, 1989

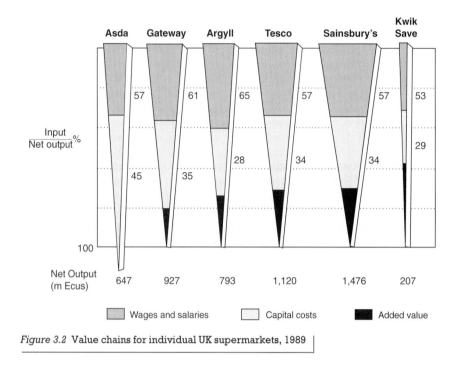

Figure 3.2 Value chains for individual UK supermarkets, 1989

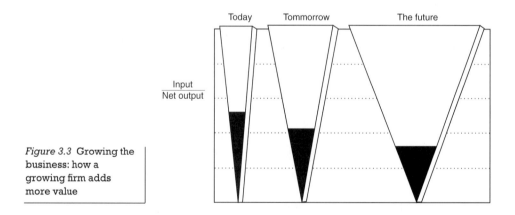

Figure 3.3 Growing the business: how a growing firm adds more value

what their doctors think is a better product and in many geographic markets much of the cost is in any case borne by the government or by insurers. Glaxo's competitive advantage in this market will diminish as other drugs become available and more familiar and as the end of patent protection allows more direct competition from generic versions of Zantac itself. But for the moment, Glaxo's competitive advantage remains strong.

Not all firms succeed in adding value. Table 3.3 shows the added value statement for the Dutch electrical giant Philips. Each Ecu of Philips's output cost it 1.08 Ecus to produce. It was unable to cover the full costs of its activities in the competitive markets it faced. Philips is a striking case because it is a firm with enormous strengths and clear distinctive capabilities. Its record of innovation in consumer electronics is second to none

Table 3.3 Added value statement: Philips, 1990 (m Ecus)

Revenues	24,247
Wages and salaries	7,666
Capital costs	2,932
Materials	15,716
Added value	(2,067)

Source: Philips NV annual reports and accounts

– the company invented the compact cassette and pioneered the compact disc (CD) and video-cassette recorder (VCR). Yet it has repeatedly failed to translate these innovations into its own commercial success. The contrast between Glaxo and Philips, like that between Glaxo and EMI, is a measure of the importance of strategy in translating distinctive capability into competitive advantage.

EUROPEAN WINNERS

By the criterion of added value, Glaxo is a success, and Philips a failure. Table 3.4 shows the European Community's 'top ten' firms of the 1980s measured by the ratio of added value to net output. Most of the companies in that list are household names. Benetton is famous for its knitwear, sold through franchised outlets around the world. Reuters began as a news service, providing syndicated material to newspapers, but its principal operations and profits are now derived from providing on-screen information in financial markets. Petrofina is Belgium's oil company with a range of upstream and downstream interests. LVMH is a French conglomerate focused on luxury goods. The company's title reflects three, Louis Vuitton luggage, Moët et Chandon champagne, and Hennessey cognac. Guinness produces not only the famous Irish stout, but also controls many leading brands of Scotch whisky – Johnnie Walker, Bell's – and other branded drinks such as Gordon's Gin.

Cable and Wireless is a British-based international telecommunications company. It holds the franchise for local telephone services in Hong Kong, owns Mercury, the second licensed public telecommunications operator in the UK, and provides international services around the world. BTR is an acquisitive, wide-ranging manufacturing conglomerate which

Table 3.4 Europe's most successful companies, 1981–1990

Position	Company	Activity	Country	Costs per unit of net output	Sales (m Ecus)
1	Glaxo	Pharmaceuticals	UK	.54	3,498
2	Benetton	Textile	Italy	.57	1,019
3	Reuters	Information	UK	.67	1,206
4	Petrofina	Oil	Belgium	.67	13,979
5	Kwik Save	Food Retailing	UK	.68	1,609
6	LVMH	Luxury Goods	France	.70	2,583
7	Guinness	Drinks	UK	.71	3,875
8	Cable and Wireless	Telecom	UK	.72	1,959
9	BTR	Conglomerate	UK	.74	7,404
10	Marks & Spencer	Retailing	UK	.74	7,678

Source: Own calculations based on Euroequities database (chosen from non-financial companies with sales in excess of 1 billion Ecus)

has earned large returns both by trading in businesses and by squeezing additional profits from the firms it has taken over. Marks & Spencer is a British retailer, now increasing its operations in continental Europe, most famous for its range of reliable clothing at value for money prices.

The list contains a disproportionate number of UK companies and Table 3.5 attempts to redress this balance by identifying the leading companies in each of the main regions of the European Community. Some common characteristics are clearly apparent among the companies represented in both the overall European list, and in these regional lists – brands and reputation, customer and supplier relationships, market dominance and control of strategic assets. These are key elements in successful strategies [. . .]

Corporate success is not measured by size, or market dominance. Coroporate success is not simply about the magnitude of profits. Shell and British Telecom earned much larger profits than any company in Table 3.4 but they did so because they are very large companies. But nor is success just about the rate of return on capital. You can run a drug company with very little capital employed but not an oil business or a telephone network. Size, market share, and profitability are aspects of corporate success, but success is not any one of these alone. The reason I believe it is appropriate to describe Glaxo as the most successful European company of the 1980s is that, more than any other major company, Glaxo added value to the resources it used. It is that achievement in adding value which underpins the financial returns, provides the basis for its future development, and explains the remarkable returns which its shareholders have enjoyed. [. . .]

Table 3.5 European companies by region, 1981–1990

Position	Company	Activity	Costs per unit of net output	Sales (m Ecus)
UK/Ireland				
1	Glaxo	Pharmaceuticals	.54	3,498
2	Reuters	Information	.67	1,206
3	Kwik Save	Food Retailing	.68	1,609
Italy				
1	Benetton	Textile	.57	1,019
2	Eridania	Food	.88	3,449
3	Mondadori	Printing	.90	1,092
Benelux				
1	Petrofina	Oil	.67	13,979
2	Hunter Douglas	Household Goods	.82	1,001
3	Unilever UK	Consumer Goods	.85	31,992
Spain/Portugal				
1	Tabacalera	Tobacco	.91	3,780
2	Cepsa	Oil	.92	4,235
Germany				
1	Wella	Toiletries	.83	1,091
2	BMW	Cars	.84	11,079
3	Porsche	Cars	.85	1,558
France				
1	LVMH	Luxury Goods	.70	2,583
2	Bongrain	Food	.83	1,065
3	Pernod Ricard	Drinks	.84	1,699

Source: Own calculations based on Euroequities database

Table 3.6 Value of the Ecu at 1 January 1992

Australia	$1.76
Austria	14.3 Sch.
Belgium	41.9 Fr.
Canada	$1.55
Denmark	7.93 Kr.
France	6.95 FF
Germany	2.04 DM
Greece	235 Dr.
Ireland	£0.766
Italy	1542 Lire
Japan	Y169
The Netherlands	2.29 Guilder
New Zealand	$2.48
Norway	8.02 Kr.
Spain	138 Peseta
Sweden	7.45 Kr.
Switzerland	1.82 SFr.
UK	£0.716
USA	$1.34

All jurisdictions require corporations to file annual financial statements. Stock market performance is widely tracked and the listing requirements of the principal stock exchanges impose further obligations to provide data. (US requirements are particularly stringent and many large European companies have now obtained US quotations for their shares.) European company legislation generally requires firms to disclose overall employee remuneration and other information about their workforce and employment practices. US and Japanese firms do not have similar obligations, and this restricts analysis of the structure of their added value using published information. Several commercial databases provide standardized company analyses, mainly directed at potential investors. The high-quality database maintained by Euroequities formed the basis of the analysis of Europe's most successful companies described in Tables 3.4 and 3.5 [. . .].

NOTE

* This chapter hass been adapted from, Kay, J. (1993) *Foundations of Corporate Success*, ch. 2, Oxford, Oxford University Press.
1 The most appropriate means of charging for capital costs is a complex question. The calculations in this chapter simply impose a rate of return on operating assets of 10%.

4

COMPETING ON CAPABILITIES*

George Stalk, Philip Evans and Lawrence Shulman

In the 1980s, companies discovered time as a new source of competitive advantage. In the 1990s, they will learn that time is just one piece of a more far-reaching transformation in the logic of competition.

Companies that compete effectively on time – speeding new products to market, manufacturing just in time, or responding promptly to customer complaints – tend to be good at other things as well: for instance, the consistency of their product quality, the acuity of their insight into evolving customer needs, the ability to exploit emerging markets, enter new businesses, or generate new ideas and incorporate them in innovations. But all these qualities are mere reflections of a more fundamental characteristic: a new conception of corporate strategy that we call capabilities-based competition.

FOUR PRINCIPLES OF CAPABILITIES-BASED COMPETITION

In industry after industry, established competitors are being outmaneuvered and overtaken by more dynamic rivals. In the years after World War II, Honda was a modest manufacturer of a 50cc engine designed to be attached to a bicycle. Today it is challenging General Motors and Ford for dominance of the global automobile industry. Xerox invented xerography and the office copier market. But between 1976 and 1982, Canon introduced more than 90 new models, cutting Xerox's share of the midrange copier market in half. Today Canon is a key competitor not only in midrange copiers but also in high-end color copiers.

The greatest challenge to department store giants like Macy's comes neither from other large department stores nor from small boutiques but from The Limited, a $5.25 billion design, procurement, delivery, and retailing machine that exploits dozens of consumer segments with the agility of many small boutiques. Citicorp may still be the largest US bank in terms of assets, but Banc One has consistently enjoyed the highest return on assets in the US banking industry and now enjoys a market capitalization greater than Citicorp's.

These examples represent more than just the triumph of individual companies. They signal a fundamental shift in the logic of competition, a shift that is revolutionizing corporate strategy.

When the economy was relatively static, strategy could afford to be static. In a world characterized by durable products, stable customer needs, well-defined national and regional markets, and clearly identified competitors, competition was a 'war of position' in which companies occupied competitive space like squares on a chessboard, building and defending market share in clearly defined product or market segments. The key to competitive advantage was *where* a company chose to compete. *How* it chose to compete was also important but secondary, a matter of execution.

Few managers need reminding of the changes that have made this traditional approach obsolete. As markets fragment and proliferate, 'owning' any particular market segment becomes simultaneously more difficult and less valuable. As product life cycles accelerate, dominating existing product segments becomes less important than being able to create new products and exploit them quickly. Meanwhile, as globalization breaks down barriers between national and regional markets, competitors are multiplying and reducing the value of national market share.

In this more dynamic business environment, strategy has to become correspondingly more dynamic. Competition is now a 'war of movement' in which success depends on anticipation of market trends and quick response to changing customer needs. Successful competitors move quickly in and out of products, markets, and sometimes even entire businesses – a process more akin to an interactive video game than to chess. In such an environment, the essence of strategy is not the structure of a company's products and markets but the dynamics of its behavior. And the goal is to identify and develop the hard-to-imitate organizational capabilities that distinguish a company from its competitors in the eyes of customers.

Companies like Wal-Mart, Honda, Canon, The Limited, or Banc One have learned this lesson. Their experience and that of other successful companies suggest four basic principles of capabilities-based competition:

- The building blocks of corporate strategy are not products and markets but business processes.
- Competitive success depends on transforming a company's key processes into strategic capabilities that consistently provide superior value to the customer.
- Companies create these capabilities by making strategic investments in a support infrastructure that links together and transcends traditional strategic business units (SBUs) and functions.
- Because capabilities necessarily cross functions, the champion of a capabilities-based strategy is the chief executive officer (CEO).

A capability is a set of business processes strategically understood. Every company has business processes that deliver value to the customer. But few think of them as the primary object of strategy. Capabilities-based competitors identify their key business processes, manage them centrally, and invest in them heavily, looking for a long-term payback.

What transforms a set of individual business processes into a strategic capability? The key is to connect them to real customer needs. A capability is strategic only when it begins and ends with the customer. Of course, just about every company these days claims to be 'close to the customer.' But there is a qualitative difference in the customer focus of capabilities-driven competitors. These companies conceive of the organization as a giant feed-back loop that begins with identifying the needs of the customer and ends with satisfying them.

As managers have grasped the importance of time-based competition, for example, they have increasingly focused on the speed of new product *development*. But as a unit of analysis, new product development is too narrow. It is only part of what is necessary to satisfy a customer and, therefore, to build an organizational capability. Better to think in terms of new product *realization*, a capability that includes the way a product is not only developed but also marketed and serviced. The longer and more complex the string of business processes, the harder it is to transform them into a capability – but the greater the value of that capability once built because competitors have more difficulty imitating it.

Weaving business processes together into organizational capabilities in this way also mandates a new logic of vertical integration. At a time when cost pressures are pushing many companies to outsource more and more activities, capabilities-based competitors are integrating vertically to ensure that they, not a supplier or distributor, control the performance of key business processes. Even when a company doesn't actually own every link of the capability chain, the capabilities-based competitor works to tie these parts into its own business systems.

Another attribute of capabilities is that they are collective and cross functional – a small part of many people's jobs, not a large part of a few. This helps explain why most companies underexploit capabilities-based competition. Because a capability is 'everywhere and nowhere,' no one executive controls it entirely. Moreover, leveraging capabilities requires a panoply of strategic investments across SBUs and functions far beyond what traditional cost-benefit metrics can justify. Traditional internal accounting and control systems often miss the strategic nature of such investments. For these reasons, building strategic capabilities cannot be treated as an operating matter and left to operating managers, to corporate staff, or still less to SBU heads. It is the primary agenda of the CEO. The prize will be companies that combine scale and flexibility to outperform the competition along five dimensions:

1 *Speed* The ability to respond quickly to customer or market demands and incorporate new ideas and technologies quickly into products.
2 *Consistency* The ability to produce a product that unfailingly satisfies customers' expectations.
3 *Acuity* The ability to see the competitive environment clearly and thus to anticipate and respond to customers' evolving needs and wants.
4 *Agility* The ability to adapt simultaneously to many different business environments.
5 *Innovativeness* The ability to generate new ideas and to combine existing elements to create new sources of value.

BECOMING A CAPABILITIES-BASED COMPETITOR

Few companies are fortunate enough to begin as capabilities-based competitors. For most, the challenge is to become one.

The starting point is for senior managers to undergo the fundamental shift in perception that allows them to see their business in terms of strategic capabilities. Then they can begin to identify and link together essential business processes to serve customer needs. Finally, they can reshape the organization – including managerial roles and responsibilities – to encourage the new kind of behavior necessary to make capabilities-based competition work.

The experience of a medical-equipment company we'll call Medequip illustrates this change process. An established competitor, Medequip recently found itself struggling to regain market share it had lost to a new competitor. The rival had introduced a lower-priced, lower-performance version of the company's most popular product. Medequip had developed a similar product in response, but senior managers were hesitant to launch it. Their reasoning made perfect sense according to the traditional competitive logic. As managers saw it, the company faced a classic no-win situation. The new product was lower priced but also lower profit. If the company promoted it aggressively to regain market share, overall profitability would suffer.

But when Medequip managers began to investigate their competitive situation more carefully, they stopped defining the problem in terms of static products and markets. Increasingly, they saw it in terms of the organization's business processes. Traditionally, the company's functions had operated autonomously. Manufacturing was separate from sales, which was separate from field service. What's more, the company managed field service the way most companies do – as a classic profit center whose resources were deployed to reduce costs and maximize profitability. For instance, Medequip assigned full-time service personnel only to those customers who bought enough equipment to justify the additional cost.

However, a closer look at the company's experience with these steady customers led to a fresh insight: at accounts where Medequip had placed one or more full-time service representatives on-site, the company renewed its highly profitable service contracts at three times the rate of its other accounts. When these accounts needed new equipment, they chose Medequip twice as often as other accounts did and tended to buy the broadest mix of Medequip products as well. The reason was simple. Medequip's on-site service representatives had become expert in the operations of their customers. They knew what equipment mix best suited the customer and what additional equipment the customer needed. So they had teamed up informally with Medequip's salespeople to become part of the selling process. Because the service reps were on-site full-time, they were also able to respond quickly to equipment problems. And of course, whenever a competitor's equipment broke down, the Medequip reps were on hand to point out the product's shortcomings.

This new knowledge about the dynamics of service delivery inspired top managers to rethink how their company should compete. Specifically, they redefined field service from a stand-alone function to one part of an integrated sales and service capability. They crystallized this new approach in three key business decisions.

First, Medequip decided to use its service personnel not to keep costs low but to maximize the life-cycle profitability of a set of targeted accounts. This decision took the form of a dramatic commitment to place at least one service rep on-site with selected customers – no matter how little business each account currently represented.

The decision to guarantee on-site service was expensive, so choosing which customers to target was crucial; there had to be potential for considerable additional business. The company divided its accounts into three categories: those it dominated, those where a single competitor dominated, and those where several competitors were present. Medequip protected the accounts it dominated by maintaining the already high level of service and by offering attractive terms for renewing service contracts. The company ignored those customers dominated by a single competitor – unless the competitor was having serious problems. All the remaining resources were focused on those accounts where no single competitor had the upper hand.

Next Medequip combined its sales, service, and order entry organizations into cross-functional teams that concentrated almost exclusively on the needs of the targeted accounts. The company trained service reps in sales techniques so they could take full responsibility for generating new sales leads. This freed up the sales staff to focus on the more strategic role of understanding the long-term needs of the customer's business. Finally, to emphasize Medequip's new commitment to total service, the company even taught its service reps how to fix competitor's equipment.

Once this new organizational structure was in place, Medequip finally introduced its new low-price product. The result: the company has not only stopped its decline in market share but also *increased* share by almost 50 percent. The addition of the lower-priced product has reduced profit margins, but the overall mix still includes many higher-priced products. And absolute profits are much higher than before.

This story suggests four steps by which any company can transform itself into a capabilities-based competitor.

Shift the strategic framework to achieve aggressive goals

At Medequip, managers transformed what looked like a no-win situation – either lose share or lose profits – into an opportunity for a major competitive victory. They did so by abandoning the company's traditional function, cost, and profit-center orientation and by identifying and managing the capabilities that link customer need to customer satisfaction. The chief expression of this new capabilities-based strategy was the decision to provide on-site service reps to targeted accounts and to create cross-functional sales and service teams.

Organize around the chosen capability and make sure employees have the necessary skills and resources to achieve it

Having set this ambitious competitive goal, Medequip managers next set about reshaping the company in terms of it. Rather than retaining the existing functional structure and trying to encourage coordination through some kind of matrix, they created a brand new organization – Customer Sales and Service – and divided it into 'cells' with overall responsibility for specific customers. The company also provided the necessary training so that employees could understand how their new roles would help achieve new business goals. Finally, Medequip created systems to support employees in their new roles. For example, one information system uses CD-ROMs to give field-service personnel quick access to information about Medequip's product line as well as those of competitors.

Make progress visible and bring measurements and reward into alignment

Medequip also made sure that the company's measurement and reward systems reflected the new competitive strategy. Like most companies, the company had never known the profitability of individual customers. Traditionally, field-service employees were measured on overall service profitability. With the shift to the new approach, however, the company had to develop a whole new set of measures – for example, Medequip's 'share-by-customer-by-product,' the amount of money the company invested in servicing a particular customer, and the customer's current and estimated lifetime profitability. Team members' compensation was calculated according to these new measures.

Do not delegate the leadership of the transformation

Becoming a capabilities-based competitor requires an enormous amount of change. For that reason, it is a process extremely difficult to delegate. Because capabilities are cross-functional, the change process can't be left to middle managers. It requires the hands-on guidance of the CEO and the active involvement of top line managers. At Medequip, the heads of sales service, and order entry led the subteams that made the actual recommendations, but it was the CEO who oversaw the change process, evaluated their proposals, and made the final decision. His leading role ensured senior management's commitment to the recommended changes.

This top-down change process has the paradoxical result of driving business decision making down to those directly participating in key processes – for example, Medequip's sales and service staff. This leads to a high measure of operational flexibility and an almost reflexlike responsiveness to external change.

Box 4.1 How capabilities differ from the core competencies: the case of Honda

In their influential 1990 HBR article, 'The Core Competencies of the Corporation,' [. . .] Gary Hamel and C.K. Prahalad mount an attack on traditional notions of strategy that is not so dissimilar from what we are arguing here. For Hamel and Prahalad, however, the central building block of corporate strategy is 'core competence.' How is a competence different from a capability, and how do the two concepts relate to each other?

Hamel and Prahalad define core competence as the combination of individual technologies and production skills that underly a company's myriad product lines. Sony's core competence in miniaturization, for example, allows the company to make everything from the Sony Walkman to videocameras to notebook computers. Canon's core competencies in optics, imaging, and microprocessor controls have enabled it to enter markets as seemingly diverse as copiers, laser printers, cameras, and image scanners.

As the above examples suggest, Hamel and Prahalad use core competence to explain the ease with which successful competitors are able to enter new and seemingly unrelated businesses. But a closer look reveals that competencies are not the whole story.

Consider Honda's move from motorcycles into other businesses, including lawn mowers, outboard motors, and automobiles. Hamel and Prahalad attribute Honda's success to its underlying competence in engines and power trains. While Honda's engine competence is certainly important, it alone cannot explain the speed with which the company has successfully moved into a wide range of businesses over the past 20 years. After all, General Motors (to take just one example) is also an accomplished designer and manufacturer of engines. What distinguishes Honda from its competitors is its focus on capabilities.

One important but largely invisible capability is Honda's expertise in 'dealer management' – its ability to train and support its dealer network with operating procedures and policies for merchandising, selling floor planning, and service management. First developed for its motorcycle business, this set of business processes has since been replicated in each new business the company has entered.

Another capability central to Honda's success has been its skill at 'product realization.' Traditional product development separates planning, proving, and executing into three sequential activities: assessing the market's needs and whether existing products are meeting those needs; testing the proposed product; then building a prototype. The end result of this process is a new factory or organization to introduce the new product. This traditional approach takes a long time – and with time goes money.

Honda has arranged these activities differently. First, planning and proving go on continuously and in parallel. Second, these activities are clearly separated from execution. At Honda, the highly disciplined execution cycle schedules major product revisions every four years and minor revisions every two years. The 1990 Honda Accord, for example, which is the first major redesign of that model since 1986, incorporates a power train developed two years earlier and first used in the 1988 Accord. Finally, when a new product is ready, it is released to existing factories and organizations, which dramatically shortens the amount of time needed to launch it. As time is reduced, so are cost and risk.

Consider the following comparison between Honda and GM. In 1984, Honda launched its Acura division; one year later, GM created Saturn. Honda chose to integrate Acura into its existing organization and facilities. In Europe, for example, the Acura Legend is sold through the same sales force as the Honda Legend. The Acura division now makes three models – the Legend, Integra, and Vigor – and is turning out 300,000 cars a year. At the end of 1991 seven years after it was launched, the division had produced a total of 800,000 vehicles. More important, it had already introduced eight variations of its product line.

By contrast, GM created a separate organization and a separate facility for Saturn. Production began in late 1990, and 1991 will be its first full model year. If GM is lucky, it will be producing 240,000 vehicles in the next year or two and will have two models out.

As the Honda example suggests, competencies and capabilities represent two different but complementary dimensions of an emerging paradigm for corporate strategy. Both concepts emphasize 'behavioural' aspects of strategy in contrast to the traditional structural model. But whereas core competence emphasizes technological and production expertise at specific points along the value chain, capabilities are more broadly based, encompassing the entire value chain. In this respect, capabilities are visible to the customer in a way that core competencies rarely are.

Like the 'grand unified theory' that modern-day physicists are searching for to explain physical behaviour at both the subatomic level and that of the entire cosmos, the combination of core competence and capabilities may define the universal model for corporate strategy in the 1990s and beyond.

A NEW LOGIC OF GROWTH: THE CAPABILITIES PREDATOR

Once managers reshape the company in terms of its underlying capabilities, they can use these capabilities to define a growth path for the corporation. At the center of capabilities-based competition is a new logic of growth.

In the 1960s, most managers assumed that when growth in a company's basic business slowed, the company should turn to diversification. This was the age of the multibusiness conglomerate. In the 1970s and 1980s, however, it became clear that growth through diversification was difficult. And so, the pendulum of management thinking swung once again. Companies were urged to 'stick to their knitting' – that is, to focus on their core business, identify where the profit was, and get rid of everything else. The idea of the corporation became increasingly narrow.

Competing on capabilities provides a way for companies to gain the benefits of both focus and diversification. Put another way, a company that focuses on its strategic capabilities can compete in a remarkable diversity of regions, products, and businesses and do it far more coherently than the typical conglomerate can. Such a company is a 'capabilities predator' – able to come out of nowhere and move rapidly from nonparticipant to major player and even to industry leader.

Capabilities-based companies grow by transferring their essential business processes – first to new geographic areas and then to new businesses. Wal-Mart CEO David Glass alludes to this method of growth when he characterizes Wal-Mart as 'always pushing from the inside out; we never jump and backfill.'

Strategic advantages built on capabilities are easier to transfer geographically than more traditional competitive advantages. Honda, for example, has become a manufacturer in Europe and the United States with relatively few problems. The quality of its cars made in the United States is so good that the company is exporting some of them back to Japan.

But the big payoff for capabilities-led growth comes not through geographical expansion but through rapid entry into whole new businesses. Capabilities-based companies do this in at least two ways. The first is by 'cloning' their key business processes. Again, Honda is a typical example.

Most people attribute Honda's success to the innovative design of its products or the way the company manufactures them. These factors are certainly important. But the company's growth has been spearheaded by less visible capabilities. For example, a big part of Honda's original success in motorcycles was due to the company's distinctive capability in 'dealer management,' which departed from the traditional relationship between motorcycle manufacturers and dealers. Typically, local dealers were motorcycle enthusiasts who were more concerned with finding a way to support their hobby than with building a strong business. They were not particularly interested in marketing, parts-inventory management, or other business systems.

Honda, by contrast, managed its dealers to ensure that they would become successful businesspeople. The company provided operating procedures and policies for merchandising, selling, floor planning, and service management. It trained all its dealers and their entire staffs in these new management systems and supported them with a computerized dealer-management information system. The part-time dealers of competitors were no match for the better prepared and better financed Honda dealers.

Honda's move into new businesses, including lawn mowers, outboard motors, and automobiles, has depended on recreating this same dealer-management capability in each new sector. Even in segments like luxury cars, where local dealers are generally more service oriented than those in the motorcycle business, Honda's skill at managing its dealers is transforming service standards. Honda dealers consistently receive the highest ratings for customer satisfaction among auto companies selling in the United States. One reason is that Honda gives its dealers far more automony to decide on the spot whether a needed repair is covered by the warranty (see Box 4.1).

But the ultimate form of growth in the capabilities-based company may not be cloning business processes so much as creating processes so flexible and robust that the same set can serve many different businesses.

THE FUTURE OF CAPABILITIES-BASED COMPETITION

For the moment, capabilities-based companies have the advantage of competing against rivals still locked into the old way of seeing the competitive environment. But such a situation won't last forever. As more and more companies make the transition to capabilities-based competition, the simple fact of competing on capabilities will become less important than the specific capabilities a company has chosen to build. Given the necessary long-term investments, the strategic choices managers make will end up determining a company's fate.

NOTE

* This chapter has been adapted from, Stalk, G., Evans, P. and Shulman, I. (1992) *Harvard Business Review*, March/April.

REFERENCE

Prahalad, C.K. and Hamel, G. (1990) 'The Core Competence of the Corporation' *Harvard Business Review*, May/June, pp. 79–91.

5

THE VALUE CHAIN AND COMPETITIVE ADVANTAGE*

Michael Porter

Competitive advantage cannot be understood by looking at a firm as a whole. It stems from the many discrete activities a firm performs in designing, producing, marketing, delivering, and supporting its product. Each of these activities can contribute to a firm's relative cost position and create a basis for differentiation. A cost advantage, for example, may stem from such disparate sources as a low-cost physical distribution system, a highly efficient assembly process, or superior sales force utilization. Differentiation can stem from similarly diverse factors, including the procurement of high quality raw materials, a responsive order entry system, or a superior product design.

A systematic way of examining all the activities a firm performs and how they interact is necessary for analyzing the sources of competitive advantage. In this chapter, I introduce the *value chain* as the basic tool for doing so. The value chain disaggregates a firm into its strategically relevant activities in order to understand the behavior of costs and the existing and potential sources of differentiation. A firm gains competitive advantage by performing these strategically important activities more cheaply or better than its competitors.

A firm's value chain is embedded in a larger stream of activities that I term the *value system*, illustrated in Figure 5.1. Suppliers have value chains (*upstream value*) that create and deliver the purchased inputs used in a firm's chain. Suppliers not only deliver a product but also can influence a firm's performance in many other ways. In addition, many products pass through the value chains of channels (*channel value*) on their way to the buyer. Channels perform additional activities that affect the buyer, as well as influence the firm's own activities. A firm's product eventually becomes part of its *buyer's value chain*. The ultimate basis for differentiation is a firm and its product's role in the buyer's value chain, which determines buyer needs. Gaining and sustaining competitive advantage depends on understanding not only a firm's value chain but how the firm fits in the overall value system.

The value chains of firms in an industry differ, reflecting their histories, strategies, and success at implementation. One important difference is that a firm's value chain may differ in *competitive scope* from that of its competitors, representing a potential source of competitive advantage. Serving only a particular industry segment may allow a firm to tailor its value chain to that segment and result in lower costs or differentiation in serving that segment

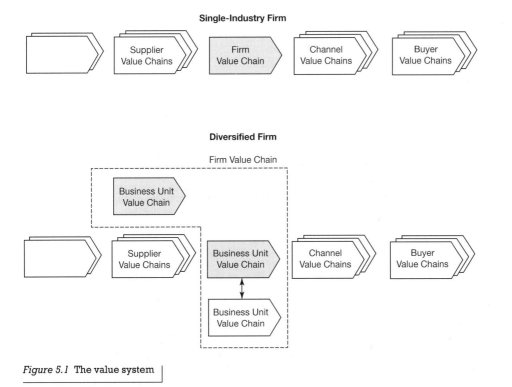

Figure 5.1 The value system

compared to competitors. Widening or narrowing the geographic markets served can also affect competitive advantage. The extent of integration into activities plays a key role in competitive advantage. Finally, competing in related industries with coordinated value chains can lead to competitive advantage through interrelationships. A firm may exploit the benefits of broader scope internally or it may form coalitions with other firms to do so. Coalitions are long-term alliances with other firms that fall short of outright merger, such as joint ventures, licenses, and supply agreements. Coalitions involve coordinating or sharing value chains with coalition partners that broadens the effective scope of the firm's chain.

This chapter describes the fundamental role of the value chain in identifying sources of competitive advantage. I begin by describing the value chain and its component parts. Every firm's value chain is composed of nine generic categories of activities which are linked together in characteristic ways. The generic chain is used to demonstrate how a value chain can be constructed for a particular firm, reflecting the specific activities it performs. I also show how the activities in a firm's value chain are linked to each other and to the activities of its suppliers, channels, and buyers, and how these linkages affect competitive advantage. I then describe how scope of a firm's activities affects competitive advantage through its impact on the value chain. [. . .] The value chain can be used as a strategic tool to analyze relative cost position, differentiation, and the role of competitive scope in achieving competitive advantage.

THE VALUE CHAIN

Every firm is a collection of activities that are performed to design, produce, market, deliver, and support its product. All these activities can be represented using a value chain, shown

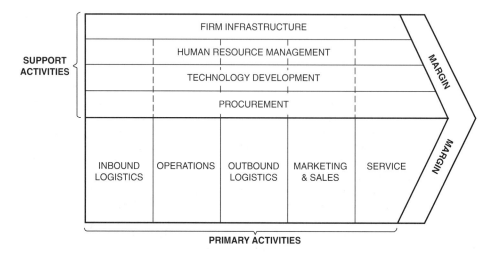

Figure 5.2 The generic value chain

in Figure 5.2. A firm's value chain and the way it performs individual activities are a reflection of its history, its strategy, its approach to implementing its strategy, and the underlying economics of the activities themselves.[1]

The relevant level for constructing a value chain is a firm's activities in a particular industry (the business unit). An industry- or sector-wide value chain is too broad, because it may obscure important sources of competitive advantage. Though firms in the same industry may have similar chains the value chains of competitors often differ. People Express and United Airlines both compete in the airline industry, for example, but they have very different value chains embodying significant differences in boarding gate operations, crew policies, and aircraft operations. Differences among competitor value chains are a key source of competitive advantage. A firm's value chain in an industry may vary somewhat for different items in its product line, or different buyers, geographic areas, or distribution channels. The value chains for such subsets of a firm are closely related, however, and can only be understood in the context of the business unit chain.[2]

In competitive terms, value is the amount buyers are willing to pay for what a firm provides them. Value is measured by total revenue, a reflection of the price a firm's product commands and the units it can sell. A firm is profitable if the value it commands exceeds the costs involved in creating the product. Creating value for buyers that exceeds the cost of doing so is the goal of any generic strategy. Value, instead of cost, must be used in analyzing competitive position since firms often deliberately raise their cost in order to command a premium price via differentiation.

The value chain displays total value, and consists of *value activities* and *margin*. Value activities are the physically and technologically distinct activities a firm performs. These are the building blocks by which a firm creates a product valuable to its buyers. Margin is the difference between total value and the collective cost of performing the value activities. Margin can be measured in a variety of ways. Supplier and channel value chains also include a margin that is important to isolate in understanding the sources of a firm's cost position, since supplier and channel margin are part of the total cost borne by the buyer.

Every value activity employs *purchased inputs*, *human resources* (labor and management), and some form of *technology* to perform its function. Each value activity also uses and creates *information*, such as buyer data (order entry), performance parameters (testing), and product failure statistics. Value activities may also create financial assets such as inventory and accounts receivable, or liabilities such as accounts payable.

Value activities can be divided into two broad types, *primary* activities and *support* activities. Primary activities, listed along the bottom of Figure 5.2, are the activities involved in the physical creation of the product and its sale and transfer to the buyer as well as after-sale assistance. In any firm, primary activities can be divided into the five generic categories shown in Figure 5.2. Support activities support the primary activities and each other providing purchased inputs, technology, human resources, and various firmwide functions. The dotted lines reflect the fact that procurement, technology development, and human resource management can be associated with specific primary activities as well as support the entire chain. Firm intrastructure is not associated with particular primary activities but supports the entire chain.

Value activities are therefore the discrete building blocks of competitive advantage. How each activity is performed combined with its economics will determine whether a firm is high or low cost relative to competitors. How each value activity is performed will also determine its contribution to buyer needs and hence differentiation. Comparing the value chains of competitors exposes differences that determine competitive advantage.[3]

An analysis of the value chain rather than value added is the appropriate way to examine competitive advantage. Value added (selling price less the cost of purchased raw materials) has sometimes been used as the focal point for cost analysis because it was viewed as the area in which a firm can control costs. Value added is not a sound basis for cost analysis, however, because it incorrectly distinguishes raw materials from the many other purchased inputs used in a firm's activities. Also, the cost behavior of activities cannot be understood without simultaneously examining the costs of the inputs used to perform them. Moreover, value added fails to highlight the linkages between a firm and its suppliers that can reduce cost or enhance differentiation.

Identifying value activities

Identifying value activities requires the isolation of activities that are technologically and strategically distinct. Value activities and accounting classifications are rarely the same. Accounting classifications (e.g., burden, overhead, direct labor) group together activities with disparate technologies, and separate costs that are all part of the same activity.

Primary activities

There are five generic categories of primary activities involved in competing in any industry, as shown in Figure 5.2. Each category is divisible into a number of distinct activities that depend on the particular industry and firm strategy:

- *Inbound logistics* Activities associated with receiving, storing, and disseminating inputs to the product, such as material handling, warehousing, inventory control, vehicle scheduling, and returns to suppliers.
- *Operations* Activities associated with transforming inputs into the final product form, such as machining, packaging, assembly, equipment maintenance, testing, printing, and facility operations.
- *Outbound logistics* Activities associated with collecting, storing, and physically distributing the product to buyers, such as finished goods warehousing, material handling, delivery vehicle operation, order processing, and scheduling.
- *Marketing and Sales* Activities associated with providing a means by which buyers can

purchase the product and inducing them to do so, such as advertising, promotion, sales force, quoting, channel selection, channel relations, and pricing.
- *Service* Activities associated with providing service to enhance or maintain the value of the product, such as installation, repair, training, parts supply, and product adjustment.

Each of the categories may be vital to competitive advantage depending on the industry. For a distributor, inbound and outbound logistics are the most critical. For a service firm providing the service on its premises such as a restaurant or retailer, outbound logistics may be largely nonexistant and operations the vital category. For a bank engaged in corporate lending, marketing and sales are a key to competitive advantage through the effectiveness of the calling officers and the way in which loans are packaged and priced. For a high speed copier manufacturer, service represents a key source of competitive advantage. In any firm, however, all the categories of primary activities will be present to some degree and play some role in competitive advantage.

Support activities

Support value activities involved in competing in any industry can be divided into four generic categories, also shown in Figure 5.2. As with primary activities, each category of support activities is divisible into a number of distinct value activities that are specific to a given industry. In technology development, for example, discrete activities might include component design, feature design, field testing, process engineering, and technology selection. Similarly, procurement can be divided into activities such as qualifying new suppliers, procurement of different groups of purchased inputs, and ongoing monitoring of supplier performance.

Procurement

Procurement refers to the *function* of purchasing inputs used in the firm's value chain, not to the purchased inputs themselves. Purchased inputs include raw materials, supplies, and other consumable items as well as assets such as machinery, laboratory equipment, office equipment, and buildings. Though purchased inputs are commonly associated with primary activities, purchased inputs are present in every value activity including support activities. For example, laboratory supplies and independent testing services are common purchased inputs in technology development, while an accounting firm is a common purchased input in firm infrastructure. Like all value activities, procurement employs a "technology," such as procedures for dealing with vendors, qualification rules, and information systems.

Procurement tends to be spread throughout a firm. Some items such as raw materials are purchased by the traditional purchasing department, while other items are purchased by plant managers (e.g., machines), office managers (e.g., temporary help), salespersons (e.g., meals and lodging), and even the chief executive officer (e.g., strategic consulting). I use the term procurement rather than purchasing because the usual connotation of purchasing is too narrow among managers. The dispersion of the procurement function often obscures the magnitude of total purchases, and means that many purchases receive little scrutiny.

A given procurement activity can normally be associated with a specific value activity or activities which it supports, though often a purchasing department serves many value activities and purchasing policies apply firmwide. The cost of procurement activities themselves usually represents a small if not insignificant portion of total costs, but often has a large impact on the firm's overall cost and differentiation. Improved purchasing practices can strongly affect the cost and quality of purchased inputs, as well as of other activities associated with receiving and using the inputs, and interacting with suppliers. In chocolate manufacturing and electric utilities, for example, procurement of cocoa beans and fuel respectively is by far the most important determinant of cost position.

Technology development

Every value activity embodies technology, be it know-how, procedures, or technology embodied in process equipment. The array of technologies employed in most firms is very broad, ranging from those technologies used in preparing documents and transporting goods to those technologies embodied in the product itself. Moreover, most value activities use a technology that combines a number of different subtechnologies involving different scientific disciplines. Machining, for example, involves metallurgy, electronics, and mechanics.

Technology development consists of a range of activities that can be broadly grouped into efforts to improve the product and the process. I term this category of activities technology development instead of research and development because R&D has too narrow a connotation to most managers. Technology development tends to be associated with the engineering department or the development group. Typically, however, it occurs in many parts of a firm, although this is not explicitly recognized. Technology development may support any of the numerous technologies embodied in value activities, including such areas as telecommunications technology for the order entry system, or office automation for the accounting department. It does not solely apply to technologies directly linked to the end product. Technology development also takes many forms, from basic research and product design to media research, process equipment design, and servicing procedures. Technology development that is related to the product and its features supports the entire chain, while other technology development is associated with particular primary or support activities.

Technology development is important to competitive advantage in all industries, holding the key in some. In steel, for example, a firm's process technology is the single greatest factor in competitive advantage.

Human resource management

Human resource management consists of activities involved in the recruiting, hiring, training, development, and compensation of all types of personnel. Human resource management supports both individual primary and support activities (e.g., hiring of engineers) and the entire value chain (e.g., labor negotiations). Human resource management activities occur in different parts of a firm, as do other support activities, and the dispersion of these activities can lead to inconsistent policies. Moreover, the cumulative costs of human resource management are rarely well understood nor are the tradeoffs in different human resource management costs, such as salary compared to the cost of recruiting and training due to turnover.

Human resource management affects competitive advantage in any firm, through its role in determining the skills and motivation of employees and the cost of hiring and training. In some industries it holds the key to competitive advantage. The world's leading accounting firm Arthur Andersen, for example, draws a significant competitive advantage from its approach to recruiting and training its tens of thousands of professional staff. Arthur Andersen has bought a former college campus near Chicago, and has invested heavily in codifying its practice and regularly bringing staff from around the world to its college for training in the firmwide methodology. Having a deeply understood methodology throughout the firm not only makes all engagements more effective but also greatly facilitates the servicing of national and multinational clients.

Firm infrastructure

Firm infrastructure consists of a number of activities including general management, planning, finance, accounting, legal, government affairs, and quality management. Infrastructure, unlike other support activities, usually supports the entire chain and not individual activities. Depending on whether a firm is diversified or not, firm infrastructure may be self-contained or divided between a business unit and the parent corporation.[4] In diversified firms, infrastructure activities are typically split between the business unit and corporate levels (e.g., financing is often done at the corporate level while quality management is done at the business unit level). Many infrastructure activities occur at both the business unit and corporate levels, however.

Firm infrastructure is sometimes viewed only as "overhead," but can be a powerful source of competitive advantage. In a telephone operating company, for example, negotiating and maintaining ongoing relations with regulatory bodies can be among the most important activities for competitive advantage. Similarly, proper management information systems can contribute significantly to cost position, while in some industries top management plays a vital role in dealing with the buyer.

Activity types

Within each category of primary and support activities, there are three activity types that play a different role in competitive advantage:

- *Direct* Activities directly involved in creating value for the buyer, such as assembly, parts machining, sales force operation, advertising, product design, recruiting, etc.
- *Indirect* Activities that make it possible to perform direct activities on a continuing basis, such as maintenance, scheduling, operation of facilities, sales force administration, research administration, vendor record keeping, etc.
- *Quality assurance* Activities that ensure the quality of other activities, such as monitoring, inspecting, testing, reviewing, checking, adjusting, and reworking. Quality assurance is *not* synonymous with quality management, because many value activities contribute to quality [. . .].

Every firm has direct, indirect, and quality assurance value activities. All three types are present not only among primary activities but also among support activities. In technology development, for example, actual laboratory teams are direct activities, while research administration is an indirect activity.

The role of indirect and quality assurance activities is often not well understood, making the distinction among the three activity types an important one for diagnosing competitive advantage. In many industries, indirect activities represent a large and rapidly growing proportion of cost and can play a significant role in differentiation through their effect on direct activities. Despite this, indirect activities are frequently lumped together with direct activities when managers think about their firms, though the two often have very different economics. There are often tradeoffs between direct and indirect activities – more spending on maintenance lowers machine costs. Indirect activities are also frequently grouped together into "overhead" or "burden" accounts, obscuring their cost and contribution to differentiation.

Quality assurance activities are also prevalent in nearly every part of a firm, though they are seldom recognized as such. Testing and inspection are associated with many primary activities. Quality assurance activities outside of operations are often less apparent though equally prevalent. The cumulative cost of quality assurance activities can be very large, as recent attention to the cost of quality has demonstrated. Quality assurance activities often affect the cost or effectiveness of other activities, and the way other activities are performed in turn affects the need for and types of quality assurance activities. The possibility of simplifying or eliminating the need for quality assurance activities through performing other activities better is at the root of the notion that quality can be "free."

Defining the value chain

To diagnose competitive advantage, it is necessary to define a firm's value chain for competing in a particular industry. Starting with the generic chain, individual value activities are identified in the particular firm. Each generic category can be divided into discrete activities, as illustrated for one generic category in Figure 5.3. An example of a complete value chain is shown in Figure 5.4, the value chain of a copier manufacturer.

Defining relevant value activities requires that activities with discrete technologies and economics be isolated. Broad functions such as manufacturing or marketing must be subdivided into activities. The product flow, order flow or paper flow can be useful in doing so. Subdividing activities can proceed to the level of increasingly narrow activities that are to some degree discrete. Every machine in a factory, for example, could be treated as a separate activity. Thus the number of potential activities is often quite large.

The appropriate degree of disaggregation depends on the economics of the activities and the purposes for which the value chain is being analyzed. [. . .] The basic principle is that activities should be isolated and separated that (1) have different economics, (2) have a high potential impact of differentiation, or (3) represent a significant or growing proportion of cost. In using the value chain, successively finer disaggregations of some activities are

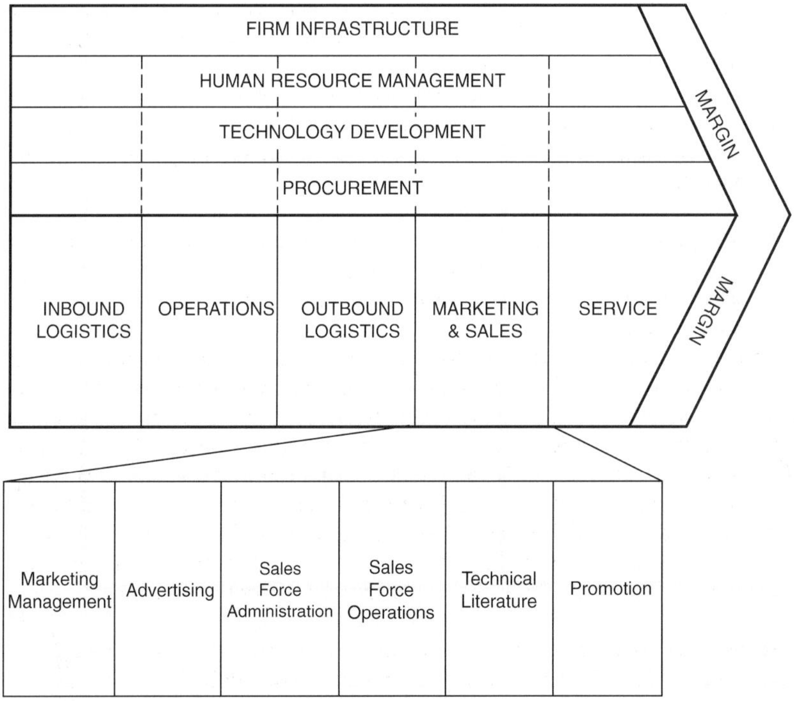

Figure 5.3 Subdividing a generic value chain

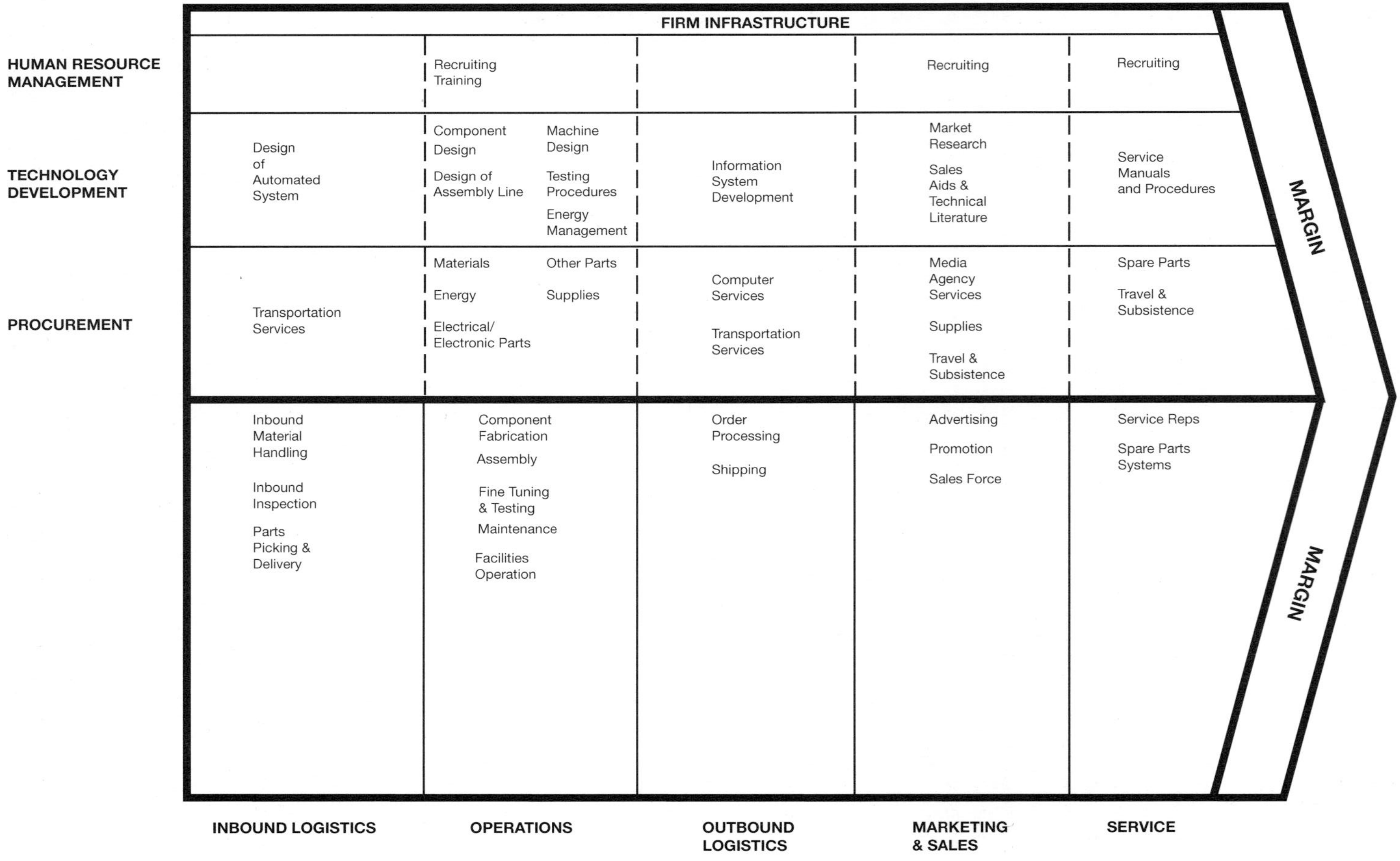

Figure 5.4 Value chain for a copier manufacturer

made as the analysis exposes differences important to competitive advantage; other activities are combined because they prove to be unimportant to competitive advantage or are governed by similar economics.

Selecting the appropriate category in which to put an activity may require judgment and can be illuminating in its own right. Order processing, for example, could be classified as part of outbound logistics or as part of marketing. In a distributor, the role of order processing is more a marketing function. Similarly, the sales force often performs service functions. Value activities should be assigned to categories that best represent their contribution to a firm's competitive advantage. If order processing is an important way in which a firm interacts with its buyers, for example, it should be classified under marketing. Similarly, if inbound material handling and outbound material handling use the same facilities and personnel, then both should probably be combined into one value activity and classified wherever the function has the greatest competitive impact. Firms have often gained competitive advantage by redefining the roles of traditional activities – Vetco, an oil field equipment supplier, uses customer training as a marketing tool and a way to build switching costs, for example.

Everything a firm does should be captured in a primary or support activity. Value activity labels are arbitrary and should be chosen to provide the best insight into the business. Labeling activities in service industries often causes confusion because operations, marketing, and after-sale support are often closely tied. Ordering of activities should broadly follow the process flow, but ordering is judgmental as well. Often firms perform parallel activities, whose order should be chosen to enhance the intuitive clarity of the value chain to managers.

Linkages within the value chain

Although value activities are the building blocks of competitive advantage, the value chain is not a collection of independent activities but a system of interdependent activities. Value activities are related by linkages within the value chain. Linkages are relationships between the way one value activity is performed and the cost or performance of another. For example, purchasing high-quality, precut steel sheets can simplify manufacturing and reduce scrap. In a fast food chain, the timing of promotional campaigns can influence capacity utilization. Competitive advantage frequently derives from linkages among activities just as it does from the individual activities themselves.

Linkages can lead to competitive advantage in two ways: optimization and coordination. Linkages often reflect tradeoffs among activities to achieve the same overall result. For example, a more costly product design, more stringent materials specifications, or greater in-process inspection may reduce service costs. A firm must optimize such linkages reflecting its strategy in order to achieve competitive advantage.

Linkages may also reflect the need to coordinate activities. On-time delivery, for example, may require coordination of activities in operations, outbound logistics, and service (e.g., installation). The ability to coordinate linkages often reduces cost or enhances differentiation. Better coordination, for example, can reduce the need for inventory throughout the firm. Linkages imply that a firm's cost or differentiation is not merely the result of efforts to reduce cost or improve performance in each value activity individually. Much of the recent change in philosophy towards manufacturing and towards quality – strongly influenced by Japanese practice – is a recognition of the importance of linkages.

Linkages are numerous, and some are common to many firms. The most obvious linkages are those between support activities and primary activities represented by the dotted lines on the generic value chain. Product design usually affects the manufacturing cost of a product, for example, while procurement practices often affect the quality of purchased

LIBRARY
BISHOP BURTON COLLEGE
BEVERLEY HU17 8QG

inputs and hence production costs, inspection costs, and product quality. More subtle linkages are those between primary activities. For example, enhanced inspection of incoming parts may reduce quality assurance costs later in the production process, while better maintenance often reduces the downtime of a machine. An interactive order entry system may reduce salesperson time required per buyer because salespersons can place orders faster and are freed from the need to follow up on inquiries and problems. More thorough inspection of finished goods often improves the reliability of products in the field, reducing servicing costs. Finally, frequent deliveries to buyers may reduce inventory and accounts receivable. Linkages that involve activities in different categories or of different types are often the most difficult to recognize.

Linkages among value activities arise from a number of generic causes, among them the following:

- *The same function can be performed in different ways* For example, conformance to specifications can be achieved through high quality purchased inputs, specifying close tolerances in the manufacturing process, or 100 percent inspection of finished goods.
- *The cost or performance of direct activities is improved by greater efforts in indirect activities* For example, better scheduling (an indirect activity) reduces sales force travel time or delivery vehicle time (direct activities); or better maintenance improves the tolerances achieved by machines.
- *Activities performed inside a firm reduce the need to demonstrate, explain, or service a product in the field* For example, 100 percent inspection can substantially reduce service costs in the field.
- *Quality assurance functions can be performed in different ways* For example, incoming inspection is a substitute for finished goods inspection.

Though linkages within the value chain are crucial to competitive advantage, they are often subtle and go unrecognized. The importance of procurement in affecting manufacturing cost and quality may not be obvious, for example. Nor is the link between order processing, manufacturing scheduling practices, and sales force utilization. Identifying linkages is a process of searching for ways in which each value activity affects or is affected by others. The generic causes of linkages discussed above provide a starting point. The disaggregation of procurement and technology development to relate them to specific primary activities also helps to highlight linkages between support and primary activities.

Exploiting linkages usually requires information or information flows that allow optimization or coordination to take place. Thus, information systems are often vital to gaining competitive advantages from linkages. Recent developments in information systems technology are creating new linkages and increasing the ability to achieve old ones. Exploiting linkages also frequently requires optimization or coordination that cuts across conventional organization lines. Higher costs in the manufacturing organization, for example, may result in lower costs in the sales or service organization. Such tradeoffs may not be measured in a firm's information and control systems. Managing linkages thus is a more complex organizational task than managing value activities themselves. Given the difficulty of recognizing and managing linkages, the ability to do so often yields a *sustainable* source of competitive advantage. [. . .]

Vertical linkages

Linkages exist not only within a firm's value chain but between a firm's chain and the value chains of suppliers and channels. These linkages, which I term vertical linkages, are similar to the linkages within the value chain – the way supplier or channel activities are performed affects the cost or performance of a firm's activities (and vice versa). Suppliers produce a product or service that a firm employs in its value chain, and suppliers' value chains also influence the firm at other contact points. A firm's procurement and inbound logistics activities interact with a supplier's order entry system, for example, while a supplier's applications engineering staff works with a firm's technology development and manufacturing activities. A supplier's product characteristics as well as its other contact points with a firm's value chain can significantly affect a firm's cost and differentiation. For example, frequent supplier shipments can reduce a firm's inventory needs, appropriate packaging of supplier products can lower handling cost, and supplier inspection can remove the need for incoming inspection by a firm.

The linkages between suppliers' value chains and a firm's value chain provide opportunities for the firm to enhance its competitive advantage. It is often possible to benefit both the firm and suppliers by influencing the configuration of suppliers' value chains to jointly optimize the performance of activities, or by improving coordination between a firm's and suppliers' chains. Supplier linkages mean that the relationship with suppliers is *not a zero sum game* in which one gains only at the expense of the other, but a relationship in which both can gain. By agreeing to deliver bulk chocolate to a confectionery producer in tank cars instead of solid bars, for example, an industrial chocolate firm saves the cost of molding and packaging while the confectionery manufacturer lowers the cost of in-bound handling and melting. The division of the benefits of coordinating or optimizing linkages between a firm and its suppliers is a function of suppliers' bargaining power and is reflected in suppliers' margins. Supplier bargaining power is partly structural and partly a function of a firm's purchasing practice. [. . .] Thus *both* coordination with suppliers and hard bargaining to capture the spoils are important to competitive advantage. One without the other results in missed opportunities.

Channel linkages are similar to supplier linkages. Channels have value chains through which a firm's product passes. The channel markup over a firm's selling price (which I term channel value) often represents a large proportion of the selling price to the end user – it represents as much as 50 percent or more of selling price to the end user in many consumer goods, such as wine. Channels perform such activities as sales, advertising, and display that may substitute for or complement the firm's activities. There are also multiple points of contact between a firm's and channels' value chains in activities such as the sales force, order entry, and outbound logistics. As with supplier linkages, coordinating and jointly optimizing with channels can lower cost or enhance differentiation. The same issues that existed with suppliers in dividing the gains of coordination and joint optimization also exist with channels.

Vertical linkages, like linkages within a firm's value chain, are frequently overlooked. Even if they are recognized, independent ownership of suppliers or channels or a history of an adversary relationship can impede the coordination and joint optimization required to exploit vertical linkages. Sometimes vertical linkages are easier to achieve with coalition partners or sister business units than with independent firms, though even this is not assured. As with linkages within the value chain, exploiting vertical linkages requires information and modern information systems are creating many new possibilities. [. . .]

The buyer's value chain

Buyers also have value chains, and a firm's product represents a purchased input to the buyer's chain. Understanding the value chains of industrial, commercial, and institutional buyers is intuitively easy because of their similarities to that of a firm. Understanding households' value chains is less intuitive, but nevertheless important. Households (and the individual consumers within them) engage in a wide range of activities, and products purchased by households are used in conjunction with this stream of activities. A car is used for the trip to work and for shopping and leisure, while a food product is consumed as part of the process of preparing and eating meals. Though it is quite difficult to construct a value chain that encompasses everything a household and its occupants do, it is quite possible to construct a chain for those activities that are relevant to how a particular product is used. Chains need to be constructed for every household, but chains for representative households can provide an important tool for use in differentiation analysis [. . .].

A firm's differentiation stems from how its value chain relates to its buyer's chain. This is a function of the way a firm's physical product is used in the particular buyer activity in which it is consumed (e.g., a machine used in the assembly process) as well as *all* the other points of contact between a firm's value chain and the buyer's chain. Many of a firm's activities interact with some buyer activities. In opto-electronic parts, for example, a firm's product is assembled into the buyer's equipment – an obvious point of contact – but the firm also works closely with the buyer in designing the part, providing ongoing technical assistance, troubleshooting, order processing, and delivery. Each of these contact points is a potential source of differentiation. "Quality" is too narrow a view of what makes a firm unique, because it focuses attention on the product rather than the broader array of value activities that impact the buyer.

Differentiation, then, derives fundamentally from creating value for the buyer through a firm's impact on the buyer's value chain. Value is created when a firm creates competitive advantage for its buyer – lowers its buyer's cost or raises its buyer's performance.[5] The value created for the buyer must be perceived by the buyer if it is to be rewarded with a premium price, however, which means that firms must communicate their value to buyers through such means as advertising and the sales force. How this value is divided between the firm (a premium price) and the buyer (higher profits or more satisfaction for the money) is reflected in a firm's margin, and is a function of industry structure. [. . .]

COMPETITIVE SCOPE AND THE VALUE CHAIN

Competitive scope can have a powerful effect on competitive advantage, because it shapes the configuration and economics of the value chain. There are four dimensions of scope that affect the value chain:[6]

- *Segment scope* The product varieties produced and buyers served.
- *Vertical scope* The extent to which activities are performed in-house instead of by independent firms.
- *Geographic scope* The range of regions, countries, or groups of countries in which a firm competes with a coordinated strategy.
- *Industry scope* The range of related industries in which the firm competes with a coordinated strategy.

Broad scope can allow a firm to exploit the benefits of performing more activities internally. It may also allow the firm to exploit interrelationships between the value chains that serve different segments, geographic areas or related industries. [. . .] For example, a shared sales force may sell the products of two business units, or a common brand name may be employed worldwide. Sharing and integration have costs, however, that may nullify their benefits.

Narrow scope can allow the tailoring of the chain to serve a particular target segment, geographic area or industry to achieve lower cost or to serve the target in a unique way. Narrow scope in integration may also improve competitive advantage through the firm's purchasing activities that independent firms perform better or cheaper. The competitive advantage of a narrow scope rests on *differences* among product varieties, buyers, or geographic regions within an industry in terms of the value chain best suited to serve them, or on differences in resources and skills of independent firms that allow them to perform activities better.

The breadth or narrowness of scope is clearly relative to competitors. In some industries, a broad scope involves only serving the full range of product and buyer segments within the industry. In others, it may require both vertical integration and competing in related industries. Since there are many ways to segment an industry and multiple forms of interrelationships and integration, broad and narrow scope can be combined. A firm may create competitive advantage by tuning its value chain to one product segment and exploiting geographic interrelationships by serving that segment worldwide. It may also exploit interrelationships with business units in related industries. [. . .]

Segment scope

Differences in the needs or value chains required to serve different product or buyer segments can lead to a competitive advantage of focusing. For example, the value chain required to serve sophisticated minicomputer buyers with in-house servicing capabilities is different from that required to serve small business users. They need extensive sales assistance, less demanding hardware performance, user-friendly software, and service capability.

Just as differences among segments favor narrow scope, however, interrelationships between the value chains serving different segments favor broad scope. General Motors' value chain for large cars is different from that for small cars, for example, but many value activities are shared. This creates a tension between tailoring the value chain to a segment and sharing it among segments. This tension is fundamental to industry segmentation and to the choice of focus strategies [. . .].

Vertical scope

Vertical integration defines the division of activities between a firm and its suppliers, channels, and buyers. A firm may purchase components rather than fabricate them itself, for example, or contract for service rather than maintain a service organization. Similarly, channels may perform many distribution, service, and marketing functions instead of a firm. A firm and its buyers can also divide activities in differing ways. One way a firm may be able to differentiate itself is by assuming a greater number of buyer activities. In the extreme case, a firm completely enters the buyer's industry.

When one views the issue of integration from the perspective of the value chain, it becomes apparent that opportunities for integration are richer than is often recognized. Vertical integration tends to be viewed in terms of physical products and replacing whole supplier relationships rather than in terms of activities, but it can encompass both. For example, a firm may rely on a supplier's applications engineering and service capability, or it may perform these activities internally. Thus there are many options regarding what value activities a firm performs internally and what value activities it purchases. The same principles apply to channel and buyer integration.

Whether or not integration (or de-integration) lowers cost or enhances differentiation depends on the firm and the activity involved. [. . .] The value chain allows a firm to identify more clearly the potential benefits of integration by highlighting the role of vertical linkages. The exploitation of vertical linkages does not require vertical integration, but integration may sometimes allow the benefits of vertical linkages to be achieved more easily.

Geographic scope

Geographic scope may allow a firm to share or coordinate value activities used to serve different geographic areas. Canon develops and manufactures copiers primarily in Japan, for example, but sells and services them separately in many countries. Canon gains a cost advantage from sharing technology development and manufacturing instead of performing these activities in each country. Interrelationships are also common among partially distinct value chains serving geographic regions in a single country. For example, food service distributors such as Monarch and SISCO have many largely distinct operating units in major metropolitan areas that share firm infrastructure, procurement, and other support value activities.

Geographic interrelationships can enhance competitive advantage if sharing or coordinating value activities lowers cost or enhances differentiation. There may be costs of coordination as well as differences among regions or countries that reduce the advantage of sharing, however. [. . .] The same principles apply to national or regional coordination of value chains.

Industry scope

Potential interrelationships among the value chains required to compete in related industries are widespread. They can involve any value activity, including both primary (e.g., a shared service organization) and support activities (e.g., joint technology development or shared procurement of common inputs). Interrelationships among business units are similar in concept to geographic interrelationships among value chains.

Interrelationships among business units can have a powerful influence on competitive advantage, either by lowering cost or enhancing differentiation. A shared logistical system may allow a firm to reap economies of scale, for example, while a shared sales force offering related products can improve the salesperson's effectiveness with the buyer and thereby enhance differentiation. All interrelationships do not lead to competitive advantage. Not all activities benefit from sharing. There are also always costs of sharing activities that must be offset against the benefits, because the needs of different business units may not be the same with respect to a value activity. [. . .]

Coalitions and scope

A firm can pursue the benefits of a broader scope internally, or enter into *coalitions* with independent firms to achieve some or all of the same benefits. Coalitions are long-term agreements among firms that go beyond normal market transactions but fall short of outright mergers. Examples of coalitions include technology licenses, supply agreements, marketing agreements, and joint ventures. Coalitions are ways of broadening scope without broadening the firm, by contracting with an independent firm to perform value activities (e.g., a supply agreement) or teaming up with an independent firm to share activities (e.g., a marketing joint venture). Thus there are two basic types of coalition – vertical coalitions and horizontal coalitions.

Coalitions can allow sharing of activities without the need to enter new industry segments, geographic areas, or related industries. Coalitions are also a means of gaining the cost or differentiation advantages of vertical linkages without actual integration, but overcoming the difficulties of coordination among purely independent firms. Because coalitions involve long-term relationships, it should be possible to coordinate more closely with a coalition partner than with an independent firm, though not without some cost. Difficulties in reaching coalition agreements and in ongoing coordination among partners may block coalitions or nullify their benefits.

Coalition partners remain independent firms and there is the question of how the benefits of a coalition are to be divided. The relative bargaining power of each coalition partner is thus central to how the gains are shared, and determines impact of the coalition on a firm's competitive advantage. A strong coalition partner may appropriate all the gains of a shared marketing organization through the terms of the agreement. [. . .]

Competitive scope and business definition

The relationship between competitive scope and the value chain provides the basis for defining relevant business unit boundaries. Strategically distinct business units are isolated by weighing the benefits of integration and de-integration and by comparing the strength of interrelationships in serving related segments, geographic areas, or industries to the differences in the value chains best suited for serving them separately. If differences in geographic areas or product and buyer segments require very distinct value chains, then segments define business units. Conversely, strong and widespread benefits of integration or geographic or industry interrelationships widen the relevant boundaries of business units. Strong advantages to vertical integration widen the boundaries of a business unit to encompass upstream or downstream activities, while weak advantages to integration imply that each stage is a distinct business unit. Similarly, strong advantages to worldwide coordination of the value chains imply that the relevant business unit is global, while strong country or regional differences necessitating largely distinct chains imply narrower geographic business unit boundaries. Finally, strong interrelationships between one business unit and another may imply that they should merge into one. Appropriate business units can be defined, then, by understanding the optimal value chain for competing in different arenas and how the chains are related. [. . .]

The value chain and industry structure

Industry structure both shapes the value chain of a firm and is a reflection of the collective value chains of competitors. Structure determines the bargaining relationships with buyers and suppliers that is reflected in both the configuration of a firm's value chain and how margins are divided with buyers, suppliers, and coalition partners. The threat of substitution to an industry influences the value activities desired by buyers. Entry barriers bear on the sustainability of various value chain configurations.

The array of competitor value chains is, in turn, the basis for many elements of industry structure. Scale economies and proprietary learning, for example, stem from the technology employed in competitors' value chains. Capital requirements for competing in an industry are the result of the collective capital required in the chain. Similarly, industry product differentiation stems from the way firms' products are used in buyers' value chains. Thus many elements of industry structure can be diagnosed by analyzing the value chains of competitors in an industry.

THE VALUE CHAIN AND ORGANIZATIONAL STRUCTURE

The value chain is a basic tool for diagnosing competitive advantage and finding ways to create and sustain it [. . .]. However, the value chain can also play a valuable role in designing organizational structure. Organizational structure groups certain activities together under organizational units such as marketing or production. The logic of those groupings is that activities have similarities that should be exploited by putting them together in a department; at the same time, departments are separated from other groups of activities because of their differences. This separation of like activities is what organizational theorists call "differentiation." With separation of organizational units comes the need to coordinate them, usually termed "integration." Thus integrating mechanisms must be established in a firm to ensure that the required coordination takes place. Organizational structure balances the benefits of separation and integration. [. . .]

The value chain provides a systematic way to divide a firm into its discrete activities, and thus can be used to examine how the activities in a firm are and could be grouped. [. . .] Organizational boundaries are often not drawn around the groups of activities that are most similar in economic terms. Moreover, organizational units such as the purchasing and R&D departments frequently contain only a fraction of the similar activities being performed in a firm.

The need for integration among organizational units is a manifestation of linkages. There are often many linkages within the value chain, and organizational structure often fails to provide mechanisms to coordinate or optimize them. The information necessary for coordinating or optimizing linkages is also rarely collected throughout the chain. Managers of support activities such as human resource management and technology development often do not have a clear view of how they relate to the firm's overall competitive position, something the value chain highlights. Finally, vertical linkages are often not well provided for in organizational structure.

A firm may be able to draw unit boundaries more in tune with its sources of competitive advantage and provide for the appropriate types of coordination by relating its organizational structure to the value chain, and the linkages within it and with suppliers or channels. An organizational structure that corresponds to the value chain will improve a firm's ability to create and sustain competitive advantage. [. . .]

NOTES

*   This chapter has been adapted from, Porter, M.E. (1985) *Competitive Advantage*, ch. 2, New York, Free Press.

1   The business system concept, developed by McKinsey and Company, captures the idea that a firm is a series of functions (e.g., R&D, manufacturing, marketing, channels), and that analyzing how each is performed relative to competitors can provide useful insights. McKinsey also stresses the power of redefining the business system to gain competitive advantage, an important idea. The business system concept addresses broad functions rather than activities, however, and does not distinguish among types of activities or show how they are related. The concept is also not linked specifically to competitive advantage nor to competitive scope. [. . .]

2   The notion of a strategic business unit as the relevant entity for strategy formulation is well accepted, and grows out of work by many scholars and consultants. Business units are often poorly defined, however, a problem exposed by value chain analysis to which I will return below.

3   Economists have characterized the firm as having a production function that defines how inputs are converted into outputs. The value chain is a theory of the firm that views the firm as being a collection of discrete but related production functions, if production functions are defined as activities. The value chain formulation focuses on how these activities create value and what determines their cost, giving the firm considerable latitude in determining how activities are configured and combined.

4   There may also be infrastructure activities at the group or sector level.

5   Unlike a firm, which can measure value in terms of price or profit, a consumer's measure of value is complex and relates to the satisfaction of needs. [. . .]

6   The term scope of the firm is used in economic theory to reflect the boundary between the activities a firm performs internally and those it obtains in market transactions – e.g., vertical integration [. . .]. Competitive scope is used here to refer to a broader conception of the scope of a firm's activities, encompassing industry segment coverage, integration, geographic markets served, and coordinated competition in related industries.

SECTION 3: CUSTOMER PROCESSING

INTRODUCTION

The purpose of sections 3 and 4 is to illustrate the principles introduced in sections 1 and 2 by considering in detail some examples of organisational activities. There are many different kinds of activities that are undertaken in the myriad of business organisations that exist. There is insufficient space in this book to provide a comprehensive consideration of all possible business activities. Consequently we have been forced to make choices in considering which business processes to focus on. We have decided to focus on two types of business processes that are important in many organisations. Section 3 examines customer processing activities, and section 4 considers materials processing activities.

Section 3 concentrates on customer processing activities. These include processes to acquire customers, processes to service their needs and processes to retain those customers over the longer term. A recurrent theme in all three chapters is that of the importance of an organisation using its processes to add value for its customers.

In chapter 6, Kotler *et al.* introduce the concept of marketing. They note that marketing is commonly misinterpreted as being only about selling, whereas it encompasses market research, product development, distribution, pricing, advertising, and many other activities in addition to selling. They define marketing as 'a social and managerial process by which individuals and groups obtain what they need and want through creating and exchanging products and value with others'. We see it more simply as a process by which organisations acquire customers. To be attractive to customers, the products and services offered must above all else provide value. Customers normally have at least some degree of choice. In exercising that choice they will choose the product that they expect to give them the greatest value. Thus the essence of marketing is the provision of value to customers.

Once acquired, organisations interact with customers when providing them with the product offering they seek. In chapter 7, Johnston presents a framework for understanding a typical customer processing operation. Customer processing operations are service operations. In service operations, the quality of the service they experience will be a major determining factor in whether customers believe they have received added value. The framework is particularly helpful as it assesses the activities of the service delivery system from the customer's standpoint, by considering the points of contact that the customer has with the service system. The chapter echoes the marketing concept described in chapter 6, by declaring that in service operations, quality is all about satisfying customers. Customer satisfaction depends on whether customers perceive that the quality of the service they receive at least meets or, better still exceeds their expectations.

In chapter 8, Buttle discusses the growing interest in developing ways that organisations can retain their customers by building long-term relationships with them. An enduring relationship between an organisation and its customers that can not be duplicated by competitors can provide a source of sustainable competitive advantage. Buttle argues that this current interest in relationship marketing is merely redressing the marketing balance between creating and retaining customers. For too long, Buttle argues, the former has received most attention. The chapter goes on to assess the economic benefits to the organisation of relationship marketing. These are twofold. First, retaining existing customers is much less costly than winning new ones. Second, the longer the association between the organisation and its customer, the more profitable the relationship is likely to be. The chapter notes that relationship marketing has been practised in some industries for many years, particularly in industrial marketing (i.e. business to business). However in recent years suppliers in mass markets with very large numbers of customers have also been adopting relationship marketing. Clearly there are great difficulties in trying to establish meaningful relationships with many thousands or even millions of customers. However some companies now make use of direct mail or the internet in an attempt to do just that. Relationship marketing is characterised by a genuine concern to meet or exceed customer expectations, and if performed well can enhance an organisation's ability to add value for its customers.

6

MARKETING IN A CHANGING WORLD*

Philip Kotler, Gary Armstrong, John Saunders and Veronica Wong

MARKETING TOUCHES OUR DAILY LIFE

Marketing touches all of us every day of our lives. We wake up to the bleep of a Sanyo radio alarm clock. It plays a track from a Chris Rea album and then a commercial advertising ZZ Top concert tickets. Then we brush our teeth with Colgate, some of us shave with a Gillette Sensor razor, gargle with Scope and use a range of toiletries and appliances produced by manufacturers around the world. We put on our Levi jeans and Nike shoes and head for the kitchen, where we have a pot of Danone breakfast yoghurt and wash down a bowl of Kellogg's Fruit n' Fibre with a mug of Kenco coffee.

We consume oranges grown in Spain and tea imported from Sri Lanka, read a newspaper made of Canadian wood pulp and tune in to international news coming from as far away as America. We fetch our mail to find an Air Miles handbook, direct mail from the RSPCA inviting donations to help save animals' lives, a letter from a Prudential insurance agent and coupons offering discounts on our favourite branded items in our local grocery superstore. We step out of the door and drive our made-in-Genk Ford to the IKEA superstore to fetch some do-it-yourself shelves for the apartment. We may stop at a Marks & Spencer to fetch some special St Michael fresh tropical fruits and gourmet party food. We buy Madonna's latest album at Virgin Megastore, grab a Big Mac at McDonald's and book a trip to EuroDisney at a Thomas Cook travel agency.

The *marketing system* has made all this possible with little effort on our part. It has given us a standard of living that our ancestors could not have imagined.

INTRODUCTION

The marketing system that delivers our high standard of living consists of many large and small companies, all seeking success. Many factors contribute to making a business successful – great strategy, dedicated employees, good information systems, excellent implementation. However, today's successful companies at all levels have one thing in common – they are strongly customer-focused and heavily committed to marketing. These companies share an absolute dedication to sensing, serving and satisfying the needs of customers in well-understood markets. They motivate everyone in the organization to deliver high quality and value for their customers.

Many people think that only large companies operating in highly developed economies use marketing, but marketing actually occurs both inside and outside the business sector, in small and large organizations and in all kinds of countries. In the business sector, marketing first spread most rapidly in consumer packaged-goods companies, consumer durables companies and industrial equipment companies. Within the past few decades, however, consumer service firms, especially airline, insurance and financial services companies, have also adopted modern marketing practices. The latest business groups to take an interest in marketing are professionals such as lawyers, accountants, physicians and architects, who now have begun to advertise and to price their services aggressively.

Marketing also has become a vital component in the strategies of many *non-profit* organizations, such as schools, churches, hospitals, museums, performing arts groups and even police departments. Consider the following developments:

> Many universities, facing declining enrolments and rising competition and costs, are using marketing to compete for students and funds. They are defining target markets, improving their communication and promotion, and responding better to student needs and wants.
>
> To stem the failing number of church-goers, many of Britain's church groups are seeking more effective ways to attract members and maintain financial support. Increasingly, and despite the controversy, preachers are using the press, television and radio to advertise religion to the general public. They are conducting marketing research to better understand member needs and are redesigning their 'service offerings' accordingly. Some evangelical groups are even starting their own radio and television stations. The Vatican has been known to have appointed the advertising agency, Saatchi and Saatchi, to run a £2.5m television campaign.[1]
>
> Cuts in funding for the performing arts are forcing museum and gallery managers to be more customer-oriented. To attract customers and boost income, many are taking steps to employ marketing techniques, ranging from sponsorships, advertising and direct mail to more aggressive shop merchandising and catering for corporate hospitality.[2]
>
> Finally, many longstanding non-profit organisations – the YMCA, the Red Cross, the Salvation Army, the Girl Scouts – are striving to modernise their missions and 'products' to attract more, members and donors.[3]

Even government agencies have shown an increased interest in marketing. For example, various government agencies are now designing *social marketing campaigns* to encourage energy conservation and concern for the environment, or to discourage smoking, excessive drinking and drug use.[4]

Finally, marketing is practised widely all over the world. Most countries in North and South America, Western Europe and the Far East have well-developed marketing systems. Even in Eastern Europe and the former Soviet republics, where marketing has long had a bad name, long-endured economic stagnation has caused nations to move towards market-oriented economies. Dramatic political and social changes have created new market opportunities and left business and government leaders in most of these nations eager to learn everything they can about modern marketing practices.

Sound marketing is critical to the success of every organization – whether large or small, for profit or non-profit, domestic or global. In this chapter, we define marketing and its core concepts, describe the central philosophies of marketing thinking and practice, explain the goals of the marketing system, and discuss some of the significant new challenges that marketers now face.

WHAT IS MARKETING?

What does the term *marketing* mean? Marketing must be understood not in the old sense of making a sale – 'selling' – but in the new sense of *satisfying customer needs*. Many people mistakenly think of marketing only as selling and promotion. And no wonder, for every day we are bombarded with television commercials, newspaper ads, direct mail and sales calls. Someone is always trying to sell us something. It seems that we cannot escape death, taxes or selling!

Therefore, many students are surprised to learn that selling is only the tip of the marketing iceberg; it is but one of several marketing functions, and often, not the most important one. If the marketer does a good job of identifying customer needs, develops good products and prices, distributes and promotes them effectively, these goods will sell very easily.

Everyone knows something about 'hot' products. When Sony designed its first Walkman cassette and disc players, when Nintendo first offered its improved video game console, and when The Body Shop introduced animal-cruelty-free cosmetics and toiletries, these manufacturers were swamped with orders. They had designed the 'right' products: not 'me-too' products, but ones offering new benefits. Peter Drucker, a leading management thinker, has put it this way: 'The aim of marketing is to make selling superfluous. The aim is to know and understand the customer so well that the product or service fits . . . and sells itself.'[5]

This does not mean that selling and promotion are unimportant. Rather, it means that they are part of a larger **marketing mix** – a set of marketing tools that work together to affect the marketplace. We define **marketing** as: *a social and managerial process by which individuals and groups obtain what they need and want through creating and exchanging products and value with others.*[6] To explain this definition, we examine the following important terms: *needs, wants, and demands; products; value and satisfaction; exchange, transactions and relationships;* and *markets.* Figure 6.1 shows that these core marketing concepts are linked, with each concept building on the one before it.

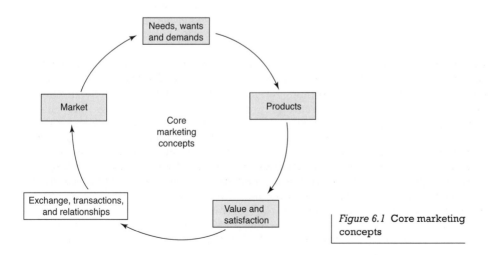

Figure 6.1 Core marketing concepts

Needs, wants, and demands

The most basic concept underlying marketing is that of human needs. A **human need** is a state of felt deprivation. Humans have many complex needs. These include basic *physical* needs for food, clothing, warmth and safety; *social* needs for belonging and affection; and *individual* needs for knowledge and self-expression. These needs are not invented by marketers, they are a basic part of the human make-up. When a need is not satisfied, a person will do one of two things:

1 look for an object that will satisfy it; or
2 try to reduce the need.

People in industrial societies may try to find or develop objects that will satisfy their desires. People in less-developed societies may try to reduce their desires and satisfy them with what is available.

Human wants are the form taken by human needs as they are shaped by culture and individual personality. A hungry person in Bahrain may want a vegetable curry, mango chutney and lassi. A hungry person in Eindhoven may want a ham and cheese roll, salad and a beer. A hungry person in Hong Kong may want a bowl of noodles, char siu pork and jasmine tea. Wants are described in terms of objects that will satisfy needs. As a society evolves, the wants of its members expand. As people are exposed to more objects that arouse their interest and desire, producers try to provide more want-satisfying products and services.

People have narrow, basic needs (e.g. for food or shelter), but almost unlimited wants. However, they also have limited resources. They therefore want to choose products that provide the most satisfaction for their money. When backed by an ability to pay – that is, buying power – wants become **demands**.

Consumers view products as bundles of benefits and choose products that give them the best bundle for their money. Thus a Ford Fiesta means basic transportation, low price and fuel economy. A Mercedes means comfort, luxury and status. Given their wants and resources, people choose the product with the benefits that add up to the most satisfaction.

Products

People satisfy their needs and wants with products. A **product** is anything that can be offered to a market to satisfy a need or want. Usually, the word *product* suggests a physical object, such as a car, a television set or a bar of soap. However, the concept of product is not limited to physical objects – anything capable of satisfying a need can be called a product. The importance of physical goods lies not so much in owning them as in the benefits they provide. We don't buy food to look at, but because it satisfies our hunger. We don't buy a microwave to admire, but because it cooks our food.

Marketers often use the expressions *goods* and *services* to distinguish between physical products and intangible ones. Moreover, consumers obtain benefits through other vehicles, such as *persons*, *places*, *organizations*, *activities* and *ideas*. Consumers decide which entertainers to watch on television, which places to visit on vacation, which organizations to support through contributions and which political party to vote for. Thus the term *product* covers physical goods, services and a variety of other vehicles that can satisfy consumers' needs and wants. If at times the term *product* does not seem to fit, we could substitute other terms such as *satisfier*, *resource* or *offer*.

Many sellers make the mistake of paying more attention to the physical products they offer than to the benefits produced by these products. They see themselves as selling a product rather than providing a *solution* to a need. A manufacturer of drill bits may think that the customer needs a drill bit, but what the customer *really* needs is a hole. These sellers may suffer from 'marketing myopia'.[7] They are so taken with their products that they focus only on existing wants and lose sight of underlying customer needs. They forget that a physical product is only a tool to solve a consumer problem. These sellers have trouble if a new product comes along that serves the need better or less expensively. The customer with the same *need* will *want* the new product.

Value and satisfaction

Consumers usually face a broad array of products that might satisfy a given need. How do they choose among these many products? Consumers make buying choices based on their perceptions of a product's value.

Suppose you need to travel three miles each day to work. A variety of products could satisfy this need, ranging from roller skates, a bicycle or motorcycle to a car, taxi or bus. Besides simply getting to work, you also have several additional needs: you want to get there easily, quickly, safely and economically. Each product has a different capacity to satisfy these various needs. The bicycle would require more effort, and is slower and less safe, although more economical, than the car. You must decide which product delivers the most total satisfaction.

The guiding concept is **customer value**. You will estimate the capacity of each product to satisfy your total needs. You might rank the products from the most need-satisfying to the least need-satisfying. If you were to imagine the *ideal* product for this task, you might answer that it would get you to work in a split second with complete safety, no effort and zero cost. Of course, no such product exists. Still, you will value each existing product according to how close it comes to your ideal product. Suppose you are mostly interested in the speed and ease of getting to work. If all of the products were free, we would predict that you would choose the car. But therein lies the rub. Because each product does involve a cost, and because the car costs much more than any of the other products, you will not necessarily buy the car. You will end up choosing the product that gives the most benefit for the money spent – the greatest value.

Today, consumer-behaviourists have gone far beyond narrow economic assumptions about how consumers form value judgements and make product choices. [. . .]

Exchange, transactions and relationships

Marketing occurs when people decide to satisfy needs and wants through exchange. **Exchange** is the act of obtaining a desired object from someone by offering something in return. Exchange is only one of many ways people can obtain a desired object. For example, hungry people can find food by hunting, fishing or gathering fruit. They could beg for food or take food from someone else. Finally, they could offer money, another good or a service in return for food.

As a means of satisfying needs, exchange has much in its favour. People do not have to prey on others or depend on donations. Nor must they possess the skills to produce every necessity, for themselves. They can concentrate on making things they are good at making and trade them for needed items made by others. Thus exchange allows a society to produce much more than it would with any alternative system.

Exchange is the core concept of marketing. For an exchange to take place, several conditions must be satisfied. Of course, at least two parties must participate and each have something of value to offer to the other. Each party also must want to deal with the other party and each must be free to accept or reject the other's offer. Finally each party must be able to communicate and deliver.

These conditions simply make exchange *possible*. Whether exchange actually *takes place* depends on the parties' coming to an agreement. If they agree, we must conclude that the act of exchange has left both of them better off or, at least, not worse off. After all, each was free to reject or accept the offer. In this sense, exchange creates value just as production creates value. It gives people more consumption choices or possibilities.

Whereas exchange is the core concept of marketing, a transaction is marketing's unit of measurement. A **transaction** consists of a trading of values between two parties. In a transaction, we must be able to say that one party gives X to another party and gets Y in return. For example, you pay a retailer £300 for a television set or the hotel £90 a night for a room. This is a classic **monetary transaction**, but not all transactions involve money. In a barter transaction, you might trade your old refrigerator in return for a neighbour's secondhand television set. A **barter transaction** also can involve services as well as goods: for example, when a lawyer writes a will for a doctor in return for a medical examination [. . .]. A transaction involves at least two things of value, conditions that are agreed upon, a time of agreement and a place of agreement.

In the broadest sense, the market tries to bring about a response to some offer. The response may be more than simply 'buying' or 'trading' goods and services. A political candidate, for instance, wants a response called 'votes', a church wants 'membership', and a social-action group wants 'idea acceptance'. Marketing consists of actions taken to obtain a desired response from a target audience towards some product, service, idea or other object.

Transaction marketing is part of the larger idea of **relationship marketing**. Smart marketers work at building long-term relationships with valued customers, distributors, dealers and suppliers. They build strong economic and social ties by promising and consistently delivering high-quality products, good service and fair prices. Increasingly, marketing is shifting from trying to maximize the profit on each individual transaction to maximizing mutually beneficial relationships with consumers and other parties. The operating assumption is: *build good relationships and profitable transactions will follow*.

Markets

The concept of transactions leads to the concept of a market. A **market** is the set of actual and potential buyers of a product. To understand the nature of a market, imagine a primitive economy consisting of only four people: a fisherman, a hunter, a potter and a farmer. Figure 6.2 shows the three different ways in which these traders could meet their needs:

1 *Self-sufficiency* They gather the needed goods for themselves. Thus, the hunter spends most of the time hunting, but also must take time to fish, make pottery, and farm to obtain the other goods. The hunter is thereby less efficient at hunting and the same is true of the other traders.
2 *Decentralized exchange* Each person sees the other three as potential 'buyers' who make up a market. Thus, the hunter may make separate trips to trade meat for the goods of the fisherman, the potter and the farmer.
3 *Centralized exchange* A new person called a *merchant* appears and locates in a central area called, a *marketplace*. Each trader brings goods to the merchant and trades for other needed goods. Thus, rather than transacting with the other providers, the hunter transacts with one 'market' to obtain all the needed goods. Merchants and central marketplaces greatly reduce the total number of transactions needed to accomplish a given volume of exchange.[8]

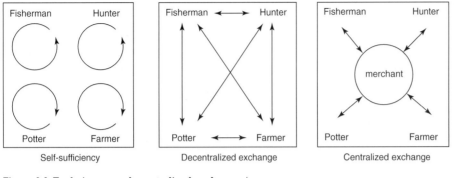

Self-sufficiency   Decentralized exchange   Centralized exchange

Figure 6.2 Evolution towards centralized exchange

As the number of persons and transactions increases in a society, the number of merchants and marketplaces also increases. In advanced societies, markets need not be physical locations where buyers and sellers interact. With modern communications and transportation, a merchant easily can advertise a product on a late evening television programme, take orders from thousands of customers over the phone, and mail the goods to the buyers on the following day without having had any physical contact with them.

A market can grow up around a product, a service or anything else of value. For example, a *labour market* consists of people who are willing to offer their work in return for wages or products. In fact, various institutions, such as employment agencies and job-counselling firms, will grow up around a labour market to help it function better. The *money market* is another important market that emerges to meet the needs of people so that they can borrow, lend, save and protect money. The *donor market* has emerged to meet the financial needs of non-profit organizations.

Marketing

The concept of markets finally brings us full circle to the concept of marketing. **Marketing** means working with markets to bring about exchanges for the purpose of satisfying human needs and wants. Thus, we return to our definition of marketing as a process by which individuals and groups obtain what they need and want by creating and exchanging products and value with others.

Exchange processes involve work. Sellers must:

- search for buyers;
- identify their needs;
- design good products;
- promote them;
- store and deliver these products; and
- set prices for them.

Activities such as product development, research, communication, distribution, pricing and service are core marketing activities.

Although we normally think of marketing as being carried on by sellers, buyers also carry on marketing activities. Consumers do 'marketing' when they search for the goods they need at prices they can afford. Company purchasing agents do 'marketing' when they track down sellers and bargain for good terms. A *sellers' market* is one in which sellers have more power and buyers must be the more active 'marketers'. In a *buyers' market*, buyers have more power and sellers have to be more active 'marketers'.

In recent decades, the supply of goods has grown faster than the demand for them. Today, most markets have become buyers' markets, and marketing has become identified with sellers seeking out buyers. [. . .]

MARKETING MANAGEMENT

Most people think of marketing management as finding enough customers for the company's current output, but this is too limited a view. The organization has a desired level of demand for its products. At any point in time, there may be no demand, adequate demand, irregular demand or too much demand, and marketing management must find ways to deal with these different demand states. Marketing management is concerned not only with finding and increasing demand, but also with changing or even reducing it. Thus marketing management seeks to affect the level, timing and nature of demand in a way that helps the organization achieve its objectives. Simply put, marketing management is *demand management*. Marketing managers in different organizations might face any of the following states of demand. The marketing task is to manage demand states effectively.

Negative demand

A large part of the market dislikes the product and may even pay to avoid it. Examples are vaccinations, dental work, cancer screenings and seat belts. Marketers must analyse why the market dislikes the product, and whether product redesign, lower prices or more positive promotion can change the consumer attitudes.

No demand

Target consumers may be uninterested in the product. Thus farmers may not care about a new farming method and consumers may not be interested in three-wheeled electric cars. The marketer must find ways to connect the product's benefits with the market's needs and interests.

Latent demand

Consumers have a want that is not satisfied by any existing product or service. There is strong latent demand for nonharmful cigarettes, safer neighbourhoods, biodegradable packages and more fuel-efficient cars. The marketing task is to measure the size of the potential market and develop effective goods and services that will satisfy the demand.

Falling demand

Sooner or later, every organization faces falling demand for one of its products. Churches have seen their membership decline and dairy farmers have seen consumption of full-cream milk fall. The marketer must find the cause of market decline and restimulate demand by finding new markets, changing product features or creating more effective communications.

Irregular demand

Demand varies on a seasonal, daily or even hourly basis, causing problems of idle or overworked capacity. In mass transit, much equipment is idle during slow travel hours and too little is available during peak hours. Museums are undervisited during weekdays and overcrowded during weekends. Marketers must find ways to change the time pattern of demand through flexible pricing, promotion and other incentives.

Full demand

The organization has just the amount of demand it wants and can handle. The marketer works to maintain the current level of demand in the face of changing consumer preferences and increasing competition. The organization maintains quality and continually measures consumer satisfaction to make sure it is doing a good job.

Overfull demand

Demand is higher than the company can or wants to handle. For example, many motorways carry more traffic than they are built for and Disney World is overcrowded in the summertime. Utilities, bus companies, restaurants and other businesses often face overfull demand at peak times. The marketing task, called *demarketing*, is to find ways to reduce the demand temporarily or permanently. Demarketing involves actions such as raising prices and reducing promotion and service. Demarketing does not aim to destroy demand, but selectively to reduce it.

We define **marketing management** as the analysis, planning, implementation and control of programmes designed to create, build and maintain beneficial exchanges with target buyers for the purpose of achieving organizational objectives. Marketing managers include sales managers and salespeople, advertising executives, sales-promotion people, marketing researchers, product managers, pricing specialists and others.

MARKETING MANAGEMENT PHILOSOPHIES

We describe marketing management as carrying out tasks to achieve desired exchanges with target markets. What *philosophy* should guide these marketing efforts? What weight should be given to the interests of the organization, customers and society? Very often these interests conflict. Invariably, the organization's marketing management philosophy influences the way it approaches its buyers.

There are five alternative concepts under which organizations conduct their marketing activities: the production, product, selling, marketing, and societal marketing concepts.

The production concept

The **production concept** holds that consumers will favour products that are available and highly affordable and that management therefore should focus on improving production and distribution efficiency. This concept is one of the oldest philosophies that guides sellers.

The production concept is a useful philosophy in two types of situations. The first occurs when the demand for a product exceeds the supply. Here, management should look for ways to increase production. The second situation occurs when the product's cost is too high and improved productivity is needed to bring it down. For example, Henry Ford's whole philosophy was to perfect the production of the Model T so that its cost could be reduced and more people could afford it. He joked about offering people a car of any colour as long as it was black. Today, Texas Instruments (TI) follows this philosophy of increased production and lower costs in order to bring down prices. The company won a big share of the handcalculator market with this philosophy. But when it used the same strategy in the digital watch market, TI failed. Although TI's watches were priced low, customers did not find them very attractive. In its drive to bring down prices, TI lost sight of something else that its customers wanted – namely, *attractive*, affordable digital watches.

The product concept

Another important concept guiding sellers, the **product concept**, holds that consumers will favour products that offer the most quality, performance and innovative features, and that an organization should thus devote energy to making continuous product improvements. Some manufacturers believe that if they can build a better mousetrap, the world will beat a path to their door.[9] But they are often rudely shocked. Buyers may well be looking for a better solution to a mouse problem, but not necessarily for a better mousetrap. The solution might be a chemical spray, an exterminating service or something that works better than a mousetrap. Furthermore a better mousetrap will not sell unless the manufacturer designs, packages and prices it attractively; places it in convenient distribution channels; and brings it to the attention of people who need it and convinces them that it is a better product. A product orientation leads to obsession with technology because managers believe that technical superiority is the key to business success.

The product concept also can lead to 'marketing myopia'. For instance, railway management once thought that users wanted *trains* rather than *transportation* and overlooked the growing challenge of airlines, buses, trucks and cars. Building bigger and better trains would not solve consumers' demand for transportation, but creating other forms of transportation and extending choice would.

The selling concept

Many organizations follow the **selling concept**, which holds that consumers will not buy enough of the organization's products unless it undertakes a large-scale selling and promotion effort. The concept is typically practised with **unsought goods** – those that buyers do not normally think of buying, such as encyclopaedias and funeral plots. These industries must be good at tracking down prospects and selling them on product benefits.

The selling concept is also practised in the non-profit area. A political party, for example, will vigorously sell its candidate to voters as a fantastic person for the job. The candidate works hard at selling himself – shaking hands, kissing babies, meeting donors and making speeches. Much money also has to be spent on radio and television advertising, posters and mailings. Candidate flaws are often hidden from the public because the aim is to get the sale, not to worry about consumer satisfaction afterwards.

A selling-oriented organization thus focuses on short-term results – profits via sales now – rather than on longer-term market and financial benefits created by satisfied customers who want more of the goods or services offered by the organization.

The marketing concept

The **marketing concept** holds that achieving organizational goals depends on determining the needs and wants of target markets and delivering the desired satisfactions more effectively and efficiently than competitors do. Surprisingly, this concept is a relatively recent business philosophy. The marketing concept has been stated in colourful ways such as 'Find a need and fill it' (Kaiser Sand & Gravel); 'To fly, to serve' (British Airways); and 'We're not satisfied until you are' (GE).

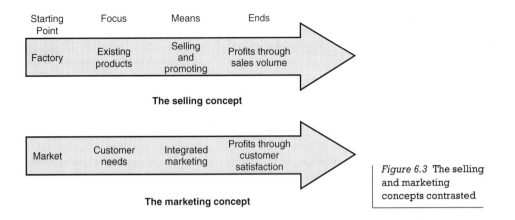

Figure 6.3 The selling and marketing concepts contrasted

The selling concept and the marketing concept are frequently confused. Figure 6.3 compares the two concepts. The selling concept takes an *inside-out* perspective. It starts with the factory, focuses on the company's existing products and calls for heavy selling and promotion to obtain profitable sales. In contrast, the marketing concept takes an *outside-in* perspective. It starts with a well-defined market, focuses on customer needs, coordinates all the marketing activities affecting customers and makes profits by creating customer satisfaction. Under the marketing concept, companies produce what consumers want, thereby satisfying consumers and making profits.

Many successful and well-known global companies have adopted the marketing concept. IKEA, Marks & Spencer, Procter & Gamble, Marriott, Nordström and McDonald's follow it faithfully [. . .]. Toyota, the highly successful Japanese car manufacturer, is also a prime example of an organization that takes a customer- and marketing-oriented view of its business.

Toyota openly publicizes its intent on getting deep into the hearts and minds of its customers, to establish precisely what they want and subsequently find ways to fulfil their wishes. In Japan, Toyota has built the Amlux, a 14-storey building resembling a blue and black striped rocket, which it uses to attract millions of visitors. These could be potential customers or people with ideas on how the company should respond to consumers' vehicle requirements. These visitors are allowed to spend as much time as they want designing their own vehicles on computer/TV screen in the vehicle-design studio. There is a two-way information centre where visitors obtain specific information about the company, its dealers or products. The visitors are also allowed to expound, at length, on what they think Toyota should be doing or making. Meanwhile, Toyota's attentive note-taking staff ensure that the entire Amlux complex is dedicated to involving potential customers who can give them close insights into how their car needs can be satisfied.

In marketing-led organizations, the entire workforce share the belief that the customer is all-important and that building lasting relationships is the key to customer retention. The following quotes reflect the level of dedication successful marketing organizations devote to customers:

We believe that real customers focus has to start from the top down and the bottom up, and it has to be totally accepted by the whole workforce. Otherwise, the lines of communication will fail.

(Divisional Director of the adventure park, Alton Towers, UK)

We put the same amount of energy into attracting existing customers as we do attracting new customers. Within the mentality of each store is the realisation that the existing customer is all-important to today's business.

(Chris Moore, Domino's Pizza)

We don't rely on buying customer loyalty, we believe we have to earn customer loyalty, and we do that by making sure that the products we offer and the service . . . meet exactly what the customer requires from us.

(Peter Whinney, Operations Manager, Land Rover)

Many companies claim to practise the marketing concept, but do not. They have the *forms* of marketing – such as a marketing director, product managers, marketing plans and marketing research – but this does not mean that they are *market-focused* and *customer-driven* companies. The question is whether they are finely tuned to changing customer needs and competitor strategies. Formerly great Western companies – Philips, General Motors, IBM, General Electric Company – all lost substantial market share because they failed to adjust their marketing strategies to the changing marketplace. Several years of hard work are needed to turn a sales-oriented company into a marketing-oriented company. The goal is to build customer satisfaction into the very fabric of the firm. Customer satisfaction is no longer a fad. As one marketing analyst notes: 'It's becoming a way of life . . . as embedded into corporate cultures as information technology and strategic planning.'[10]

Why is it supremely important to satisfy customers? A company's sales come from two groups: *new* customers and *repeat* customers. It usually costs more to attract new customers than to retain current customers. Therefore, customer *retention* is often more critical than customer *attraction*. The key to customer retention is *customer satisfaction*. A satisfied customer buys more, stays 'loyal' longer, talks favourably to others, pays less attention to competing brands and advertising, is less price sensitive and costs less to serve than a first time customer.

However, the marketing concept does not mean that a company should try to give *all* consumers *everything* they want. Marketers must balance creating more value for customers against making profits for the company:

The purpose of marketing is not to *maximise* customer satisfaction. The shortest definition of marketing I know is 'meeting needs profitably'. The purpose of marketing is to generate customer value [at a profit]. The truth is [that the relationship with a customer] will break up if value evaporates. You've got to continue to generate more value for the consumer but not give away the house. It's a very delicate balance.[11]

The societal marketing concept

The **societal marketing concept** holds that the organization should determine the needs, wants and interests of target markets. It should then deliver the desired satisfactions more effectively and efficiently than competitors in a way that maintains or improves the consumer's *and the society's* well-being. The societal marketing concept is the newest of the five marketing management philosophies.

The societal marketing concept questions whether the pure marketing concept is adequate in an age of environmental problems, resource shortages, worldwide economic problems and neglected social services. It asks if the firm that senses, serves and satisfies individual wants is always doing what's best for consumers and society in the long run. According to the societal marketing concept, the pure marketing concept overlooks possible conflicts between short-run consumer *wants* and long-run consumer *welfare*.

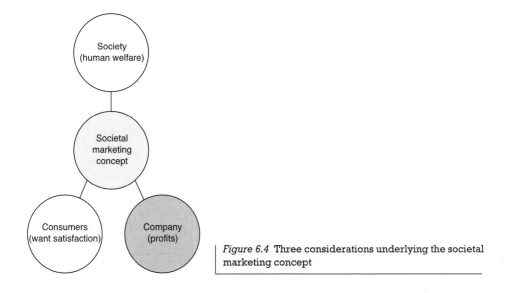

Figure 6.4 Three considerations underlying the societal marketing concept

Consider the Coca-Cola Company. Most people see it as a highly responsible corporation producing fine soft drinks that satisfy consumer tastes. Yet certain consumer and environmental groups have voiced concerns that Coke has little nutritional value, can harm people's teeth, contains caffeine and adds to the litter problem with disposable bottles and cans.

Such concerns and conflicts led to the societal marketing concept. As Figure 6.4 shows, the societal marketing concept calls upon marketers to balance three considerations in setting their marketing policies: company profits, consumer wants, and society's interests. Originally, most companies based their marketing decisions largely on short-run company profit. Eventually, they began to recognize the long-run importance of satisfying consumer wants and the marketing concept emerged. Now many companies are beginning to think of society's interests when making their marketing decisions.

One such company is the international corporation, Johnson & Johnson, that stresses community and environmental responsibility. J&J's concern for societal interests is summarized in a company document called 'Our Credo', which stresses honesty, integrity and putting people before profits. Under this credo, Johnson & Johnson would rather take a big loss than ship a bad batch of one of its products. And the company supports many community and employee programmes that benefit its consumers and workers, and the environment. J&J's chief executive puts it this way: 'If we keep trying to do what's right, at the end of the day we believe the market-place will reward us.'[12]

The company backs these words with actions. Consider the tragic tampering case in which eight people died from swallowing cyanide-laced capsules of Tylenol, a Johnson & Johnson brand. Although J&J believed that the pills had been altered in only a few stores, not in the factory, it quickly recalled all of its product. The recall cost the company $240 million in earnings. In the long run, however, the company's swift recall of Tylenol strengthened consumer confidence and loyalty, and Tylenol remains the leading brand of pain reliever in the US market. In this and other cases, J&J management has found that doing what's right benefits both consumers and the company. Says the chief executive: 'The Credo should not be viewed as some kind of social welfare program . . . it's just plain good business.'[13] Thus over the years, Johnson & Johnson's dedication to consumers and community service has made it one of America's most admired companies, *and* one of the most profitable.

Increasingly, firms also have to meet the expectations of society as a whole. For example, society expects businesses to uphold basic ethical and environmental standards. Not only should they have ethics and environmental policies, they must also genuinely uphold these standards. Consider, for instance, the bad publicity The Body Shop received during the early 1990s when the company came under attack in 1992 over its environmental standards. Some critics who researched the company's ethical and environmental practices charged that the high standards which it claims to uphold might be less genuine than it would like the world to think. The critics also expressed a broader concern – that the company persistently appears to exaggerate its involvement in worthy causes. Such charges cannot be ignored by the company's management, particularly its founder, Anita Roddick, and chairman, Gordon Roddick, who have long been involved in promoting ethical and environmental causes within the business world. Any tarnishing of The Body Shop's image removes the organization's point of differentiation and, therefore, increases its vulnerability to competition, like Boots in the United Kingdom and Bath & Body Works, the US natural toiletries group, which is expanding into global markets.[14]

THE GOALS OF THE MARKETING SYSTEM

Our marketing system consists of the collective marketing activities of tens of thousands of profit and non-profit organizations at home and around the globe. This marketing system affects everyone – buyers, sellers and many public groups with common characteristics. The goal of these groups may conflict.

Buyers want good-quality products at reasonable prices in convenient locations. They want wide brand and feature assortments; helpful, pleasant and honest salespeople; and strong warranties backed by good follow-up service. The marketing system can greatly affect buyer satisfaction.

Sellers face many challenging decisions when preparing an offer for the market. What consumer groups should be targeted? What do target consumers need and how should products be designed and priced to give the greatest value? What wholesalers and retailers should be used? What advertising, personal selling and sales promotion would help sell the product? The market demands a lot. Sellers must apply modern marketing thinking in order to develop an offer that attracts and satisfies customers.

Legislators, public interest groups and other *publics* have a strong interest in the marketing activities of business. Do manufacturers make safe and reliable products? Do they describe their products accurately in ads and packaging? Is competition working in the market to provide a reasonable range of quality and price choice? Are manufacturing and packaging activities hurting the environment? The marketing system has a significant impact on the quality of life, and various groups of citizens want to make the system work as well as possible. They act as watchdogs of consumer interests and favour consumer education, information and protection.

The marketing system affects so many people in so many ways that it inevitably stirs controversy. Some people intensely dislike modern marketing activity, charging it with ruining the environment, bombarding the public with senseless ads, creating unnecessary wants, teaching greed to youngsters and committing several other 'sins'. Consider the following:

> For the past 6,000 years the field of marketing has been thought of as made up of fast-buck artists, con-men, wheeler-dealers, and shoddy-goods distributors. Too many of us have been 'taken' by the touts or con-men; and all of us at times have been prodded into buying all sorts of 'things' we really did not need, and which we found later on we did not even want.[15]

Others vigorously defend marketing:

> Aggressive marketing policies and practices have been largely responsible for the high material standard of living in the west. Today through mass, low-cost marketing we enjoy products which once were considered luxuries, and which still are so classified in many foreign countries.[16]

What should a society seek from its marketing system? Four goals have been suggested: maximize consumption, maximize consumer satisfaction, maximize choice, and maximize quality of life.

Maximize consumption

Many business executives believe that marketing's job should be to stimulate maximum consumption, which in turn will create maximum production, employment and wealth. This view has been promoted by slogans such as 'Who says you can't have it all?' (Michelob); or 'The costliest perfume in the world' (Joy); or 'Greed is good' (from the movie *Wall Street*). The assumption is that the more people spend, buy, and consume the happier they are. 'More is better' is the war cry. Yet some people doubt that increased material goods mean more happiness: They see too many affluent people leading unhappy lives. Their philosophy is 'less is more' and 'small is beautiful'.

Maximize consumer satisfaction

Another view holds that the goal of the marketing system is to maximize consumer satisfaction, not simply the quantity of consumption. Buying a new car or owning more clothes counts only if this adds to the buyer's satisfaction.

Unfortunately, consumer satisfaction is difficult to measure. First, nobody has discovered how to measure the total satisfaction created by a particular product or marketing activity. Second, the satisfaction that some individual consumers get from the 'goods' of a product or service must be offset by the 'evils', such as pollution and environmental damage. Third, the satisfaction that some people get from consuming certain goods, such as status goods, depends on the fact that few other people have these goods. Thus, evaluating the marketing system in terms of how much satisfaction it delivers is difficult. Companies, however, can develop ways to evaluate the level of satisfaction offered to customers. Consider the following example:

> The international courier company, Federal Express, tried to rate not only the quality of their existing services, but also what it could be delivering. In both the US and European markets, FedEx went beyond its customer satisfaction index to improve its basic offering, while growing its customer base. FedEx discovered from its customer satisfaction surveys that it had been providing customers with a 'more than satisfactory' level of service. The firm decided that 'good enough' was not good enough. It examined its entire package delivery and billing process, charting the costs and activities at each step from the customer's perspective. It offers to its 20,000 or so key customers 'Powership', a computer terminal which generates address labels with routing instructions and automatic billing in the form of an invoice that hits the computer screen when the package arrives. FedEx uses its customer knowledge to upgrade and improve its core services. It claims that its employees understand their customers' needs better than the customers themselves. As a result, customer loyalty is strengthened, with customers forming an even closer relationship with the company. Customer satisfaction levels have soared, so has customer spending.[17]

Maximize choice

Some marketers believe that the goal of a marketing system should be to maximize product variety and consumer choice. This system would enable consumers to find goods that satisfy their tastes exactly. Consumers would be able to realize their lifestyle fully, and could therefore maximize their overall satisfaction.

Unfortunately, maximizing consumer choice comes at a cost. First, the price of goods and services rises because producing great variety increases production and inventory costs. In turn, higher prices reduce consumers' real income and consumption. Second, the increase in product variety will require greater consumer search and effort: consumers have to spend more time learning about and evaluating the different products. Third, the existence of more products, will not necessarily increase the consumer's real choice. For example, hundreds of brands of beer are sold worldwide, but most of them taste about the same. So when a product category contains many brands with few differences, consumers face a choice that is really no choice at all. Finally, not all consumers welcome great product variety. For some consumers, too much choice leads to confusion and frustration.

Maximize life quality

Many people believe that the goal of a marketing system should be to improve the *quality of life*. This also includes not only the quality, quantity, availability and cost of goods, but also the quality of the physical and cultural environments. Advocates of this view would judge marketing systems not only by the amount of direct consumer satisfaction, but also by the impact of marketing on the quality of the environment. Most people would agree that quality of life is a worthwhile goal for the marketing system. But they might also agree that quality is hard to measure and that it means different things to different people.

MARKETING CHALLENGES IN THE 1990s

Marketing operates within a dynamic global environment. Every decade calls upon marketing managers to think freshly about their marketing objectives and practices. Rapid changes can quickly make yesterday's winning strategies out of date. As management thought-leader Peter Drucker once observed, a company's winning formula for the last decade will probably be its undoing in the next decade.

What are the marketing challenges of the 1990s? Today's companies are wrestling with increased global competition, environmental decline, economic stagnation, and a host of other economic, political and social problems. In the European Union (EU), as the concept of nationally separate markets vaporizes, competition among sellers will further intensify. There is increasing pressure on individual firms within member countries to adjust to evolving deregulation and advancement of universal trading standards within the single market. However, these problems also provide marketing opportunities.

We now look more deeply into three key forces that are changing the marketing landscape and challenging marketing strategy: rapid globalization, the changing world economy, and the call for more socially responsible actions.

Rapid globalization

The world economy has undergone radical change during the past two decades. Geographical and cultural distances have shrunk with the advent of jet planes, fax machines, global computer and telephone hook-ups, world television satellite and cable broadcasts, and other technical advances. This has allowed companies to greatly expand their geographical market coverage, purchasing, and manufacturing. Many companies are trying to create a global structure to move ideas swiftly around the world. The picture is one of a vastly more complex marketing environment for both companies and consumers.

Today, almost every company, large or small, is touched in some way by global competition. European and US firms, for example, are being challenged at home by the skilful marketing of Japanese and other Asian multinationals. Companies like Toyota, Honda, Fujitsu, Sony and Samsung have often outperformed their Western competitors in overseas markets. Similarly, Western companies in a wide range of industries have found new opportunities abroad. Glaxo, Asea Brown Boveri, Coca-Cola, IKEA, Toys 'R' Us, Club Mediterranean and many others have developed global operations, making and selling their products worldwide. The following are just a few of the countless examples of Western companies taking advantage of international marketing opportunities:

IKEA, the Swedish home furnishings retailer, grew from one store in 1958 to more than 100 stores, stretched over 22 countries, by the early 1990s. IKEA's European expansion has hit the fortunes of traditional furniture retailers and manufacturers in supposedly staid furniture markets. Some have not survived the onslaught. [The UK's Habitat] was later acquired by IKEA. IKEA has successfully spread into the North American, Far Eastern and Australian markets. It practises its four-pronged philosophy – attention to product quality, value (low prices and 'more for your money'), innovative style and service – which it has successfully transferred to markets world-wide. Over the years, IKEA has built, and capitalised on, its 'affordable style' mass market positioning. IKEA's international expansion has raised its fortunes in what competition claims to be a traditionally dull and fragmented market. IKEA has proven that, with the right marketing approach, fortunes can be grown even in staid, old markets.

Coca-Cola and Pepsi, fierce competitors in the global soft drinks market, recently have watched the domestic (US) soft-drink market go flat, growing at only about 1 percent per year. Thus, both now have created new marketing strategies to attack Western Europe, a market growing at an 8 percent clip. Coca-Cola invested millions of dollars in marketing at the Barcelona Olympics and in the opening of EuroDisney. Coke makes about 80 percent of its profits outside of America and it has always led Pepsi abroad. Still, Pepsi thinks that it can compete successfully with Coke in Europe. It is investing almost $500 million in European businesses during the mid-nineties in what both companies view as their new big battleground.

Toys 'R' Us spent several years slogging through the swamps of Japanese bureaucracy before it was allowed to open the very first large US discount store in Japan, the world's No. 2 toy market behind the United States. The entry of this foreign giant has Japanese toymakers and retailers edgy. The typical small Japanese toy store stocks only 1,000 to 2,000 items, whereas Toys 'R' Us stores carry as many as 15,000. And the discounter will likely offer toys at prices 10 percent to 15 percent below those of competitors. The opening of the first Japanese store was 'astonishing', attracting more than 60,000 visitors in the first three days. Toys 'R' Us plans to open ten new Japanese stores each year from now through the end of the decade. If the company's invasion of Japan succeeds as well as its recent entry into Europe, Japanese retailers will have their hands full. Toys 'R' Us began with just five European stores in 1985 but now has over 76 and growing. European sales, now about $800 million, are growing at triple the rate of total sales.

After ten years of relentless growth in America, Music Television's (MTV) home market has become saturated. Now the company is looking abroad for growth. It recently set up MTV Europe, which reaches 27 countries and 25 million homes. It is 'aggressively pan-European' – its programming and advertising are the same throughout Europe, and they are all in English. Initially, MTV has to convince advertisers that a true 'Euro-consumer' exists.'[8]

Today, companies are not only trying to sell more of their locally produced goods in international markets, they are also buying or making more components and obtaining supplies abroad. Increasingly, international firms have to coordinate more and more functional operations across borders and to increase efficiency [. . .]. Consequently, many domestically purchased goods and services are 'hybrids', with design, material purchases, manufacturing, and marketing taking place in several countries. British consumers who decide to 'buy British' might reasonably decide to avoid Sony televisions and purchase Amstrad's. Imagine their surprise when they learn that the Amstrad TV was actually made from parts and components imported from the Far East, whereas the Sony product was assembled in the United Kingdom from British-made parts.

Thus managers in countries around the world are asking: Just what is global marketing? How does it differ from domestic marketing? How do global competitors and forces affect our business? To what extent should we 'go global'? Many companies are forming strategic alliances with foreign companies, even competitors, who serve as suppliers or marketing partners. The past few years have produced some surprising alliances between competitors such as Mazda and Ford, Rover and Honda, General Electric and Matsushita, Philips and Siemens, and Daimler Benz and United Technologies of the United States. Winning companies in the 1990s may well be those that have built the best global networks.[19]

The changing world economy

A sluggish world economy has resulted in more difficult times for both consumers and marketers. Around the world, people's needs are greater than ever, but in many areas, people lack the means to pay for needed goods. Markets, after all, consist of people with needs *and* purchasing power. In many cases, the latter currently is lacking. In the developed Western and Asian economies, although wages have risen, real buying power has declined, especially for the less skilled members of the workforce. Many households have managed to maintain their buying power only because both spouses work. However, many workers have lost their jobs as manufacturers have automated to improve productivity or 'downsized' to cut costs.

Current economic conditions create both problems and opportunities for marketers. Some companies are facing declining demand and see few opportunities for growth. Others, however, are developing new solutions to changing consumer problems. Stronger businesses have recognized and taken advantage of recent developments in communications and related technologies. These developments have raised customers' expectations of product quality, performance and durability. They no longer accept or tolerate shoddy products. Power and control also have shifted from brand manufacturers to channel members who have become as sophisticated at marketing and exploiting technology as producers themselves. Many are finding ways to offer consumers 'more for less', like Sweden's IKEA and America's Toys 'R' Us. Heavy discounters are emerging to offer consumers quality merchandise at everyday low prices. These days, customers want value and more value. Increasingly marketers must deliver offerings that delight, not merely satisfy, customers. Toyota has succeeded in doing that: its highly acclaimed Lexus luxury line offers consumers all the technology (gadgetry) and comfort they can ever dream of, and at about £44,000, is considered exceptionally good value for money, compared to rival offerings in its class.

The call for more ethics and social responsibility

A third factor in today's marketing environment is the increased call for companies to take responsibility for the social and environmental impact of their actions. Corporate ethics has become a hot topic in almost every business arena, from the corporate boardroom to the business school classroom. And few companies can ignore the renewed and very demanding environmental movement.

The ethics and environmental movements will place even stricter demands on companies in the future. Consider recent environmental developments. The West was shocked, after the fall of communism, to find out about the massive environmental negligence of the former Eastern bloc governments. In these and many Asian countries, air, water and soil pollution has added to our environmental concerns. These concerns led to representatives from more than one hundred countries attending the Earth Summit in Rio de Janeiro in 1992 to consider how to handle such problems as the destruction of rain forests, global warming, endangered species and other environmental threats. The pressure is on to 'clean up' our environment. Clearly, in the future, companies will be held to an increasingly higher standard of environmental responsibility in their marketing and manufacturing activities.

More specifically, in the EU, the toughening up of environmental rules should drive nonconformers out of business, while others who are committed to 'cleaning up' or 'greening' their practices and operations will emerge the stronger. Specialist industries for environmental goods and services (e.g. paper, bottle and tyre recyclers) have expanded quickly in recent years. As they say, 'there is money in Europe's muck'.[20]

The new marketing landscape

The past decade taught business firms everywhere a humbling lesson. Domestic companies learned that they can no longer ignore global markets and competitors. Successful firms in mature industries learned that they cannot overlook emerging markets, technologies and management approaches. Companies of every sort learned that they cannot remain inwardly focused, ignoring the needs of their customers.

Prominent Western multinationals of the 1970s, including Philips, Volvo, General Motors and RCA, that floundered at marketing are all struggling to revive their fortunes today. They failed to understand their changing marketplace, their customers and the need to provide value. Today, General Motors is still trying to figure out why so many consumers around the world have switched to Japanese and European cars. In the consumer electronics industry, Philips has lost its way, losing share to Japanese competitors that have been more successful in turning expensive technologies into mass consumer products. Volvo, which has long capitalized on its safety positioning, has, of late, lost this unique selling point to other car manufacturers who have turned the safety benefit into a universal feature: many large European and Japanese car producers now offer, as standard features, driver and passenger airbags, antilock braking system and other safety devices. RCA, inventor, of so many new products, never quite mastered the art of marketing and now puts its name on products largely imported from Asia.

Today, companies must become customer-oriented and market driven in all that they do. It's not enough to be product or technology driven – too many companies still design their products without customer input, only to find them rejected in the marketplace. It is not enough to be good at winning new customers – too many companies forget about customers after the sale, only to lose their future business. Not surprisingly, we have seen a flood of books with titles such as *The Customer Driven Company, Keep the Customer, Customers for Life, Total Customer Service: The ultimate weapon,* and *The Only Thing that Matters: Bringing the customer into the center of your business.*[21] These books emphasize that for the 1990s and beyond, the key to success will be a strong focus on the marketplace and a total marketing commitment to providing value to customers.

LIBRARY
BISHOP BURTON COLLEGE
BEVERLEY HU17 8QG

SUMMARY

Marketing touches everyone's life. It is the means by which a standard of living is developed and delivered to a people. Many people confuse marketing with *selling*, but in fact, marketing occurs both before and after the selling event. Marketing actually combines many activities – marketing research, product development, distribution, pricing, advertising, personal selling and others – designed to sense, serve and satisfy consumer needs while meeting the organization's goals.

Marketing is human activity directed at satisfying needs and wants through *exchange processes*. The core concepts of marketing are *needs, wants, demands, products, exchange, transactions* and *markets*.

Marketing management is the analysis, planning, implementation and control of programmes designed to create, build and maintain beneficial exchanges with target markets in order to achieve organizational objectives. Marketers must be good at managing the level, timing, and composition of demand because actual demand can be different from what the organization wants.

Marketing management can be guided by five different philosophies. The *production concept* holds that consumers favour products which are available at low cost and that management's task is to improve production efficiency and bring down prices. The *product concept* holds that consumers favour quality products and that little promotional effort is thus required. The *selling concept* holds that consumers will not buy enough of the company's products unless stimulated through heavy selling and promotion. The *marketing concept* holds that a company should research the needs and wants of a well-defined target market and deliver the desired satisfactions. The *societal marketing concept* holds that the company should generate customer satisfaction and long-run societal well-being as the key to achieving both its goals and its responsibilities.

Marketing practices have a considerable impact on people in our society. Different goals have been proposed for a marketing system, such as maximizing *consumption, consumer satisfaction, consumer choice,* or *quality of life.* Marketing operates within a dynamic global environment. Rapid changes can quickly make yesterday's winning strategies obsolete. Marketers are facing many new challenges and opportunities in the 1990s. With the end of the Cold War, today's companies are wrestling with increased global competition, a sluggish world economy, a call for greater social responsibility, and a host of other economic, political and social problems. However, these problems also offer marketing opportunities. The future for adaptive organizations will always look bright. To be successful, they will have to be strongly market focused.

REFERENCES

*   This chapter has been adapted from excerpts from, P. Kottler *et al., Principles of Marketing (European Edition)* (London: Prentice Hall).

1   Martin Wroe, 'Ministries, missions and markets', *Marketing Business* (October 1993), 8–11.

2   'Balancing act', *Marketing Business* (October 1991), 41–3.

3   For more examples, see Philip Kotler and Karen Fox, *Strategic Marketing for Educational Institutions* (Englewood Cliffs, NJ: Prentice Hall, 1985); Bradley G. Morrison and Julie Gordon Dalgleish, *Waiting in the Wings: A larger audience for the arts and how to develop it* (New York: ACA Books, 1987); and Norman Shawchuck Philip Kotler, Bruce Wren and Gustav Rath, *Marketing for Congregations: Choosing to serve people more effectively* (Nashville, TN: Abingdon Press, 1993).

4   Philip Kotler and Eduardo Roberto, *Social Marketing: Strategies for changing public behaviour* (New York: Free Press, 1990).

5 Peter F. Drucker, *Management: Tasks, responsibilities, practices* (New York: Harper & Row, 1973), 64–5.

6 Here are some other definitions: 'Marketing is the performance of business activities that direct the flow of goods and services from producer to consumer or user'. 'Marketing is selling goods that don't come back to people that do'. 'Marketing is getting the right goods and services to the right people at the right place at the right time at the right price with the right communication and promotion'. 'Marketing is the creation and delivery of a standard of living'. 'Marketing is the creation of time, place and possession utilities'. The American Marketing Association approved the definition: 'Marketing is the process of planning and executing the conception, pricing, promotion, and distribution of ideas, goods, and services to create exchanges that satisfy individual and organizational objectives'. As you can see, there is no single, universally agreed definition of marketing. There are definitions that emphasize marketing as a process, a concept or philosophy of business, or an orientation. The diversity of views adopted by authors is reflected in the wide selection of marketing definitions in common use. See Michael J. Baker, *Macmillan Dictionary of Marketing & Advertising*, 2nd edn (London: Macmillan, 1990), 148–9.

7 See Theodore Levitt's classic article, 'Marketing myopia', *Harvard Business Review* (July–August 1960), 45–56.

8 The number of transactions in a decentralized exchange system is given by $N (N\text{-}1)/2$. With four persons, this means $4(4\text{-}1)/2 = 6$ transactions. In a centralized exchange system, the number of transactions is given by N, here 4. Thus a centralized exchange system reduces the number of transactions needed for exchange.

9 Ralph Waldo Emerson offered this advice: 'If a man . . . makes a better mousetrap . . . the world will beat a path to his door'. Several companies, however, have built better mousetraps yet failed. One was a laser mousetrap costing $1,500. Contrary to popular assumptions, people do not automatically learn about new products, believe product claims, or willingly pay higher prices.

10 Howard Schlossberg, 'Customer satisfaction: not a fad, but a way of life', *Marketing News* (10 June 1991), 18.

11 Thomas E. Caruso, 'Kotler: future marketers will focus on customer data base to compete globally', *Marketing News* (8 June 1992), 21–2.

12 See 'Leaders of the Most Admired', *Fortune* (29 January 1990), 40–54.

13 Ibid. 54.

14 Andrew Jack and Neil Buckley, 'Halo slips on the raspberry bubbles', *Financial Times* (27–28 August 1994), 8.

15 Richard N. Farmer. 'Would you want your daughter to marry a marketing man?', *Journal of Marketing* (January 1967), 1.

16 William J. Stanton and Charles Futrell, *Fundamentals of Marketing*, 8th edn (New York: McGraw-Hill, 1987), 7.

17 The Boston Consulting Group, 'Discovering how to maximise customer share', *Marketing Business* (September 1993), 13.

18 For these and other examples, see J. Reynolds, 'IKEA: a competitive company with style', *Retail and Distribution Management*, **16**, 3 (1988); B. Saporito, 'IKEA's got 'em lining up', *Fortune*, **123**, 5 (1991); 'Soda-pop celebrity', *The Economist* (14 September 1991), 75–6; 'MTV: rock on', *The Economist* (3 August 1991), 66; Robert Neff, 'Guess who's selling barbies in japan now?', *Business Week* (9 December 1991), 72–6; Patrick Oster; 'Toys "R" Us making Europe its playpen', *Business Week* (20 January 1992), 88–91; Julie Skur Hill, 'Toys "R" Us seeks global growth', *Advertising Age* (30 March 1992), 33; and Kevin Cote, 'Toys "R" Us grows in Europe', *Advertising Age* (27 April 1992), 1–16.

19 For more on strategic alliances, see Jordan D. Lewis, *Partnerships for Profit: Structuring and managing strategic alliances* (New York: Free Press, 1990); Peter Lorange and Johan Roos, *Strategic Alliances: Formation, implementation and evolution* (Cambridge, MA: Blackwell, 1992);

and Frederick E. Webster, Jr., 'The changing role of marketing in the corporation', *Journal of Marketing* (October 1992), 1–17.

20 'The money in Europe's muck', *The Economist* (20 November 1993), 109–10.

21 Richard C. Whitely, *The Customer Driven Company* (Reading, MA: Addison-Wesley, 1991); Robert L. Desanick, *Keep the Customer* (Boston: Houghton Mifflin, 1990); Charles Sewell, *Customers for Life: How to turn the one-time buyer into a lifetime customer* (New York: Pocket Books, 1990); William H. Davidow and Bro Uttal, *Total Customer Service: The ultimate weapon* (New York: Harper & Row, 1989); and Karl-Albrecht, *The Only Thing that Matters: Bringing the customer into the center of your business* (New York: Harper Business, 1992).

7

A FRAMEWORK FOR DEVELOPING A QUALITY STRATEGY IN A CUSTOMER PROCESSING OPERATION*

Robert Johnston

INTRODUCTION

The service economy is undergoing substantial growth. Three strategies have been identified by Voss *et al.*[1] by which service industries can gain advantage over competitors and capitalise on this growth. They are: the development of decentralised and localised multi-site operations; the creation of cost advantages through economies of scale; and the creation of service differentials. This article focuses on the third strategy and examines how an organisation can differentiate its service from that of the competition by improving its quality of service provision in the front office (the part of the operation where contact and interaction with the customer takes place).[2] To achieve improved service quality, this article considers what is meant by service quality, why as a potential weapon it can prove difficult to use and how a quality strategy can be developed. The article then looks specifically at the creation of service quality from a customer's perspective by providing a framework that identifies the significant points and activities in a service system that impact on service quality.

QUALITY OF SERVICE

Wyckoff[3] defines quality as the "degree of excellence intended, and the control of variability in achieving that excellence, in meeting a customer's requirements". In service industries there are two elements to quality. Firstly there is the quality of the products; the tangible items that are provided for the customers's use or consumption in the system or removal from the system. Secondly there is the quality of the service; the intangibles – the way the products are provided and the way the customer is dealt with. This article focuses on the quality of service and examines the relationship between the intended degree of excellence and customer requirements, and how this relationship can be managed to produce a differentiated service.

QUALITY OF SERVICE – THE DIFFICULTIES

The following observations have been made by several writers on service operations that suggest that as a weapon, service quality can be difficult to master.

- Organisations find it easier to measure product-related criteria rather than service-related.[4]
- Service is difficult to measure because it is not always clearly definable.[1]
- Quality only exists to the extent that a product or service meets customer requirements.[3]

The above observations suggest that the difficulty stems from an inability to define the service to be provided, to the extent that many organisations only control product-related criteria. The starting point for the development of a quality strategy must be an understanding of customer requirements in order to define the service required.

- Quality is determined by the expectations and perceptions of the customer which are different for each and every customer.[1]

Because customer requirements and expectations may vary from customer to customer, a quality strategy must be able to be responsive enough to deal with a range of customer requirements and expectations and/or be able to limit that range. Also important is the need for a quality strategy to manage the individual customer's perception of service quality as he/she progresses through the system. In order to do this a quality strategy must be able to identify all the significant elements in the service system that create the perception of quality.

- Quality tends to be measured after the event not during it.[4]
- If quality is measured during the event it interferes with the process.[5]

The control of quality after the event may only benefit future users of the system. A quality strategy must deal with mismatches between expectations and perceptions at the time, in a way that enhances rather than interferes with the process.

- The provision of quality varies adversely with the amount of individual judgement exercised by the server.[6]
- Contact staff must have the desire to provide good quality; it is not achieved by throwing more supervision at it.[6]
- A service of high quality is the result of a total system of quality throughout every aspect of the firm.[3]

A quality expectation and commitment by every part of the organisation, contact staff, non-contact staff and supplier is central to the provision of service quality.

A quality strategy must overcome these difficulties. It has to make service quality easier to understand, define, provide and control. It would seem that the management of customer expectations and perceptions is fundamental to the development of a quality strategy. I believe that a customer's view of service is based upon the degree of fit between his/her expectations of the way he/she will be treated and his/her perceptions of the way he/she was treated. It matters little whether his/her expectations were "low" or "high", provided that his/her expectations were matched by his/her perception that the quality of service was adequate. If the perception was lower than expectation then service is seen to have been inadequate and poor; if above, then good or even outstanding service has occurred.

QUALITY STRATEGY

A quality strategy, therefore, is a set of plans and policies to harness operational resources in order to match the expectations of the customers in the segment of the market that is being served, with their perceptions of the service provided. The purpose of a quality strategy is to provide the business with a distinct advantage in the market place.

As such a quality strategy involves:

1   an understanding of how customer expectations are created before entry to the service system, so that quality of service can be defined;
2   an understanding of how expectations and perceptions of service quality can be managed during and after the provision of service;
3   the definition of standards, based on customer expectations and operational abilities at each part of the process;
4   the creation of procedures to meet the quality standards;
5   the communication of those standards and procedures to employees and the training of them to achieve them;
6   the monitoring and control of those standards.

This article focuses on the first two parts of the development of a quality strategy by providing a framework that can be used to understand the process of matching customer expectations to their perceptions of quality of service provision.

There are two stages in the creation of a framework for the development of a quality strategy. The first stage is to identify the significant points and activities that occur in the treatment or processing of a customer. The second stage is to examine the factors at each point and activity that impact upon the development of customer expectations or the creation of customer perceptions of the quality of service.

THE CUSTOMER PROCESSING OPERATION FRAMEWORK

A service operation could be considered as a customer processing operation, where the customer is processed through a series of stages. These stages are identified in the Customer Processing Operation (CPO) framework in Figure 7.1. This is a simple framework that identifies the significant points and activities for the customer, before, during and after the service delivery system.

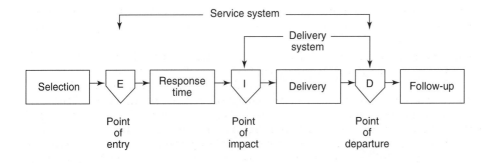

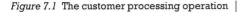

Figure 7.1 The customer processing operation

The significant activities in the CPO with which the customer is involved are selection, response time, delivery and follow-up. The critical points are the points of entry, impact and departure.

Selection

Selection is the act of choosing between competing service organisations. A customer will base this choice upon his/her understanding of them. Such understanding will be based on:

1 the customer's previous experiences, if any;
2 the experience of other people known to the customer;
3 the marketing image created by the organisation's advertising and promotions efforts;
4 independent media coverage.

Point of entry (POE)

Having selected a service organisation, the customer chooses the moment to enter or interact with the service system. This is the point of entry. Examples of such might be an entrance door or the start of a telephone call.

Response time

Having entered the system, the customer usually has to wait for someone to respond to his/her presence and wait to be dealt with. This time is the response time and is usually spent in a queue. Queues may be of several forms; a physical visible line of people waiting for service; an invisible queue of incoming telephone calls; or a remote queue of customers in several locations waiting for a service to arrive.

Point of impact (POI)

When a service contact worker first acknowledges and responds to the customer in the service system, the process of service delivery begins. This first point of personal contact is the point of impact, referred to as a "moment of truth" by Normann.[7]

Delivery

The point of impact (POI) is the entrance to the delivery system. This is the activity during which the services and associated products are provided and will involve many further points of personal contact.

Point of departure (POD)

On completion of the service delivery, the customer leaves the service system. This is the point of departure.

Follow-up

The customer, having received the service and left the service system, may choose to reflect upon it and react to it. Thereby adding to his/her own understanding of that service operation which may then be communicated to friends or acquaintances.

CPOs in series and in parallel

Most service systems are complex operations and may involve a combination of CPOs in series and in parallel. Frequently a delivery system will include several service subsystems in series within it, each with points of entry, responses, points of impact and delivery subsystems as shown in Figure 7.2.

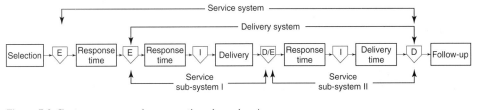

Figure 7.2 Customer processing operations in series

At the point of entry to a service system there may be alternative parallel service systems as shown in Figure 7.3.

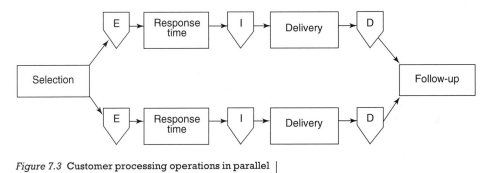

Figure 7.3 Customer processing operations in parallel

FACTORS INFLUENCING THE PROVISION AND PERCEPTION OF QUALITY OF SERVICE

This section will examine how the significant points and activities before, during and after the service delivery system, identified by the CPO framework, impact upon the development of customer expectations and perceptions and thus identify the factors that influence the provision of service quality.

Selection

A customer's expectations of the quality of service will be based upon his/her understanding of the image of the operation. That image will be created by his/her own previous experiences, the experiences of others, and the organisation's marketing efforts. To ensure that inadequate service quality is not perceived, the image of the operation must be matched by the abilities and limitations of that operation. The marketing team must therefore understand the operation. Not only the creation of products but the way the customers are processed, thereby developing an understanding of the range of expectations that the operation can provide for. This will help identify the appropriate market segment and thus the appropriate market image to select customers with achievable expectations. Also, operations staff must test the match between customer expectations and perceptions (see "Point of departure" above) and deal with mismatches, either by a change of methods of operation and quality standards employed or by an adjustment to market image to improve customer selection.

Point of entry

The development of perceptions about the quality of service begins at the point of entry into the service system. One factor that will influence perceptions is the ease of entry, the degree of difficulty experienced in finding the building and the entrance, or the correct telephone number of the organisation. The customer also requires early training by the system as to where to go and how to act. Clear signposts are required to provide "handholding" for the customer to help him/her ascertain quickly and easily where to go to get the service required and how to enter and behave in any queuing system. For a first time entrant to a service organisation this can be a most unnerving time as the customer searches for clues as to what to do and how to behave. The customer's assessment of quality of service starts with his/her perception of the ease of entry into the service system.

Response time

Once the customer has entered the service system and discovered how to interact with it, several factors identified in[1] will influence his/her perception of service quality:

Time factors   Each customer may have expectations about what is an acceptable waiting time for the service. This will be influenced by:

(a) the desire or need for the service,
(b) the alternatives available,
(c) whether it is peak time or off-peak time,
(d) the waiting time relative to expected service time.

Conditions   The perceived waiting time may also be a function of the conditions experienced during the wait about which the customer may also have expectations, for example:

(a) the environmental conditions in which the customer has to wait,
(b) whether the customer's presence in the queue is acknowledged,
(c) the perceived fairness of the queue,
(d) information about the likely length of wait from the visible movement of the queue or other sources,
(e) the usefulness of the queue and activities provided during the wait,
(f) the variety or types of queue and conditions of queuing.

If the customer's expectations regarding the time and conditions of queuing are not met then the service, so far, may be perceived to have been inadequate or poor.

Point of impact

The point of impact is the moment when the customer comes face to face with a contact service worker. This first point of contact may have a considerable impact upon the customer's perception of quality as first impressions are lasting. The contact worker is expected to have a good knowledge of the service(s) available, maybe even knowledge of the customer and his/her requirements, and the ability to deal with the customer caringly and efficiently. This contact worker is seen to be representative of the whole organisation and the quality and level of service to come. Despite this, the worker at the point of impact is frequently the least knowledgeable and least paid in the whole organisation.

Delivery

On entry to the service system the customer begins to judge the quality of the process of service delivery. If the service is highly customised, the perceived quality will be a function of the ability of the customer processing staff to accurately diagnose the requirements of the customer and to negotiate not only what the service will be but how it will be provided. In a standardised service, processing staffs' social skills are vital as they will influence the degree of personalisation of the service.

Point of departure

The point of departure from the system is the point at which mismatches between expectations and perceptions need to be dealt with. Done here, it is not seen to interfere with the process itself but becomes an ancillary process demonstrating concern for the customer that if well managed should enhance the perception of quality rather than diminish it. This is an opportunity to show recognition for customers' views of quality, demonstrate that they are important and may have an impact upon either the service system or the methods of customer selection. The skills of negotiation and appeasement are central to the success of the management of the point of departure.

Follow-up

Once the customer has left the service system, two types of follow-up action may be appropriate. Firstly, having allowed time for reflection on the service, it may provide a second opportunity to assess latent mismatches between expectations and perceptions of quality. Secondly, it can be used as an opportunity to capitalise on good service to bring the customer back to the system or provide incentives to influence friends or acquaintances of the customer.

Reshaping expectations in the CPO

So far it has been implied that a customer's expectations are created before entry to the service system and that the customer's view of quality depends upon the degree of fit between those expectations and the perceived quality of service in the CPO. The reality is more complex than this as each point or activity in the CPO may influence and reshape the customer's expectations of the next part of the service. If the point of entry, response time and point of impact are managed well, for example, the customer's expectations of the standard of delivery may be raised. Poorly managed points and activities in the CPO may either confirm initial perceptions and reduce expectations thus preparing the customer for a poor delivery, or they could raise expectations so that to achieve the perception of adequate overall quality, delivery will have to be significantly better than originally expected to compensate for the "poor" service so far.

SUMMARY

Service quality has been defined as the degree of fit between the customer's expectations of the way he/she will be treated and his/her perceptions of the way he/she was treated. The purpose of a quality strategy, therefore, is to provide a set of plans and policies to manage the creation of expectations and development of perceptions that will provide the organisation with a competitive advantage in the market place. Such a differentiated service may arise by firstly reducing any mismatch by understanding or controlling the factors that create service quality and/or limiting the range of customer expectations, and secondly by providing an improved service quality by improving operational standards at the critical points and activities in the customer processing operation and correspondingly enhancing the market image.

Table 7.1 identifies the critical stages and provides a summary of the significant factors that impact upon quality at each stage in a customer processing operation. Customer expectations are created before entry to the service system and based on the image of the operation which is created by the organisation's marketing efforts based on an understanding of the abilities of the service system and customer's previous experiences. These expectations may be reshaped as the customer enters and progresses through the system as a result of his/her experiences at each critical stage in the system. At the same time the customer develops perceptions about the quality of service that are reinforced or rejected at each stage. Each stage from the point of entry, through response time, point of impact, delivery to point of departure embodies different factors that create the perception of quality.

The use of the CPO framework overcomes some of the difficulties that have been identified concerning the definition and provision of service. The framework deals specifically with the creation and development of customer expectations and perceptions of service quality. It provides a means of focusing on the provision of service quality that may lead to clearer understanding and specification of service quality.

Table 7.1 Factors influencing the provision and perception of service quality

Selection	Point of entry	Response time	Point of impact	Delivery	Point of departure	Follow-up
Creation of expectations	Re-shaping of expectations					Reflection on perceptions and expectations
			Development of perceptions			
Understanding of CPO to:						
			Staff knowledge of:		Assess mismatches	
Match operational abilities and limitations to market image	Ease of entry: Signposts Customer training	Time factors Waiting conditions	Service(s) Customer Customer's requirements	Staff ability to: Diagnose Negotiate Personalise	Demonstrate concern Recognise customer's view	Assessment of latent mismatches Capitalise on good service
Identify segment with achievable expectations			Efficient and caring handling of customer		Negotiate Appease	

The application of the CPO framework to a service organisation is the first step in the development of a quality strategy. It identifies the significant points and activities in the provision of service quality. The following stages in the development of a quality strategy involve the definition of standards at each of those points and activities, based on the understanding of customer expectations and perceptions gained from the application of the framework, the development of procedures to meet those standards, and finally procedures to ensure that those standards are attained.

NOTE

* This chapter has been adapted from, Johnston, R. "A Framework for Developing a Quality Strategy in a Customer Processing Operation", *International Journal of Quality and Reliability Management*, Vol. 4 No. 4, 1987, pp. 37–46.

REFERENCES

1 Voss, C., Armistead, C., Johnston, R. and Morris, B., *Operations Management in Service Industries and the Public Sector*, New York, Wiley, 1985, pp. 270–2.

2 Chase, R.B., "Where Does the Customer Fit in a Service Operation", *Harvard Business Review*, Vol. 56 No. 4, November–December 1978, pp. 137–42.

3 Wyckoff, D.D., "New Tools for Achieving Service Quality", *Cornell H.R.A. Quarterly*, November 1984, pp. 78–91.

4 Johnston, R. and Morris, B., "Monitoring and Control in Service Industries", *International Journal of Operations and Production Management*, Vol. 5 No. 1, 1985, pp. 32–8.

5 Armistead, C., "Quality Assurance in the Uniform Branch of the Police Service", *International Journal of Quality and Reliability Management*, Vol. 3 No. 3, 1986, pp. 8–25.

6 Heskett, J.L., *Managing in the Service Economy*, Harvard, Harvard Business School Press, 1986.

7 Normann, R., *Service Management*, New York, Wiley, 1984.

8

RELATIONSHIP MARKETING *

Francis Buttle

Harley-Davidson, whose Harley Owners club has 200,000 members worldwide, has an insurance programme, travel agency, emergency roadside service, two magazines, member competitions and 750 local chapters.

In two years from launch, British Airways' worldwide executive club grew from 100,000 to 1.3 million members. Starting as a lounge at Heathrow airport, the club is now based on card ownership and the provision of multiple benefits. The cards are linked to BA's customer database which tells the airline which seat is preferred by the customer, whether the customer is a smoker and the customer's flying history.

Renault's relationship marketing programme is mediated by the car firm's dealership network. Notes thanking owners for buying Renault, service reminders and special offers are printed on dealers' headed notepaper and personalized. Renault's UK market share rose from 3.5% in 1988 when the scheme was introduced to 5.5% in 1994.

Nestlé's French baby-food marketing programme invests heavily in relationship marketing. The firm regularly mails offers and information to young mothers. It employs qualified dieticians to operate its customer service lines and it runs a chain of baby cafés to cater for families away from home. In 1985, Nestlé's market share was 20%; in 1992 it was 40%.

These stories are indicative of the changing nature of marketing. Marketing is no longer simply about developing, selling and delivering products. It is progressively more concerned with the development and maintenance of mutually satisfying long-term relationships with customers. If the 1950s was the era of mass-marketing, and the 1970s the era of market segmentation, then the 1990s represent the genesis of personalized marketing, in which knowledge about individual customers is used to guide highly focused marketing strategies. This change is driven by several conditions: more intense, often global, competition; more fragmentation of markets; a generally high level of product quality which is forcing companies to seek competitive advantage in other ways; more demanding customers; and rapidly changing customer buying patterns. Enduring relationships with customers cannot be duplicated by competitors, and therefore provide for a unique and sustained competitive advantage.

The expression most widely used to describe this new form of marketing is relationship marketing (RM). Other terms have been used, either as substitutes for RM or to describe some close parallel – micromarketing, database marketing, one-to-one marketing, loyalty marketing, wrap-around marketing, customer partnering, symbiotic marketing and inter-active marketing.

Although the shift to RM is widespread, it is occurring more rapidly in some sectors and industries than others, facilitated by fundamental cultural shifts within organizations, powerful databases and new forms of organizational structure.

REDEFINING MARKETING

Marketing's leading international professional bodies are the Chartered Institute of Marketing and the American Marketing Association. They offer the following definitions of marketing:

> Marketing is the management process of identifying, anticipating and satisfying customer requirements profitably.
>
> (CIM)

> Marketing is the process of planning and executing conception, pricing, promotion and distribution of ideas, goods and services to create exchanges that satisfy individual and organizational objectives.
>
> (AMA)

Both these definitions reflect a traditional, transaction-orientated view of marketing. They contain no explicit recognition of the long-term value of a customer.

Theoreticians have begun to develop alternative definitions which capture the nature of the new marketing. Grönroos (1990; 1991; 1994, p. 355), for example, offers the following: 'Marketing is to establish, maintain, and enhance relationships with customers, and other partners, at a profit, so that the objectives of the parties involved are met. This is achieved by a mutual exchange and fulfilment of promises.' This definition attempts to incorporate both the transactional and the relational qualities of marketing. All marketing strategies, Grönroos (1991) tells us, lie on a continuum ranging from transactional (e.g. fast-moving consumer goods) to relational (e.g. services). Relational marketing, he claims, is charac-teristically different from transactional marketing. For example, rather than routinely employing the marketing mix's four Ps, it focuses on interactive marketing with the four Ps in a supporting role. (The four Ps (product, price, promotion, place) are the traditional tools that marketers use to manage demand. Known as the marketing mix (Borden, 1964), the four Ps have become a staple organizing construct of marketing texts since the early work of E.J. McCarthy (1975).) Rather than employing market share to assess marketing success, relational marketing measures customer retention.

Others have sought not to redefine marketing *per se* but more precisely to define the character of RM. Some have examined RM from sectoral perspectives. Berry (1983, p. 25), the first to publish work on RM, takes a service sector perspective: 'RM is attracting, maintaining and – in multi-service organizations – enhancing customer relationships.' Jackson (1985, p. 2) writes from an industrial marketing perspective: 'RM concerns attracting, developing and retaining customer relationships.' Others have attempted to characterize RM more broadly. Dwyer, Schurr and Oh (1987, p. 12) describe RM as 'longer in duration [than transactional marketing], reflecting an ongoing process'. Christopher, Payne and Ballantyne (1991) see RM as a synthesis of marketing, customer service and quality management. Sheth (1994, p. 2) describes RM as 'the understanding, explanation and management of the ongoing collaborative business relationship between suppliers and customers'. Evans and Laskin (1994, p. 440) suggest: 'RM is a customer centred approach whereby a firm seeks long-term business relations with prospective and existing customers.' Morgan and Hunt (1994, p. 22) offer the broadest definition of RM, taking neither a sectoral perspective nor specifying the need for there to be a 'customer'. Rather, 'RM refers to all marketing activities directed toward establishing, developing and maintaining successful relational exchanges'.

Some critics of the new RM have suggested that it is really no more than a series of transactions over time, and that it has no special character. However, Czepiel (1990, p. 13) retorts that a relationship possesses 'mutual recognition of some *special* status between exchange partners' (emphasis added), to which Barnes (1995, p. 1394) adds: 'a succession of interactions does not necessarily lead to a relationship any more than repeat purchasing constitutes loyalty.'

Finally, as Gummesson (1994, p. 7) has rightly observed: 'RM is currently seeking its identity. Gradually, a more general approach to marketing management, based on relationships, is gaining ground.' It may be that RM will not be firmly entrenched as standard business practice until the millennium.

WHOSE RELATIONSHIPS?

As indicated by these definitions, there is some debate about the focus of RM. The older definitions suggest that RM's focus is the external customer. The newer contributions widen its scope. Morgan and Hunt (1994) identify ten discrete forms of RM (see Table 8.1). Gummesson (1994, p. 12) goes even further. He lists 32 relationships in defining RM as 'marketing seen as relationships, networks and interaction'. Companies clearly have relationships with many different persons and organizations.

Traditionally, marketing strategies have been developed both to push product through distribution channels (trade marketing strategy) and pull consumers towards the point of sale (consumer marketing strategy). A third form of marketing strategy has gained currency recently – the internal marketing strategy. Internal marketing focuses on employees. It recognizes that every person in an organization is both a customer and a supplier. An organization's final output, be it a good or a service, is almost always the product of operations and processes performed by people in series. A principal purpose of internal marketing is to ensure that the final outputs of the organization are of suitably high, external-customer-satisfying quality. For this to happen, each operation in the series must be performed to high standards. It is therefore helpful for employees to view the next person in the series as a customer. Internal marketing is also concerned with ensuring all employees buy into the organization's mission and goals and successfully develop and execute strategies.

These three relationships – company/intermediary, company/consumer and company/employee – are at the heart of most RM practice, although the dominant focus is on external customer relationships.

New words are being employed to describe these relationships. Customers are now *associates* or *partners* enmeshed in *alliances* or *partnerships* with companies. Levitt (1983a)

Table 8.1 The relational exchanges in RM

Supplier partnerships	Lateral partnerships	Internal partnerships	Buyer partnerships
Goods suppliers Services suppliers	Competitors Non-profit organizations Government	Business units Employees Functional departments	Intermediate customers Ultimate customers

and Dwyer, Schurr and Oh (1987) both employ a marriage metaphor to describe the new marketing. Levitt (1983a, p. 111) wrote: 'the relationship between a seller and buyer seldom ends when the sale is made . . . the sale merely consummates the courtship. Then the marriage begins.' Dwyer, Schurr and Oh (1987) incorporate dating and divorce into the metaphor when they observe that supplier-customer relationships are marked by five stages: awareness, exploration, expansion, commitment and dissolution.

Marketers are now beginning to talk about share of customer (in addition to share of market), economies of scope (as well as economies of scale) and customer loyalty (instead of brand loyalty). Share of customer, a reference to the percentage of an individual's annual or lifetime purchases that is won by a company, is employed as a measure of RM performance. Economies of scope are cost savings owing to the complementarities of products. Cross-selling related services generates these economies. Customer loyalty emphasizes the interactive nature of RM, unlike brand loyalty; it is an acknowledgement of the personal nature of the commitment of the customer to the firm and/or its employees. Brand loyalty, in contrast, suggests that the commitment is to the product.

Christopher, Payne and Ballantyne (1991) have developed the idea that there is a relationship 'ladder of customer loyalty'. Initially the company's relationship is with a prospect. The relationship progresses up several rungs – customer, client, supporter and, at the top, advocate. Accordingly, the job of RM is to advance relationships to advocate status. Advocates are so deeply enmeshed in the organization that they are not only very loyal long-term purchasers but they also influence others through positive word of mouth.

Having claimed that the goal of RM is to identify and nurture mutually satisfying long-term relationships with customers, there has been an argument that RM need not necessarily focus on the long term. Grönroos (1990, p. 3), for example, stresses that

> marketing can be considered as revolving around relationships, some of which are like single transactions, narrow in scope and not involving much or any social relationship (e.g. marketing soap or breakfast cereals). Other relationships, on the other hand, are broader in scope and may involve even substantial social contacts and be continuous and enduring in nature (e.g. marketing hospitality or financial services).

He argues that 'every single customer forms a customer relationship with the seller', but that 'the emphasis should be on developing and maintaining enduring, long-term customer relationships' (p. 4).

THE ECONOMICS OF RELATIONSHIP MARKETING

The impetus for the development of RM has been a growing awareness of the long-term financial benefits it can convey. RM is not philanthropic. It is a means to an end, and it is based on two economic arguments. One: it is more expensive to win a new customer than it is to retain an existing customer. Two: the longer the association between company and customer the more profitable the relationship for the firm.

Theodore Levitt once said that the job of marketing is to create and keep customers. Historically the focus has been on creating customers; less attention has been paid to their retention. RM reverses the emphasis.

It has long been claimed that it is between five and ten times as expensive to win a new customer than it is to retain an existing one (e.g. Rosenberg and Czepiel, 1984). While the factor will differ between industries and companies, it is evident that recruiting new customers is a costly business. Not only are there the direct costs of the successful conversion of a prospect into a customer (selling costs, commission, product samples, credit-checking costs, administrative costs, database costs) but there are also the costs of unsuccessful prospecting. Some industries experience a very low conversion ratio of prospects to customers. These costs of failure also have to be recovered.

There is now a growing awareness of the lifetime value of a customer. A transaction-orientated view of the customer would consider the sales value and margin earned from a single sale. A relationship-orientated view of the customer considers the revenues and contributions earned from a long-term relationship with a customer.

Reichheld and Sasser (1990) argue that companies should attempt to improve their customer-retention performance. They have observed a cross-industry trend: sales and profits per account rise the longer a relationship lasts. As customers become more satisfied with the service they receive, the more they buy. As purchases rise, operating costs decline, because companies climb the experience curve and become more efficient. Profits therefore improve. They provide illustrative data from the credit-card industry: it costs $51 to win a new account; profits earned grow annually from $30 in year 1, through $42, $44, $49, to $55. Clearly, a customer relationship must last into the second year before break-even (profits equal to the cost of winning the account) is reached. The pattern of annually increasing profits is commonplace, and it emphasizes the benefits of retaining customers into the long term. Heskett *et al.* (1994, p. 164) estimate that the lifetime revenue stream from a loyal pizza customer can be $8,000; from a Cadillac customer it can reach $332,000; and in the case of 'a corporate purchaser of commercial aircraft literally billions of dollars'.

Reducing customer defection rates is critical for retention rates to improve. As defection rates fall the average customer-relationship lifespan increases. According to Reichheld and Sasser (1990, p. 107), 'as the credit card company cuts its defection rate from 20% to 10%, the average lifespan of its relationship with a customer doubles from 5 years to 10 and the value of the customer more than doubles – jumping from $134 to $300.'

When customers defect they not only take margin from current transactions with them but all future margin also. Additionally, if customers defect angry or dissatisfied, they are likely to utter negative word of mouth about the company, thereby reducing the prospect pool for the firm.

Several authors have therefore suggested methods of measuring the profitability of relationships (Reichheld and Sasser, 1990; Grönroos, 1992; Buck-Lew and Edvinsson 1993; Petrison, Blattberg and Wang, 1993; Pitt and Page, 1994; Payne and Rickard, 1994; Storbacka, 1994; Storbacka, Strandvik and Grönroos, 1994; Wang and Splegel, 1994; Hughes and Wang, 1995; Keane and Wang, 1995). Any attempt to compute the lifetime value of a customer requires the following data: cost of winning the customer; periodic cost of retaining the customer; gross margin earned from the first, second, third, fourth . . . nth sale to the customer; probabilities that the customer will buy a second, third, fourth . . . nth time; required rate of return for the company (in order to compute net present value); and numbers of purchases made by the customer from the company. These data can be used to compute the lifetime value of individual customers, segments of customers or of the 'average' customer. They can serve as benchmarking data and are useful to monitor the impact of customer-retention strategies.

Other authors have suggested strategies to improve customer retention rates (Hart, Heskett and Sasser, 1990; Reichheld and Sasser, 1990; Fornell, 1992; Pitt and Page, 1994; Reichheld, 1993; Rust and Zahorik, 1993; Rust, Zahorik and Keiningham, 1994). There is widespread agreement that the root causes of customer defection must be addressed, and that recovery programmes should be in place to prevent the defection of at-risk customers.

Customers have been shown to defect for a number of reasons (DeSouza, 1992 – see Table 8.2). Since not all these causes can be eliminated, there will clearly be some defections whatever actions companies take. Furthermore, companies realize that not all customers are worth retaining. Not all relationships are equally profitable. For example, Storbacka, Strandvik and Grönroos (1994, p.32) claim that 'it is not uncommon for approximately

Table 8.2 Reasons for customer defection

Type	Description
Price	Defections to a lower-priced alternative
Product	Defections to a superior product
Service	Defections owing to poor service
Market	Customers who leave the market, but not to a competitor
Technological	Defections to a product from outside the industry
Organizational	Defections owing to internal or external political considerations

50% of the customers in a retail bank's data base to be unprofitable'. Neither is it always possible to know whether a currently unprofitable account would generate a future profit stream given investment in that customer's satisfaction. One way of dealing with this problem is the use of customer profiling. This involves constructing a profile of existing profitable accounts and searching the prospect or light-user database for customers of similar profile. A close match indicates significant future potential.

MUTUAL SATISFACTION?

Traditional marketing theory places mutual satisfaction at the heart of marketing exchanges. Companies achieve their profit targets by virtue of satisfying customers. This is explicit in the CIM, AMA and Grönroos' definitions presented earlier.

As already noted, it is corporate economics that are forcing the pace of adoption of RM. The needs, wants and expectations of customers have not been of paramount importance. Indeed there is very little evidence that customers want to enter into long-term partnerships and alliances with suppliers (Barnes, 1995; Blois, 1995). There are some exceptions: clothing retailers, for instance, are building alliances with manufacturers to ensure the timely supply of goods of specified quality and design. Manufacturers are enjoying the long-term security and profitability that such relationships bring.

It is evident that customers generally seek quality, value and convenience in their transactions with suppliers. What is not clear is what else customers would expect if they were to enter into a longer-term relationship. In a close relationship customers could reasonably expect suppliers to have a better appreciation of their circumstances and require-ments; customers in turn should develop more realistic expectations of their suppliers. However, we do not even know whether all customers value the formation of relationships with suppliers. It is entirely possible that markets may be segmentable against some sort of 'relationship-proneness' variable. Neither do we know whether relationship-building is contextualized, i.e. is valued more highly in some sectors than in others. It would seem reasonable to hypothesize that relationship building would be seen as offering significant benefits when transaction costs are high.

Finally, we do not fully understand the motivations of relationship-seekers. We have some indications from research into shopping motives (Tauber, 1972; Buttle, 1992) that some shoppers value and seek out social contact. How deeply this phenomenon extends into other parts of customers' lives is unknown. Other than seeking social contact, it may be that relationship-prone customers seek to reduce risk and avoid unduly stressful arousal.

Whether entering into a discrete transaction or ongoing relationship with a supplier, customers will experience what economists call transaction costs (Milgrom and Roberts, 1992). For example, there may be search costs, negotiation costs and legal costs. These costs may be higher when a customer is selecting a supplier with whom to have a long-term relationship. The search may be more extensive and more information may be acquired and processed in order to reduce the financial and other risks associated with a long-term commitment. However, once incurred, these costs do not recur in a relationship. In contrast, where a customer switches suppliers frequently, transaction costs may be significantly higher in the long term. RM therefore does offer customers an important benefit – the control, reduction and potential elimination of transaction costs.

In sum, Grönroos (1991, p. 10) noted that 'in a transaction marketing strategy there is not much other than the core product, and sometimes the image of the firm which keeps customers attached to the seller'. The implication is that in RM there will be much more.

THE CHARACTER OF A MARKETING RELATIONSHIP

Relationships between customer and supplier have traditionally been characterized as confrontational or adversarial. The literatures on distribution-channel management and industrial marketing are typical. They have focused on issues of power, conflict and control (see, for example, O'Neal, 1989; Rosenbloom, 1991; Stern and El-Ansary, 1992). Only recently has the introduction of the concept of supply-chain management produced a more harmonious view of the relationships between retailer and supplier. Young and Wilkinson (1989) note that this emphasis in the literature has been on sick rather than healthy relationships.

RM is about healthy relationships which are characterized by concern, trust, commitment and service.

Concern

Relationship marketers are concerned for the welfare of their customers. They want to meet or, preferably exceed customer expectations, producing satisfaction or delight. KwikFit and American Express are two companies who claim to be dedicated to producing customer delight by exceeding customer expectations. The key is to understand intimately the expectations of customers. Since expectations are the product of personal needs and experience, word of mouth and marketing communications (Parasuraman, Zeithaml and Berry, 1994; Zeithaml, Parasuraman and Berry, 1994) they are dynamic. Dynamism means that it is no simple matter to understand, or to track, change in expectations. Marketers can to some degree mould expectations through mediated and interpersonal communications with customers, but only in very rare circumstances is it likely that they will be able to determine expectations.

Trust and commitment

Trust and commitment are the focus of much of the published research into RM. Moorman, Zaltman and Deshpande (1992), Gamesan (1994), Morgan and Hunt (1994) and Geyskens and Steenkamp (1995) focus on the role of trust in developing successful relationships. Morgan and Hunt (1994, p. 22) argue that

> commitment and trust are 'key' because they encourage marketers to (1) work at preserving relationship investments by cooperating with exchange partners, (2) resist attractive short-term alternatives in favour of the expected long-term benefits of staying with existing partners, and (3) view potentially high risk actions as being prudent because of the belief that their partners will not act opportunistically. When commitment and trust – not just one or the other – are present they produce outcomes that promote efficiency, productivity and effectiveness.

Morgan and Hunt (*ibid.*) describe commitment as an enduring desire to maintain a relationship, and trust as the confidence that one partner has in the other's reliability and integrity. Confidence is associated with the partner's consistency, competence, honesty, fairness, willingness to make sacrifices, responsibility, helpfulness and benevolence. Trust, they argue, is the cornerstone of relationship commitment; without it commitment flounders. Geyskens and Steenkamp (1995) conclude that there is a consensus emerging that trust encompasses two essential elements: trust in the partner's honesty and trust in the partner's benevolence. Honesty refers to the belief that the partner stands by its word, fulfils promised role obligations and is sincere. Benevolence reflects the belief that one partner is interested in the other's welfare and will not take unexpected actions to the detriment of the partner. Trust brings about a feeling of security, reduces uncertainty and creates a supportive climate.

Morgan and Hunt (1994, p. 25) provide empirical data which support the role of commitment and trust in RM success: 'First, acquiescence and propensity to leave directly flow from relationship commitment. Second, functional conflict and uncertainty are the direct results of [lack of] trust. Third, and most importantly . . . cooperation arises directly from both relationship commitment and trust.' Co-operative behaviours, they claim, are necessary for RM success whatever the context. Relationship marketers have attempted to bond customers to their companies in a number of ways (Storbacka, 1994). Social, technological, legal, economic and cultural bonds all serve as exit barriers, discouraging customers from seeking alternative suppliers. Customers may therefore remain ostensibly loyal, even though they are not satisfied with the service they receive. Bonding which is not based on trust and commitment is unlikely to persist.

The challenge for RM managers is to demonstrate their commitment to the relationship and to inculcate trust in their partner. In a service marketing context this can be particularly challenging because of the relative absence of tangible clues, and because services cannot be examined before they are produced/consumed.

Service

The outcome of this concern for customers, in an environment of relationship commitment and trust, is a desire to provide excellent service. RM requires an organization-wide commitment to providing high-quality service which is reliable, empathic and responsive.

Since RM is a means to a profitable end, relationship marketers must believe that excellent service produces improved profitability. This has been the focus of a stream of research (e.g. Rust and Zahorik, 1993; Heskett *et al.*, 1994; Rust, Zahorik and Keiningham, 1994) which broadly supports this view. Recently, for example, Storbacka, Strandvik and Grönroos (1994, p. 23) have proposed a model which hypothesizes a number of connections between service quality and profitability. Their framework incorporates this basic sequence: 'service quality leads to customer satisfaction which leads to relationship strength, which leads to relationship longevity, which leads to customer relationship profitability.'

WHERE IS RELATIONSHIP MARKETING FOUND

Although 'relationship marketing' has entered the management lexicon only recently (Berry, 1983) the practice of RM has a long history. Historical research indicates that merchants in the Middle Ages recognized that some customers were worth courting more seriously than others. Richer customers would be offered credit terms; the poor paid cash.

Industrial marketers, particularly those selling high-priced capital goods, have long known that they must take a long-term view to make a sale. Team-selling, with multiple levels of contact between seller and customer organizations, is commonplace. Sales are only closed after protracted periods involving many people, and after-sale follow-up is the norm.

Manufacturers of fast-moving consumer goods (FMCG) have also attempted to climb on the RM bandwagon. Businesses which are dependent on large numbers of customers, high sales volumes and low margins tend to have more difficulty adopting RM. Frequently, their customer databases are inadequately disaggregated; they know little about their customers at a personal level. Heinz has computed that RM is not financially worthwhile if a customer spends less than £10 on Heinz products per annum (Treather, 1994). Until the costs of communicating with customers fall, it is likely that FMCG manufacturers will be slow to move to RM.

It is, however, in the services marketing area that RM is practised most widely. Services provided by banks, hotels and healthcare organizations are particularly suitable for RM initiatives because they supply multiple services deliverable over several contacts, in person. Because of their participation in the production of services, customers come face to face with employees and are able to form an interpersonal relationship with the service provider.

Research into RM has been produced from a number of perspectives. Relationships between members of the marketing channel have been examined by several authors (Dwyer, Schurr and Oh, 1987; Anderson and Narus, 1990; Spriggs and Nevin, 1992). Dwyer, Schurr and Oh (1987) found that channel relationships exist on a continuum, ranging from discrete to relational. Channel members whose relationships take the relational form have expectations that the relationship will persist over time, exhibit mutual trust and make plans for the future.

In an industrial marketing context, RM has been studied by many authors (Håkansson, 1982; Jackson, 1985; Gummesson, 1987; Spekman, 1988; Anderson and Narus, 1991). Switching costs associated with changing supplier may be immense; manufacturing technology and processes represent long-term commitments for most producers. Hence, suppliers of critical inputs are rarely changed. Often, relationships are made more secure through joint product-development programmes.

The service marketing context provides the setting for most research (Berry and Gresham, 1986; Crosby, 1989; Crosby, Evans and Cowles, 1990; Czepiel, 1990; Grönroos, 1990; 1991; 1994). According to Ellis, Lee and Beatty (1993), published service sector research has taken two forms: those studies which focus on the individual service encounter and those which focus on the ongoing relationship between buyer and seller. Long-term relationships are composed of encounters in series and, according to Czepiel (1990), are developed in a number of stages: 1) the accumulation of satisfactory encounters; 2) active participation based on mutual disclosure and trust; 3) creation of a double bond (personal and economic); and 4) psychological loyalty to the partner. Frenzen and Davis (1990) characterized RM relationships as enduring sequences of encounters that involve indebtedness, embeddedness and rules of reciprocity.

Although Crosby, Evans and Cowles (1990) found that salesperson behaviours such as contact intensity, disclosure and co-operative intentions had a positive impact on the customer's level of satisfaction and trust, in general little is known about employee behaviours that foster long-term relationships (Ellis, Lee and Beatty, 1993).

The literatures of psychology, social psychology and communication theory have not infiltrated deeply into the marketing literature, although there is some evidence that they could contribute significantly to our understanding of RM. Martin and Sohi (1993), for example, found that trust, frequency of communication, quality of communication and relational norms impacted on the length of a relationship. Their work supports that of Heide and John (1992) who found that norms such as flexibility (mutual expectation of willingness to change), information exchange (mutual, proactive provision of information to the relationship partner) and solidarity (mutual expectation that a high value is placed on the relationship) facilitate relationship duration. Martin and Sohi (1993) also note that certain seller characteristics influence the duration of a relationship: dependability, competence, likeability and customer orientation. Dependability implies that the customer can predict how the seller will behave/perform; competence refers to the technical skill and knowledge required to satisfy customer expectations; likeability helps build rapport; and customer orientation refers to the seller's empathy towards customer needs, and willingness to prioritize those needs. These characteristics bear a remarkable resemblance to the generic dimensions of service quality identified by Parasuraman, Zeithaml and Berry (1985; 1988; 1991): reliability, responsiveness, empathy, assurance and tangibles.

An additional question concerns the locus of the relationship. Can customers develop relationships with organizations or must relationships always be interpersonal?

REQUIREMENTS FOR SUCCESSFUL RELATIONSHIP MARKETING

There appear to be a number of requirements for the successful implementation of RM programmes.

First, a supportive culture is necessary for RM to flourish. Several commentators have noted that RM represents a paradigm shift from the older, transactional way of doing business (Levitt, 1983b; Shapiro, 1991; Webster, 1992). Paradigm shifts inevitably pose threats to, and demand changes of, existing corporate culture. RM is typified by mutual co-operation and interdependence between customer and supplier (Sheth, 1994). Under a transactional regime, the relationship is better characterized as 'manipulation of customers, exploiting their ignorance' (Gummesson, 1994, p. 9). At its extreme, transactional marketing reflects P.T. Barnum's contemptuous observation: 'There's a sucker born every day.' Under RM, salespeople are likely to be replaced by relationship managers; customer retention is likely to be rewarded more highly than customer acquisition; customer satisfaction data will receive billing equal to that of financial data in management meetings; and the CEO will spend as much time with customers as with department heads. These are not the priorities in exploitative marketing settings.

Internal marketing is a second prerequisite for successful RM (Gummesson, 1987; Grönroos, 1990). The goal of internal marketing is to convert employees to the new vision of RM, to promote the development of the new culture, to persuade them that it is sensible to buy into the new vision, and to motivate them to develop and implement RM strategies. The internal market's expectations and needs must be satisfied. 'Unless this is done properly, the success of the organization's operations on its ultimate, external markets will be jeopardized' (Grönroos, 1990, p. 8). If the organization is unable to meet its employees' needs, it is likely that they will defect to other jobs before being able to build long-lasting relationships with customers.

It is also clear that the firm must understand customer expectations. This means that there must be a continuous flow of information into the business; continuity is required because expectations change over time. Work by Parasuraman, Berry and Zeithaml (1991) suggests that managers do not always have a clear understanding of customer expectations. This is a product of an inadequate marketing information system, too many levels of management between the front line and management, and communication difficulties.

A fourth requirement for successful RM is a sophisticated customer database which provides information in actionable format for the development and monitoring of RM strategy and tactics. Petrison and Wang (1993) claim that database technology is fundamental to allowing companies to get to know their customers as individuals. An example is provided by the US retail chain, Service Merchandise. Their point-of-sale system captures 100% of customers' identities and transactions down to the individual

SKU (stock-keeping unit) level. The database contains over 20 million records and each household record has over 100 fields of information. The company uses these data to communicate highly focused offers to customers, and to monitor the impacts of any RM initiatives. Relationship managers are increasingly able to use databases to track retention rates longitudinally, conduct root-cause investigations of defections, segment their markets and establish retention objectives.

Finally, new organizational structures and reward schemes may be required. The traditional marketing and sales function is organized around products or geographic markets. Under the influence of RM, organization around customers becomes more sensible. Customer, or account, managers are better placed to build long-term relationships with clients, more deeply understanding their expectations and constructing financial, social and structural links to the firm. IBM, for example, has a team of customer relationship managers. The logic of RM would suggest that the people allocated to customer acquisition should differ from those dedicated to customer retention. Different knowledge, skills and attitudes are deployed. Through their combined efforts these account managers should be able to acquire, migrate (from light-user to heavy-user status) and retain customers. Companies will also need to reconsider how they reward employees. At present, sales and marketing management is widely rewarded with a mix of basic salary and performance-related bonus or commission. Common performance criteria include sales volume and customer acquisition. Under the RM regime, customer managers are more likely to be rewarded by customer profitability, account penetration and customer retention.

SUMMARY

RM is a term which has yet to acquire uncontested status and meaning. For some, RM is simply transactional marketing dressed up in new clothes; for others, it represents a significant change in the practice of marketing. For some, RM refers to all types of internal and external organizational relationships; for others, RM is focused clearly on external customer relationships.

Companies, particularly in the service sector, are increasingly finding ways of building close, long-term relationships with external customers. These companies know that winning new customers is significantly more costly than retaining existing customers, and that when customers defect they take with them all future income stream. Their reason for practising RM is customer retention. However, the more advanced relationship marketers also know that not all customers are worth retaining. Not all contribute positively and equally to company performance.

The voice of the customer is absent from much RM. Indeed, it is not known whether customers want, in significant numbers, to enter into relationships with their suppliers. Companies routinely communicate more frequently and make special offers to their more valued customers. Whether this is seen by customers as adding value is a moot point.

At its best, RM is characterized by a genuine concern to meet or exceed the expectations of customers and to provide excellent service in an environment of trust and commitment to the relationship. To be successful relationship marketers, companies must develop a supportive organizational culture, market the RM idea internally, intimately understand customers expectations, create and maintain a detailed customer database, and organize and reward employees in such a way that the objective of RM, customer retention, is achieved.

NOTE

*   This chapter has been adapted from, Buttle, F. (1996) Relationship Marketing. In F. Buttle (ed.) *Relationship Marketing: Theory and Practice*, ch. 1, London, Prentice Hall.

REFERENCES

Anderson, J. and Narus, J. (1990) A model of distributor firm and manufacturer firm working partnerships, *Journal of Marketing*, Vol. 54, pp. 42–58.

Anderson, J. and Narus, J. (1991) Partnering as a focused market strategy, *California Management Review*, Vol. 33, pp. 95–113.

Barnes, J.G. (1995) The quality and depth of customer relationships. In M. Bergadaà (ed.) *Proceedings of the 24th EMA Conference*, ESSEC. Cergy-Pontoise.

Berry, L.L. (1983) Relationship marketing. In L.L. Berry, G.L. Shostack and G.D. Upah (eds) *Perspectives on Services Marketing*, American Marketing Association, Chicago, Ill.

Berry, L.L. and Gresham, L.G. (1986) Relationship retailing: transforming customers into clients, *Business Horizons*, Vol. 29, pp. 43–7.

Blois, K. (1995) Relationship marketing in organizational markets – what is the customer's view? In M. Bergadaà (ed.) *Proceedings of the 24th EMAC Conference*, ESSEC. Cergy-Pontoise.

Borden, N.H. (1964) The concept of the marketing mix, *Journal of Advertising Research*, June, pp. 2–7.

Buck-Lew, M. and Edvinsson, L. (1993) *Intellectual Capital at Skandia*, Skandia, Stockholm.

Buttle, F.A. (1992) Shopping motives: a constructionist perspective, *Service Industries Journal*, Vol. 12, pp. 349–67.

Christopher, M., Payne, A. and Ballantyne, D. (1991) *Relationship Marketing: Bringing Quality, Customer Service and Marketing Together*, Butterworth-Heinemann, Oxford.

Cowles, D. (1989) Putting the relations into relationship banking, *Bank Marketing*, April, pp. 38–9.

Crosby, L.A. (1989) Building and maintaining quality in the service relationship. In S.W. Brown and E. Gummesson (eds) *Quality in Services*, Lexington Books, Lexington, Mass.

Crosby, L.A., Evans, K.R. and Cowles, D. (1990) Relationship quality in services selling: an interpersonal influence perspective, *Journal of Marketing*, Vol. 54, pp. 68–81.

Czepiel, J.A. (1990) Service encounters and service relationships: implications for research, *Journal of Business Research*, Vol. 20, pp. 13–21.

DeSouza, G. (1992) Designing a customer retention plan, *Journal of Business Strategy*, March–April, pp. 24–8.

Dwyer, F.R., Schurr, P.H. and Oh, S. (1987) Developing buyer–seller relationships, *Journal of Marketing*, Vol. 51, pp. 11–27.

Ellis, K.L., Lee, J. and Beatty, S.E. (1993) Relationships in consumer marketing: directions for consumer research, AMA Marketing Educator's Summer Conference.

Evans, J.R. and Laskin, R.L. (1994) The relationship marketing process: a conceptualisation and application, *Industrial Marketing Management*, Vol. 23, pp. 439–52.

Fornell, C. (1992) A national customer satisfaction barometer: the Swedish experience, *Journal of Marketing*, Vol. 56, pp. 6–21.

Frenzen, J.K. and Davis, H.L. (1990) Purchasing behaviour in embedded markets, *Journal of Consumer Research*, Vol. 17, pp. 1–11.

Gamesan, S. (1994) Determinants of long-term orientation in buyer–seller relationships, *Journal of Marketing*, Vol. 58, pp. 1–19.

Geyskens, I. and Steenkamp, J.–B. (1995) An investigation into the joint effects of trust and interdependence on relationship commitment. In M. Bergadaà (ed.) *Proceedings of the 24th EMAC Conference*, ESSEC. Cergy-Pontoise.

Grönroos, C. (1990) Relationship approach to the marketing function in service contexts: the marketing and organization behaviour interface, *Journal of Business Research*, Vol. 20, pp. 3–11.

Grönroos, C. (1991) The marketing strategy continuum: towards a marketing concept for the 1990s, *Management Decision*, Vol. 29, pp. 7–13.

Grönroos, C. (1992) Facing the challenge of service competition: the economies of services. In P. Kunst and J. Lemmik (eds) *Quality Management in Services*, Van Gorcum, Maastricht.

Grönroos, C. (1994) Quo vadis, marketing? Toward a relationship marketing paradigm, *Journal of Marketing Management*, Vol. 10, pp. 347–60.

Gummesson, E. (1987) The new marketing – developing long-term interactive relationships, *Long Range Planning*, Vol. 20, pp. 10–20.

Gummesson, E. (1994) Making relationship marketing operational, *International Journal of Service Industry Management*, Vol. 5, pp. 5–20.

Håkansson, L. (1982) *International Marketing and Purchasing of Industrial Goods: An Interaction Approach*, Wiley, New York.

Hart, C.W.L., Heskett, J.L. and Sasser, W.E. jr (1990) The profitable art of service recovery, *Harvard Business Review*, July–August, pp. 148–56.

Heide, J.B. and John, G. (1992) Do norms matter in a marketing relationship? *Journal of Marketing*, Vol. 56, pp. 32–44.

Heskett, J.L., Jones, T.O., Loveman, G.W., Sasser, W.E. jr and Schlesinger, L.A. (1994) Putting the service profit chain to work, *Harvard Business Review*, March–April, pp. 164–74.

Hughes, A. and Wang, P. (1995) Media selection for database marketers, *Journal of Direct Marketing*, Vol. 9, pp. 79–89.

Jackson, B.B. (1985) *Winning and Keeping Industrial Customers*, Lexington Books, Lexington ,Mass.

Keane, T.J. and Wang, P. (1995) Applications of the lifetime value model in modern newspaper publishing, *Journal of Direct Marketing*, Vol. 9, pp. 59–71.

Levitt, T (1983a) *The Marketing Imagination*, Free Press, New York.

Levitt, T. (1983b) After the sale is over . . . , *Harvard Business Review*, September–October, pp. 87–93.

Martin, M.C. and Sohi, R.S. (1993) Maintaining relationships with customers: some critical factors. Unpublished paper, University of Nebraska, Lincoln.

McCarthy, E.J. (1975) *Basic Marketing: A Managerial Approach*, Irwin, Homewood, Ill.

Milgrom, P. and Roberts, J. (1992) *Economics, Organization and Management*, Prentice-Hall, Englewoods Cliffs, NJ.

Moorman, C., Zaltman, G. and Deshpande, R. (1992) Relationships between providers and users of market research: the dynamics of trust within and between organizations, *Journal of Marketing Research*, Vol. 29, pp. 314–28.

Morgan, R.M. and Hunt, S.D. (1994) The commitment-trust theory of relationship marketing, *Journal of Marketing*, Vol. 58, pp. 20–38.

O'Neal, C. (1989) JIT procurement and relationship marketing, *Industrial Marketing Management*, Vol. 18, pp. 55–63.

Parasuraman, A., Berry, L.L. and Zeithaml, V.A. (1991) Perceived service quality as a customer-based performance measure: an empirical examination of organizational barriers using an extended service quality model, *Human Resource Management*, Vol. 30, pp. 335–64.

Parasuraman, A., Zeithaml, V. and Berry, L.L. (1985) A conceptual model of service quality and its implications for future research, *Journal of Marketing*, Vol. 49, pp. 41–50.

Parasuraman, A., Zeithaml, V. and Berry, L.L. (1988) SERVQUAL: a multiple-item scale for measuring consumer perceptions of service quality, *Journal of Retailing*, Vol. 64, pp. 12–40.

Parasuraman, A., Zeithaml, V. and Berry, L.L. (1991) Refinement and reassessment of the SERVQUAL scale, *Journal of Retailing*, Vol. 67, pp. 420–50.

Parasuraman, A., Zeithaml, V. and Berry, L.L. (1994) Expectations as a comparison standard in measuring service quality: an assessment of a reassessment, *Journal of Marketing*, Vol. 58, pp. 132–9.

Payne, A. and Rickard, J. (1994) *Relationship Marketing, Customer Retention and Service Firm Profitability*, working paper, Cranfield Business School, Cranfield.

Petrison, L.A., Blattberg, R.C. and Wang, P. (1993) Database marketing: past, present and future, *Journal of Direct Marketing*, Vol. 7, pp. 27–36.

Petrison, L.A. and Wang, P. (1993) From relationships to relationship marketing: applying database technology to relationship marketing, *Public Relations Review*, Vol. 19, pp. 235–45.

Pitt, L.L. and Page, M.J. (1994) *Customer Defections Analysis and Management: A Graphic Approach*, working paper, Henley Management College, Henley on Thames.

Reichheld, F. (1993) Loyalty-based management, *Harvard Business Review*, March–April, pp. 64–73.

Reichheld, F. and Sasser, W.E. jr (1990) Zero defections: quality comes to services, *Harvard Business Review*, September–October, pp. 105–11.

Rosenberg, L.J. and Czepiel, J.A. (1984) A marketing approach to customer retention, *Journal of Consumer Marketing*, Vol. 1, pp. 45–51.

Rosenbloom, B. (1991) *Marketing Channels: A Management View*, Dryden, Hinsdale, Ill.

Rust, R.T. and Zahorik, A.J. (1993) Customer satisfaction, customer retention and market share, *Journal of Retailing*, Vol. 69, pp. 193–215.

Rust, R.T., Zahorik, J.A. and Keiningham, T.L. (1994) *Return on Quality – Measuring the Financial Impact of your Company's Quest for Quality*, Probus, Chicago, Ill.

Shapiro, B. (1991) Close encounters of four kinds: managing customers in a rapidly changing environment. In R. Dolan (ed.) *Strategic Marketing Management*, Harvard University Press, Boston, Mass.

Sheth, J.N. (1994) The domain of relationship marketing. Unpublished paper, Second Research Conference on Relationship Marketing, Center for Relationship Marketing, Emory University, Atlanta, Ga.

Spekman, R. (1988) Strategic supplier selection: understanding long-term buyer relationships, *Business Horizons*, Vol. 31, pp. 75–81.

Spriggs, M.T. and Nevin, J.R. (1992) *A Relational Contracting Framework for Understanding Exchange Relationships*, working paper, University of Oregon.

Stern, L.W. and El-Ansary, A. (1992) *Marketing Channels* (4th edn), Prentice-Hall, Englewood Cliffs, NJ.

Storbacka, K. (1994) *The Nature of Customer Relationship Probability*, Swedish School of Economics and Business Administration, Helsinki.

Storbacka, K., Strandvik, T. and Grönroos, C. (1994) Managing customer relationships for profit: the dynamic of relationship quality, *International Journal of Service Industry Management*, Vol. 5, pp. 21–38.

Tauber, E.M. (1972) Why do people shop? *Journal of Marketing*, Vol. 36, pp. 46–9.

Treather, D. (1994) Souped-up for direct attack, *Marketing*, 29 September, pp. 18–19.

Wang, P. and Splegel, T. (1994) Database marketing and its measurements of success, *Journal of Direct Marketing*, Vol. 8, pp. 73–83.

Webster, F. (1992) The changing role of marketing in the corporation, *Journal of Marketing*, Vol. 56, pp. 1–17.

Young, L.C. and Wilkinson, I.F. (1989) The role of trust and cooperation in marketing channels: a preliminary study, *European Journal of Marketing*, Vol. 23, pp. 109–22.

Zeithaml, V., Parasuraman, A. and Berry, L.L. (1994) The nature and determinants of customer expectation of service, *Journal of the Academy of Marketing Science*, Vol. 21, pp. 1–12.

SECTION 4: MATERIALS PROCESSING

INTRODUCTION

This section examines those business processes involved in processing materials. All organisations need processes to acquire material. Some might wish to change the state of that material through a manufacturing or production process. Some might wish to move that material, using logistics processes. Some may also be confronted with the need for a process to dispose of unwanted material in an environmentally safe manner.

In chapter 9, Baily considers the processes involved when an organisation purchases materials from its supply markets. Organisational purchasing is very different from most household purchasing. It is a complex process that may be lengthy and involve many different people in the organisation. The chapter compares purchasing with marketing in that both are activities primarily involving interactions with the organisation's environment. However as purchasing is concerned with inputs to the organisation rather than outputs from it, we might think of it as 'marketing in reverse'. As the chapter points out, purchasing and marketing are two sides of the same coin. In the same way that marketing seeks to identify the customers whose needs the organisation can best meet, purchasing is concerned to identify those suppliers who can best meet the organisation's needs. In a world where purchased materials can account for as much as 80% of the cost of the finished product, purchasing is clearly an important activity. Recent trends in purchasing have seen many organisations seeking to have much closer, long term relationships with many fewer suppliers. The term 'partnership sourcing' has come into currency, and is similar to many aspects of relationship marketing.

In chapter 10, Parnaby describes manufacturing as a system that processes materials, taking inputs of purchased materials and transforming them to products for use by customers. He argues that there is much to be gained from the study of different manufacturing operations from a systems perspective. Understanding the interrelationships between the various subsystems that make up an individual manufacturing system, and the part played by manufacturing as a subsystem within the wider business system can only improve the design and control of manufacturing systems. All manufacturing can be described in terms of the simple input–output model as depicted in the transformation model. In this respect manufacturing is the easiest business activity to describe in systems terms. However, this apparent uniformity is superficial. All manufacturing systems are different in that they are made up of various subsystems and are themselves part of a larger business system. Differences are bound to arise from the different ways in which any organisation combines these subsystems, and from the different interactions that it has with its environment. These factors invariably make each manufacturing system unique.

In chapter 11, Christopher argues that logistics can simultaneously add value for customers and lower costs for the organisation thereby achieving a competitive advantage. Logistics involves those business processes concerned with movement of materials, into, through and out of the organisation. Christopher views logistics as a process for fulfilling customer orders. He points out that logistics is the link between the market place and the operating activity of the organisation. Logistics spans the whole organisation from suppliers to customers, and as such we should adopt a systems perspective, in effect seeing the organisation as a series of linked processes which seek to satisfy customers. Through its use of the systems perspective, logistics offers the means of integrating activities from the supplier through the organisation and on to the customer. The adoption of a systems perspective is a key theme in all the chapters in this book.

Historically, the main concern of logistics has been the movement of materials in the direction of the customer. However, in chapter 12, Lancioni considers those occasions when products need to be moved in the opposite direction, back into the organisation. There may be two main reasons why organisations might need to undertake such reverse logistics: a requirement to reclaim material for recycling, and to recall defective products. There seems to be increasing pressure on suppliers to be able to respond to both of these demands. The objective of a reverse logistics system is not only to minimise the costs involved, but also to do so with the minimum disruption to the service provided to customers in the normal outward flow of goods. Like any normal forward logistics system, the reverse logistics system will involve actions and decisions in the areas of transport, warehousing, inventory control, materials handling and order processing. The development of an effective system will depend on all these decision areas, both individually and collectively.

9

PURCHASING*

Peter Baily

The winds of change are blowing in purchasing and supply. Continued upgrading of conformance quality standards, just-in-time approaches to material availability, long-term relationships with fewer suppliers and a win–win approach to negotiations instead of the more traditional adversarial or win–lose approach, are just some of the changes in the way procurement is managed. These changes are helping organizations to survive and succeed in a very competitive world.

Purchasing and supply is a necessary function in almost every organization, from the private household to the national government. This [chapter] is mainly about larger organizations which have purchasing and supply departments, but purchasing and supply is just as important in small organizations which do not employ full-time people to do the work [. . .].

SMALLER ORGANIZATIONS

Paul Bocuse, a world-famous French cook, employs about 50 people at his main restaurant; not enough to have a purchase department. But every day when he is in residence he shops personally at the Lyon market. According to him, 'a good cook is someone who knows how to buy produce'. Franco Taruschio, who runs what is perhaps the best restaurant in Wales, also gets to the market in Abergavenny early to buy the best on offer.

As we read in the *Good Food Guide 1985*, 'nearly all the restaurants in this book take as much care over their ingredients as they do in the cooking. They have supported local producers, cajoled people back to the land, created new jobs by providing a market for small-scale operations that would otherwise be unable to compete with big factory farms.' This close attention to buying, and to developing new supply sources if existing sources do not meet requirements, are just the sort of policies adopted by large supply departments.

THE PROCESS DEFINED

Organizational purchasing is the process by which organizations define their needs for goods and services; identify and compare the supplies and suppliers available to them; negotiate with sources of supply or in some other way arrive at agreed terms of trading; make contracts and place orders; and finally receive, accept and pay for the goods and services required.

Purchasing is closely associated with other organizational functions, such as inventory management, stores operation, and transport. Production planning and control, in manufacturing organizations, and merchandizing, in distributive organizations, have to work closely with buying. Often some or all of these functions are combined with the purchasing function under a single head, the materials manager or supply manager.

Traditionally, purchasing objectives were defined as: to obtain the right quality of goods, in the right quantity, at the right time, from the right supplier, at the right price. These five 'rights' were often thought of in the context of a static environment, so that by a series of successive approximations it would eventually be possible to arrive at the final right answer for each one.

But in highly competitive world markets the environment is not static but dynamic, tending not towards equilibrium but always towards something new. Purchasing objectives continually need to be updated and revised. Arriving at the final right answer for some old product just as it is discontinued does nothing for the competitive position of an organization.

Proactive, rather than reactive; dynamic, rather than static, is the way in which the purchasing role is now conceived. Better quality, in more suitable quantities, just in time for requirements, from better suppliers, at prices which continue to improve, are the sort of aims set by the dynamic purchasing function today.

A GLANCE BACKWARDS

Long before the large organization appeared with its functionally specialized departments, people bought and sold. Buying, that is acquiring goods and services in return for a price, dates back before the invention of written records. So also does selling, the disposal of goods and services in return for a price. It is likely that human communities have always bought and sold and that culturally and materially they have benefited from these transactions.

Archaeological evidence shows that trade occurred between the prehistoric tribes of Britain's stone age. The distinctive products of a flint axe factory at Langdale in the Lake District have been found hundreds of miles away in South Wales. Did Langdale send out travelling salesmen, or did South Wales have tribal buyers searching the land for better buys in stone age weaponry? We do not know. But what *is* known is that among the earliest things to be written down were stock records and accounts of commercial transactions. In days when literature and history were still being recited from memory, the pioneer developments in written record, whether incised on baked clay in cuneiform or carved or painted in pictographs, dealt with purchases, stocks and sales.

When books were invented, they dealt at first with higher matters than trade. Yet in the Bible itself, the oldest of all best-sellers, we read: 'It is naught, it is naught, saith the buyer; but when he is gone his way then he rejoiceth' (*Proverbs* 20.14). In Chaucer's *Canterbury Tales*, one of the oldest works in the canon of English literature, several of the horseback pilgrims are described as 'purchasours' or (since the ruling classes had previously spoken a kind of French) 'achatours'. No salesmen made the pilgrimage.

Many of Chaucer's pilgrims have occupational titles which with the passage of time have come to sound more like surnames. There was a 'manciple', for instance, described as an expert catering buyer. There was a 'reeve', who could 'better than his lord purchase', and no auditor could catch him out. The merchant was stately in bargaining, and as for the sergeant of law,

So great a purchasour was nowhere none . . .
Nowhere so busy a man as he there was,
And yet he seemed busier than he was.

There are buyers today who have never made a pilgrimage and would not know a reeve from a manciple of whom the same could be said.

THE GROWTH OF THE FIRM

Most firms start off as very small organizations, growing in size as they become more successful. The small firm consists of the entrepreneur who runs it and who usually started it, plus a number of other people to whom work is assigned which the entrepreneur either does not wish to do himself (such as perhaps packaging and despatch), or cannot do himself because he does not know how (such as, perhaps, preparation of final accounts), or else because there are not enough hours in the day to do everything. In such a small firm, major purchasing decisions are usually made by the head of the organization and minor purchasing decisions together with the detailed purchasing work fall to those in charge of any departments that exist. When a purchasing officer is appointed, his job may at first be seen as to do the legwork and the paperwork associated with purchasing, rather than to take the basic purchasing decisions.

Eventually, if the firm continues to increase in size, proper departments are set up for all major functions, and it is at this stage that management needs to delegate to purchasing the authority and responsibility to identify and evaluate purchasing problems, and to initiate, recommend and implement effective solutions.

A COMPLEX PROCESS

Organizational purchasing can be a complex process. Many people may take part, at various levels in the management hierarchy and in several functional departments. It can be a lengthy process: major 'one-off' decisions may take years to finalize. Even routine repeat orders that are placed immediately without consultation may be placed in accordance with policies previously laid down after much consultation and experiment over a lengthy period of time.

It is made more complex by its detailed involvement with other decision and control processes such as:

1 stock control policies and procedures which determine, control and replenish the range of items stocked;
2 the physical supply cycle which goods pass through as they are despatched, transported, received, stored and either issued or sold;
3 production planning and control which determines and controls the quantities of parts and materials required to meet production commitments;
4 merchandizing which decides which goods will be offered for resale and at what price.

It is when some or all of these other processes are combined in one department or under one head that the term *materials management* is used. The term *purchasing and supply* also suggests a joint consideration of purchasing with stock control and stores management, without necessarily implying that all those concerned with carrying out the relevant activities report to a single manager.

Purchasing works for every department in the business, and may be particularly involved with:

1 the specification and design of the end-product;
2 the quality control policies and procedures which set standards, assess capability, and control performance;

[. . .]

3　the finance function that pays bills and is also particularly concerned with capital expenditure, terms of credit, budgets, and stock investment.

[. . .]

THE RESPONSIBILITIES OF PURCHASING

Some organizations issue an internal charter or purchasing manual which incorporates a formal statement signed by management of what services the purchasing department is expected to provide and what its responsibilities are. Croell (1977) suggests the following:

1　Provide all materials and services that the company elects not to provide internally. In accomplishing this, purchasing must perform the following basic tasks.

(a)　Select and develop as required, vendors capable of meeting company needs.

(b)　Prepare and sign all purchase orders/contracts, so that the needs of the company and all pertinent terms and conditions related to the purchase are clearly understood by the supplier and documented accordingly.

(c)　Monitor supplier performance and related company activities during the course of the contract to assure that performance is accomplished by both parties in accordance with that originally intended.

(d)　Renegotiate or terminate purchase orders/contracts as required when changes occur, or as other conditions develop that warrant such action.

2　Provide information to and participate in management planning sessions on subjects related to purchased materials services.

3　Review purchase specifications and assist operating departments in selection of required materials and services for standardization purposes, and to assure their availability from competent suppliers at reasonable prices.

4　Protect the company from all unnecessary or unauthorized commitments which may result from inappropriate contacts or discussions with suppliers.

5　Dispose of all obsolete materials, equipment, or scrap that is no longer required for company operations.

MARKETING AND PURCHASING

The buying department and the selling department are the two departments mainly concerned with external relations, with reaching out into the supply markets and the sales markets outside the firm. To what extent does it make sense to say that both are engaged in marketing? This question is partly semantic (what words mean and how they are used) and partly about what departments do and how their work is perceived.

Definitions and discussions of marketing have certainly been dominated by selling considerations in recent years, although not in earlier periods. Consumer product manufacturers in the West which were competing for discretionary spending by consumers took to the marketing concept in a big way. The marketing concept, so called, could be described as the realization that firms need to find out what their customers want and take steps to provide it if they are to prosper; rather than producing the goods they were interested in producing, they needed to provide the goods the consumer was interested in purchasing. The marketing concept was less prevalent in industrial marketing, where many firms remained firmly and indeed proudly product-oriented rather than customer-oriented.

Industrial marketing differs from consumer marketing in several ways. Firstly, it usually sells different products. It deals in heavy equipment, such as tractors and machine tools; light equipment, such as photocopiers and hand power tools; construction, for example, of factories, docks and housing estates. It sells raw materials, such as iron ore and coal; processed materials, such as steel bar, chemicals and plywood; components, such as ball bearings and electric motors and semi-conductors; consumable supplies, such as cleaning materials and cutting oils; and a variety of services, such as those of the forwarding agent, the contract painter, or machine maintenance.

Secondly, it usually sells to different customers. Consumer marketing aims at households and individuals. Industrial marketing aims at organizations, and these have different and often much more complex buying processes. Consequently, when products such as motor cars or typewriters are sold to both consumers and to organizations the marketing approach tends to be very different for the two.

As Webster and Wind (1972) point out,

> industrial and institutional marketers have often been urged to base their strategies on careful appraisal of buying behaviour within key accounts and in principal market segments. When they search the available literature on buyer behaviour, however, they find virtually exclusive emphasis on consumers, not industrial buyers. Research findings and theoretical discussions about consumer behaviour often have little relevance for the industrial marketer.

Yet the total value of interfirm purchases of raw materials, components and semi-finished parts, finished parts, tools and supplies, is considerably greater than the total of sales to retail consumers. Rowe and Alexander (1968) quote an estimate to the effect that interfirm sales are worth about 2.5 times as much as sales to individual consumers – 3.5 times as much if sales to the government are included. They conclude that:

> resource allocation, in effect the sorting or matching of needs to supplying ability, is what marketing and selling is all about when looked at from the economist's viewpoint, and nowhere is this function more in need of being expertly carried out than in the area of interfirm transactions where industries are becoming interlocked in increasing interdependence.

This remains at least equally true if the words 'purchasing and supply' are substituted for the words 'marketing and selling'. It could indeed be said that the sorting or matching of needs to supplying ability is what purchasing is all about, and that in the area of interfirm transactions this often calls for marketing initiatives on the buying side.

This is sometimes described as 'marketing in reverse'. But one definition of 'to market', in the most popular dictionary in the United Kingdom, is 'to buy or sell in market', and the very word 'market' derives from a Latin word which means 'to buy' (*mercari*). In earlier days the merchant venturers set forth through unknown seas and distant countries in search, not so much of customers although they had to have something to trade, but more of new suppliers of new products – spices, furs, carpets, turkeys, tomatoes, oranges – as well as of new sources of known materials such as gold, diamonds and tin. Sourcing, and buying generally, was the venturesome and creative part of their marketing effort.

In the distributive industries, the selection and pricing of merchandise to sell is fundamental to marketing plans, and buying is therefore an important part of marketing for the retailer. In the manufacturing industries on the other hand, it is the selection and pricing of products to make which corresponds to this, and the procurement of parts and material to make them tends to be seen as part of the production process rather than part of the marketing process.

Even here, some buying activities call for creative and entrepreneurial skills, for commercial innovation and persuasion. [. . .] Kotler (Kotler and Levy, 1973; Kotler and

Balachandrian, 1975) for instance argues that in times of shortage the marketing problem shifts its location from selling to buying. The development of new suppliers is another example of purchasing firms marketing their buying requirements to the supply markets. And in the negotiation of major contracts (for the design and development of equipment at the frontier of the art) to meet customer requirements, the term marketing may well be equally appropriate to the proposals and arguments coming from each side (if indeed it is appropriate at all in this situation).

The increasing concentration of markets has been a noticeable feature of recent years and accounts for part of the difference between industrial marketing and consumer marketing. For example, if three detergent manufacturers sell to tens of millions of households, scientific studies can be made of the market and how it can be segmented, of marketing methods and how best to apply them. But if an industrial manufacturer sells to six major industrial customers plus a number of minor customers, the scope for science is less, and it is more a matter of art. The shotgun communications of mass media advertising are used in the first case; the sharpshooter methods of field salesmen and low budget advertising in specialist trade journals are used in the second case.

In many industries a small number of manufacturers produce most of the output; and in quite a high proportion of cases, a small number of customers take most of the output. Buying and selling are both affected by the situation; after all, every purchase is someone's sale, purchasing and marketing are the two sides of one coin. Purchase cost analysis, negotiated prices based on mutually agreed figures or cost, larger and more expert departments both for buying and for selling, are typical features.

When two or three large firms supply equivalent or interchangeable products to the same market, at prices which each is reluctant to change because of the risk of retaliation by the others, two obvious ways to increase security as well as profits are: firstly by product differentiation, and secondly by cost reduction. Product differentiation makes the products seem less equivalent or interchangeable to the customer. Cost reduction enables a manufacturer to increase profit without starting a price war.

Cost reduction initially concentrated on manufacturing costs, with much success in many firms. But as one managing director said:

we have over the years by dint of research, engineering development and good management, reduced operating costs to such an extent that now nearly 80% of total cost consists of purchased materials. Obviously it is important that buyers have an eye for more than the cheap price. Purchasing and supply have a major part to play in reducing cost and increasing profit.

Purchase transactions are made to supply various types of requirement, and several methods of purchasing are used. Types of requirement include:

1 merchandise for resale;
2 parts and material for production;
3 maintenance, repair and operating supplies;
4 capital plant and equipment;
5 services such as maintenance of equipment, cleaning, catering.

Some of these requirements are normally bought for stock, for instance merchandise. Parts and material for production are bought either for stock or else to arrive just in time to meet manufacturing schedules. Maintenance, repair and operating supplies may be bought to meet immediate needs, or else put into stock for future needs.

Purchasing methods include word-of-mouth contracts, such as purchases at auction sales, the use of standard purchase order forms, simplified order forms, purchase for cash and many others. The choice of ordering method can be affected by the type of requirement and by other things such as the type of market in which the purchase is made.

[. . .]

TYPICAL TRANSACTION STAGES

A typical purchase transaction in an organization goes through at least the four stages shown in Figure 9.1: originating, selecting, ordering, and completing. [. . .]

This chapter deals with the first two stages in the four-stage model: originating and selecting. [. . .]

ORIGINATING THE PURCHASE

For specific individual needs such as purchases for immediate use, the person requiring the item writes out a purchase requisition for it. A typical general purpose requisition form is shown in Figure 9.2. This document notifies purchasing of the requirement, authorizes the expenditure, and after processing is filed for audit and reference purposes. Anyone can make out a requisition, but no action will be taken unless it is signed by one of the few senior people who can authorize the expenditure. A list of authorized signatories is kept by purchasing, and states what sort of purchases the person concerned can authorize and any cash limit which applies; for instance, it may state that J. Brown, toolroom foreman, can

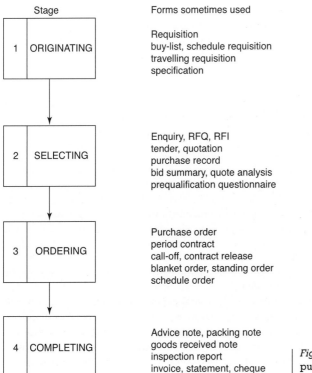

Stage	Forms sometimes used
1 ORIGINATING	Requisition buy-list, schedule requisition travelling requisition specification
2 SELECTING	Enquiry, RFQ, RFI tender, quotation purchase record bid summary, quote analysis prequalification questionnaire
3 ORDERING	Purchase order period contract call-off, contract release blanket order, standing order schedule order
4 COMPLETING	Advice note, packing note goods received note inspection report invoice, statement, cheque

Figure 9.1 Stages in typical purchase transaction

PURCHASE REQUISITION To Purchase Department Please obtain the undermentioned		Department _____ Date _____ Number _____	
Suggested supplier	Quantity and description	Price	Required for
	Requistioned by	Authorised by	

Figure 9.2 Typical purchase requisition; handwritten, one copy to the purchasing department, and second copy retained by originator

authorize expenditure on toolroom requirements up to £500 in value, and above that value the works manager must sign the requisition.

The requisition is date-stamped when received by the purchasing department and allocated to a buyer. The buyer checks the authorizing signature, and the description of the goods (which may need to be corrected or amplified), before taking action to obtain the goods required.

Capital expenditure

Capital goods include additions to or replacements of plant and machinery, such as machine tools, computers, company cars, and buildings.

Capital expenditure is treated differently from revenue expenditure in the accounts and for taxation purposes. Typically it comprises long-term investments such as new machine tools with an expected life of at least five years rather than short-term investments such as materials for immediate processing. At the bottom end of the range of capital goods, where price is not high or expected life is not long, the borderline between capital goods and revenue goods may be a bit vague, and it is for the accountants to say where it lies, with the approval of the auditors. In principle, a £5 pocket calculator expected to last for a year or two is capital expenditure, but in practice it will be written off to revenue, with no effect on the overall results as stated in final accounts. Principle and practice converge further up the range. Most firms do not regard a purchase as capital expenditure if it is below a certain figure, such as £30, or £300, or even £3000.

Special authorization rules are often used for capital expenditure. The requisition may have to be signed by a director, or approved by a sub-committee of the board of directors, with the board approval number stated on the requisition. In large organizations it may not be feasible for all capital expenditure to be approved at board level, so authority is delegated to local directors or division managers to authorize capital expenditure up to a stated cash limit. Above his limit capital expenditure proposals still go to the main board.

Capital goods are often acquired by a normal purchase transaction, but other methods are used. These include hire-purchase, leasing through a finance house or bank, and renting. Hire purchase is a system in which goods are hired or rented for a certain period of time after which they become the property of the hirer on payment of the final instalment. Leasing and renting are alternative ways of purchasing the use of capital equipment without actually buying it. Leasing is a form of rental; property is transferred by one party to another for a specified time in consideration of rent. Rent is a periodical payment to the owner for the use of goods or premises.

The main advantage of hiring, renting or leasing equipment, as compared to buying it outright, is that there is no capital outlay. Payment is made monthly or weekly in relatively small amounts instead of in one large sum at the date of acquisition. Some arrangements enable you to make the most of rapidly advancing technology by exchanging your equipment periodically for something newer.

These methods are often used for vehicles, and for electronic equipment such as computers [. . .] Rental usually includes sales and service support and maintenance.

Hiring or renting is much used in the construction industry. This is a very large industry in which at least half the capital equipment used is obtained on rental from plant hire firms [. . .]. The equipment, often highly specialized, is usually supplied with trained operators.

Vehicle hire on the other hand is often on a self-drive basis, because the operating skills are commonly available. It is of course possible to arrange for drivers to be supplied, in customized vehicles. Contract hire usually includes provision for relief vehicles, renewal of batteries and tyres, and arrangements for servicing and maintenance.

Purchases for stock

In order to replenish stock as it is used up, or (a much better way to think of the process) in order to provide for expected future demands after allowing for stock on hand, stock control will originate purchases by issuing requisitions. These may be general purpose requisitions as described earlier, but much use is also made of travelling requisitions and buy-lists or schedule requisitions.

Travelling requisitions are documents which travel from the originating department to purchasing in order to initiate a purchase, and then after transaction details have been recorded on them travel back to the originating department where they are filed for future reference and for use again the next time the item is required. They have nothing to do with travelling expenses or with requests to visit an overseas supplier. Alternative names for travelling requisitions are permanent order cards and perpetual requisitions.

An example of a travelling requisition is shown in Figure 9.3. This form is printed on heavyweight card for repeated use, unlike the general purpose requisition which is on flimsy paper for once-only use. Purchase description and other permanent data such as supplier name and address are written in. Space is provided to enter date, quantity on hand, quantity required, initials of originator and authorizer, and order number. The same card is used for years without rewriting.

Buy-lists (also known as blanket or schedule requisitions) are used when a large number of items need to be ordered at one time. This happens with some stock control systems and also with some production planning systems. No special form is used for these schedules of requirements. Often they are retained in the computer system as planned orders and not printed out as hard copy until action needs to be taken by purchasing.

In smaller organizations, the same person may be responsible for deciding what is to be ordered for stock as well as for actually ordering it – such as the buyer/first sales in a department store, the manager of a small retailer, the purchaser/stock controller in a small manufacturing firm.

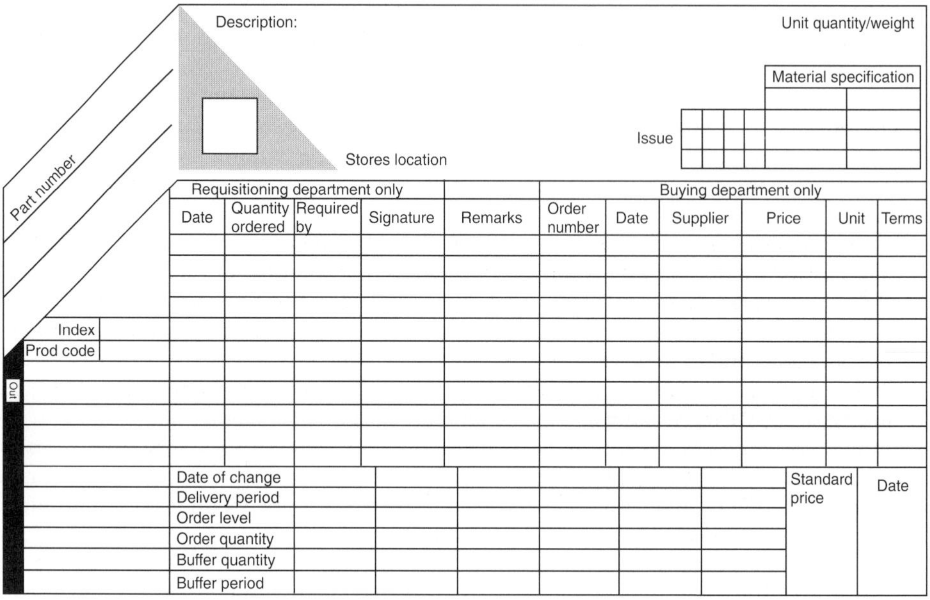

Figure 9.3 Travelling requisition, or permanent order card

Purchases for production

Parts and material required to make products to meet manufacturing schedules are normally supplied from stock, in the case of both common use and inexpensive items. For expensive or bulky items, and those used in large quantities, material requirements are planned week by week, or even day by day, and deliveries are timed so as to meet needs with little or no stock.

Material requirements for manufacturing schedules are notified to purchasing in the same way as stock requirements, by general purpose requisitions, travelling requisitions, or buy-lists, which may be retained in the computer system until they need to be actioned.

In some small organizations the purchasing and stock control department is given a master production schedule showing what end-products are due out week by week, plus parts lists for the end-products. They calculate materials requirements, adjust for stock, and place orders accordingly. This is now usually done on a computer, using MRP software.

THE SELECTION STAGE

The next stage, once the purchase department is aware that a requirement exists, is to select a supplier, and perhaps to select a brand or specification of goods. It is at this stage that the purchase department can make a major contribution to success. In most cases the specification will already have been decided and will not need to be reviewed every time a purchase transaction occurs. In many cases this will also be true of the supplier, as is shown in Figure 9.4. Reference to purchase records will show where previous orders were placed and whether supplier performance was satisfactory.

Existing purchase contracts may cover the requirement. In this case the selection stage has already been carried out. The order or call-off goes to the agreed supplier, mentioning the existing contract.

Even if there is no period contract, there may be an established supplier. Competent buyers do not change from an established supplier without good reason. As research has shown (Buckner, 1967):

1 Approximately half the persons involved in purchasing would not change from their best supplier to buy an identical product from a new supplier for a price reduction of less than 5%, that is, on average 27% increase in profitability; approximately one-fifth would not change for less than 10% reduction in price.
2 Even if an existing supplier is regarded as satisfactory, it is prudent to check the market periodically and see what any other possible sources have to offer. Research indicates that buyers in fact do check the market when the existing supplier requests a price increase or when a new supplier knocks hard at the door, but it is also desirable to check the market periodically even if trigger events of this kind have not occurred. How often? It could be three months after the last check, or three years: experience and market knowledge are the best guide.

Identifying potential suppliers

If there is no established supplier, or if the previous supplier proved unsatisfactory, or if it is considered to be time to check the market to see what alternative suppliers have to offer, then as shown in Figure 9.4 the standard procedure is:

1 Draw up a short list of potential sources.
2 Send them details of the requirement and ask for quotations.
3 Compare the quotations, obtain additional information as required, and decide.

In drawing up a short list of possible sources of supply, buyers rely on their own trade knowledge. They learn of potential suppliers from trade magazines, exhibitions and trade shows, calls by company representatives, catalogues and literature delivered by post. Colleagues in other departments may have useful information. Through personal contacts and membership of professional associations buyers may be able to consult people in other firms. Competent purchase departments keep a basic reference library including such general directories as *Kelly's Manufacturers and Merchants Directory, Sell's, Kompass, Who Owns Whom*, and perhaps the *Directory of Directors*. (There's also a *Directory of Directories*.) For particular areas, yellow pages and local business directories are useful; and for particular trades, excellent guides are published by trade magazines, trade associations and independent publishers.

These publications are usually reprinted annually, but even so the information given may be as much as 18 months out of date. Increasingly, similar information is available on computerized databases which can in principle be updated daily. Dun and Bradstreet's well-known *Business Information Reports*, which can be used to assess the credit-worthiness and financial stability of suppliers, are derived from a large database maintained by the company. This can be accessed online [. . .].

Enquiry procedures

General buyers' guides give you a long list rather than a short list of potential suppliers. This can be cut down by sending to the firms listed a preliminary enquiry giving brief details of the requirement, and asking firms, if they are able and willing to supply the requirement, to give some details about capability, performance record, financial status and other matters useful in drawing up a short list. These preliminary enquiries are usually called *requests*

LIBRARY
BISHOP BURTON COLLEGE
BEVERLEY HU17 8QG

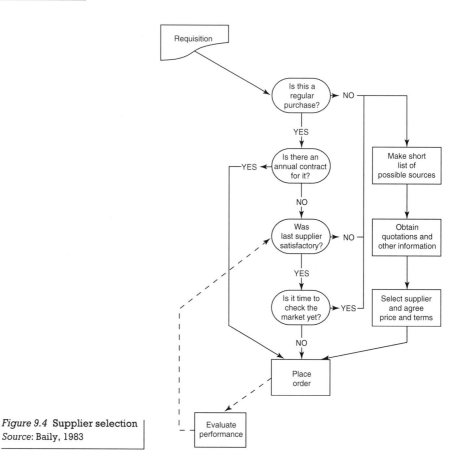

Figure 9.4 **Supplier selection**
Source: Baily, 1983

for information (RFI). In connection with construction contracts they are often called *prequalification questionnaires*, since the aim is to 'prequalify' or make a preliminary selection of potential suppliers who appear qualified to undertake the work.

Existing commitments or future plans may make it difficult for a supplier to bid for the requirement, in which case the supplier should say so. The purchaser should be pleased by this responsible attitude and keep the firm on the list of potential suppliers.

Having prepared a short list of possible suppliers, the next step is to send out formal enquiries or *requests for quotation* (RFQ), or tender forms. If a preprinted form is used it should not look like the order form and should not need to have such messages as 'This is not an order!' printed across it in large letters. It should either be a specially designed form such as the one shown in Figure 9.5, or else should be a version of the normal letterhead with such words as 'Your quotation is invited not later than . . . for the supply and delivery of the goods specified below, subject to the terms and conditions printed on the back of this form', preprinted to save typing. With the increasing use of word processors preprinted forms of this kind are used less than before.

One dictionary definition of 'quotation' is: 'amount stated as current price of stocks or commodities'. So a supplier could in principle reply to a request for quotation by saying 'we are currently selling this article at £p per thousand and delivery is usually about four weeks from receipt of order'. This is indeed a quotation but it is not an offer to sell so much as a statement of fact. Or a supplier could reply, as many do, by saying 'in reply to your enquiry

REQUEST FOR QUOTATION

ALEXANDER CONTRACTS PLC.
122 Baker Street
London WC1 3RG

TELEX 32148 & 32273
TELEPHONE 01- 222 668

Please quote this Reference in any correspondence
or Telephone call

Reference	Date	Contact
_ _ _ _ _ -		

Please quote us delivered carriage paid on the
conditions specified overleaf your lowest
fixed price for goods enumerated
below A Cash Discount of $2\frac{1}{2}$% M/A will be deducted from
invoice (unless otherwise stated in your Quotation)

Your Quotation should reach this office by:

For and on behalf of
ALEXANDER CONTRACTS PLC.

- -

Specification:

Delivery date required _____

Delivery of goods to be made to

Figure 9.5 Request for quotation

we offer to supply you with the articles specified at a price of £p per thousand for delivery four weeks from receipt of your order'. This is an offer to sell, which can be converted into a contract by acceptance, for instance by sending a order.

Or a supplier could reply in similar words on a preprinted quotation form, with a set of terms and conditions printed on the back which are not the same as the buyer's. This is also an offer to sell, but if the buyer accepts it using a purchase order form with different terms printed on it he is not in law accepting the offer but making a counter-offer. [. . .] They are regarded as relatively unimportant for a transaction which is one of a series between a regular supplier and a regular customer. They are important for an isolated transaction, for instance to build a new factory, where buyer and seller may never deal with each other again. For constructional work of this kind it is usual to use standard forms of contract which cover most of the things which could go wrong, and it is also usual for suppliers to quote for the work on tender forms.

A tender has been defined as 'a written offer to execute work or supply goods at a fixed price', and this offer is usually made on a form supplied by the purchaser, or the engineer or architect acting on behalf of the purchaser. This enquiry procedure is normal for building and civil engineering contracts [. . .].

Evaluating suppliers' quotations or tenders

The usual procedure is to keep a copy of the request for quotations in a pending file until all replies are received or until the closing date, and the quotations are then compared and analysed. It is convenient both for comparison and for subsequent reference to transfer key data from suppliers' quotations to a quotation summary sheet or bid summary – either a copy of the request for quotation form or a special form. When set-up costs or tooling charges or transport costs or payment arrangements differ, it is useful to show them on a bid summary so that direct comparison is easier. The order number and the name of the selected supplier are entered on the form before filing it away. The reason why that supplier was selected may also be shown.

Any anomalies or discrepancies between the offers and the enquiry documents should be sorted out at this stage, at least for the preferred bidders. Delivery promises should be considered in the light of past experience with the bidder or reports from other customers of actual delivery performance. Escalation clauses and, in the case of foreign sources, the possible effect of currency fluctuations should be taken into account.

Quality capability may have been examined at the previous, prequalification or RFI, stage; or it may be known from past dealings. At any rate it is certainly a key factor to be considered in comparing offers.

When everything is equal except price, the order goes to the firm which offers the lowest price. But it does not often happen that everything except price is equal, and both technical and commercial evaluation is usually required. The low bid or cheapest offer is not always the best buy.

Sometimes the low bidder turns out on investigation to be unable to meet volume requirements, or quality standards, or to be a bad risk in some other way. Buyers do not ask unsuitable suppliers to quote for major purchases. But for minor purchases they may not investigate untried suppliers unless they submit an attractive quotation. Sometimes the low bidder cannot deliver when required, and it has to be decided whether to pay another supplier more for earlier delivery.

Quoted price is only one factor in obtaining good value for money. It may be the main determinant of monetary cost, but there are other factors. Specification and design standard, delivery reliability, performance, durability and maintenance costs, and perhaps improvements in productivity are some of the factors that may affect total cost over the life of the product. Lower lifetime cost leads to better value for money even if the initial quoted price is higher.

It is a courtesy to tell unsuccessful bidders why they lost the order, with a word of thanks for their quotation and a tick against a preprinted list of reasons for failure, such as: lower quote accepted, better delivery elsewhere, other material or equipment preferred, no order placed this time, etc.

Price analysis and cost analysis

In considering quotations and tenders, some form of price analysis is used. Price may be compared with prices submitted by others, or paid in the past, or with the going rate if one exists. It may be compared with the cost of alternative materials or articles which could be used as substitutes.

When several quotations are received, it sometimes happens that one is much lower than the rest. It is wise to find out why. Perhaps the seller has made a mistake. If the low bid is 25% below the rest, the seller should be given the opportunity to correct or withdraw his offer: bankrupt suppliers and half-finished contracts are not the aim. Or perhaps the seller is short of work and is offering a price which just covers labour and materials without making full contribution to profit and overhead. This could lead to a good deal for both buyer and seller – unless the supplier is short of work because his work has been unsatisfactory. Low prices are also sometimes offered to get potential customers to give a fair trial to a new supplier. This is a legitimate ploy, since there is some risk in switching to an untried supplier. Special offers cannot be made the basis for standard prices, however.

Cost analysis is not the same as price analysis. Cost analysis is a systematic attempt to determine what a cost-based price ought to be by analysing the underlying costs of labour, materials, and overheads and adding a suitable figure for profit. This technique is particularly useful when competitive quotations do not provide a simple way to check the price.

It may be within the buyer's capability to carry out a cost analysis if it occasionally needs to be done for relatively simple articles. But the main application is in bulk regular purchases for high volume manufacturing. Here the buyer gets help from qualified estimators or cost analysts.

Suppliers are asked to submit a cost breakdown in support of their quoted price. Meanwhile qualified cost estimators in the purchase department analyse the cost of the articles. Price is settled by negotiation on a factual basis, with detailed comparison of the two price estimates, the seller's and the purchaser's. Suppliers are reluctant to do this if they have not done it before. But once one supplier agrees to it the others tend to follow. Civil engineering and building contracts based on bills of quantity are placed on a similar basis.

[. . .]

DISCOUNTS AND REBATES

A discount is normally a deduction from the list price, quoted price or usual price, or from the invoice total, which is given for a variety of reasons and is usually expressed as a percentage. However, chain discounts sometimes incorporate pluses as well as minuses. Chain discount is the term used when nominal price is subject to a series or chain of percentage adjustments, such as: £75 less 7½% plus 5% less 12½%. Consequently a discount is sometimes defined as a percentage *variation* to the nominal price rather than as a deduction.

A rebate has been defined as 'deduction from the sum to be paid, discount', and thus appears to be just another word for discount. Perhaps the term rebate is used most commonly in connection with cumulative discounts or annual rebates.

The three main kinds of discount are: settlement discounts, trade discounts, and quantity discounts, but some other kinds are encountered.

Settlement discounts are given for payment earlier than is usual. They are often called cash discounts, a term which is correctly used for discounts given for immediate payment in cash rather than on credit. They were formerly very common, typical terms being 3¾% for payment in seven days, or 2½% for payment in 30 days. This is substantial; to lose 2½% of the invoice total for taking an extra month's credit is roughly equivalent to borrowing money at about 30% interest. Rather than lose the discount, every solvent business paid on time. Some suppliers saw little point in giving a discount for standard practice, so they altered their terms of payment to net monthly account. Unfortunately, some customers saw that taking an extra month's credit without change to the invoice total was equivalent to borrowing money at zero interest; or from the supplier's viewpoint, lending money at zero interest.

Trade credit is a legitimate source of finance provided that it is taken with the supplier's consent. Cases have been reported, however, in which large purchasers have abused their position by taking up to 12 months credit despite objections from the victim. Unpaid suppliers can take their customer to court or even arrange for a liquidator to take over their affairs, but are usually reluctant to take such drastic action. The better suppliers are unlikely to look with favour on customer organizations which fail to honour agreed terms of payment. They may demand cash with order, payment in full of all previous debts before accepting further orders, 4% surcharge on bills not paid when due, or Romalpatype contract clauses under which goods supplied remain the property of the supplier until paid for.

Unless an organization has explicit terms of payment which it applies rigorously, the buyer should be authorized to negotiate terms and times of payment along with other aspects of the contract and to commit the organization to them.

Terms of payment are significant issues in major contracts likely to take several years to complete, which may provide for initial payments to finance development work, progress payments to cover work packages as they are completed month by month, contract price adjustments to cover increases in the costs of labour and materials, and retention amounts if a trial period is required to ensure that the work or equipment meets the specification. They are also important in international contracts where rate of exchange or availability of foreign currency may present problems.

Trade discount no doubt originally meant discounts given to tradesmen such as plumbers, builders and decorators, or to 'the trade' in the sense of the distribution channels used by manufacturers – wholesalers, retailers, and many others. Now it seems to mean a discount given to any special class of customer: educational discounts, OEM (original equipment manufacturer) discounts, major user discounts, etc. 'List price is the notional price, but I don't know who pays it,' one sales manager is quoted as saying. 'Everyone seems to qualify for a trade discount of some kind.'

Discount structures are often laid down formally in the case of price list goods – x% for the wholesaler, y% for the retailer for instance – but discretionary discounts are usually available in addition to these: that is, discounts available at the discretion of the sales manager or his representative. 'I always ask for a discount,' said one buyer. 'Sometimes I can think of a reason for it, sometimes not. Usually I get it.'

Price lists are applicable to standard articles sold to many customers, but not to special goods to the specification of one customer. Most of the more important purchases in most organizations are not charged by price list.

Special discounts are sometimes available to buyers who take seasonable goods out of season: road salt, antifreeze or coal in summer for instance. The advantage to the seller of these seasonal discounts is that production can be smoothed, and the cost of distribution and stock-holding may be reduced. The advantage to the buyer is a lower price, but this has to be offset against the disadvantage of higher stocks.

Quantity discounts are given for large orders or to large customers. The seller benefits from big orders which often enable direct as well as indirect costs to be reduced. Sometimes quantity discounts are expressed as percentages. Sometimes a price–quantity table is drawn up, such as the one shown below.

Alternatively, the price could be quoted as 40p kg, subject to a 5% surcharge for orders below 1000 kg, and to quantity discounts on the following scale: less 5% for orders of 2250–4999 kg, less 10% for orders of 5000–9999 kg, and less 12½% for orders of 10 000 kg or more.

Price per kg	For quantities of:
42p	Below 1000 kg
40p	1000–2249 kg
38p	2250–4999 kg
36p	5000–9999 kg
35p	10 000 kg upwards

These two ways of expressing the price–quantity relationship are arithmetically equivalent. It is a matter of preference which one the seller adopts.

Small quantity extras, small order premiums, and minimum order charges are imposed by some firms; in a sense they are the reverse of quantity discounts, but they have the same effect of charging higher prices for smaller quantities.

When offered a lower price (whether in the form of a discount or not) for ordering a larger quantity for delivery at one time, the buyer needs to weigh the advantage of a lower purchase cost against the disadvantage of carrying larger stocks than would otherwise be needed. This can sometimes be quantified [. . .]. Other possible disadvantages include: having to place all the business with a single source instead of dividing it between two suppliers; and undertaking to deal with a particular supplier for a longer period.

Buyers also take the initiative in looking for quantity discounts. Group contracts are an example of this: a group of establishments can often get a lower price if they all agree to deal with a single source for a particular item. Imaginative approaches can pay off: order quantities can be adjusted to make the most of price breaks, rebates can be requested on total annual volume of business, if it exceeds a certain figure.

NEGOTIATION

The four main price negotiation situations are:

1 An established supplier wants to increase price.
2 The buyer wants an established supplier to reduce price.
3 A potential supplier wants to get the business and oust the established supplier.
4 There is no regular supplier and this is a new purchase.

Negotiations about price changes usually turn on costs. Suppliers in a position to dictate price do not need to negotiate. Suppliers who do negotiate need to make out a reasonable case.

Buyers negotiate many other matters apart from price: terms and conditions of contract, tooling, transport, quality control arrangements, delivery and stockholding arrangements, in fact any aspect of the agreement which is not standard.

Negotiation should not be difficult between reasonable persons who want to reach a mutually satisfactory agreement quickly, upon a matter they understand. Lengthy and arduous negotiations occur mainly when one or more of the parties are not being reasonable, and when large numbers of people are affected by the result.

A common mistake is not preparing thoroughly enough. Inadequate preparation is sometimes attributed to lack of time, but everyone has all the time there is; no-one's day has more than 24 hours in it. Faulty allocation of time might be nearer the mark.

Another mistake is trying to score a great victory. 'Win–win' negotiations do not lead to the defeat of one side and the victory of the other, since buyer and supplier are not at war with each other. The aim in this kind of negotiation must be a mutually satisfactory solution. Trying to win every point is the result of not thinking the situation through. Most commercial negotiations occur between buyers and sellers who intend to continue trading with each other; whose objectives cannot rationally include leaving the other party stone cold dead in the market; who cannot therefore be said to have succeeded in achieving their objectives unless the other party is also reasonably satisfied with the outcome.

Preparation for negotiations

Objectives, and tactics, are the two areas where advance planning and preparation can pay off.

In considering objectives, the major issues and the minor issues should be spelled out. The other parties' needs should be considered: what are they really after? How can we satisfy some of their needs? What do *we* stand to lose or gain, and what do *they* stand to lose or gain, if settlement is not reached? What are the relevant facts and figures? Often these have to be collected and collated in consultation with colleagues in other departments – in finance, engineering, production or sales. Long-term objectives such as the future supply pattern should not be left out of account when planning a short-term negotiation such as the price to be paid or the supplier to be chosen for a particular contract.

In fixing objectives for a negotiation, some margin for manoeuvre should be left. We might for instance aim at a settlement price of £10 000, while hoping to settle for £8000 and being willing to agree at most to £12 000. These are precise figures but do not send the negotiator into battle with his hands tied.

In considering the tactical plan, we have to consider relative bargaining strengths. How much the seller needs the business, how sure he is of getting it, and how much time there is to reach agreement; how much the buyer needs the seller's product, what alternatives are open to him, how much time he has to develop alternatives, how much business he has to give the supplier, and what cost and price data he has; these are particularly relevant. Time and location of meeting have to be settled. The home player has a small advantage. It is hardly enough to justify booking a hotel room to make sure of a neutral meeting ground.

In fixing the tactical plan, what questions to ask, and how to word them; what approaches the other side may come up with, and how to counter them; and the order in which issues will be tackled, are the main things to plan.

Conduct of negotiations

The reasonable negotiator begins on a positive friendly note, perhaps by referring to a past history of mutually satisfactory transactions. He shows clearly that he intends if at all possible to come to a mutually satisfactory settlement of the points at issue as soon as he can. He deals systematically in succession with the various points. He concludes by recapping what has been agreed, and he confirms this in writing the following day. He does not attempt to put one over on the other side by smuggling into the confirmation matters that were not mentioned in the recap. His plain and evident intention is to reach agreement on terms which satisfy both sides. Provided that the other party is also reasonable, it is on the whole a pleasure to do business with him. It cannot, however, be denied that unreasonable negotiators sometimes enjoy an undeserved success.

Some practical advice is as follows:

1　DO give plenty of thought to the other party's probable objectives, tactics, and attitude.
2　DON'T waste time scoring debating points, proving your opponent wrong, or otherwise showing off.
3　DON'T let emotional reactions such as rage or pride cloud your thinking.
4　DON'T do all the talking; ask questions, listen to the answers.
5　DON'T keep your eyes on the papers. Watch our opponent's body language: his eyes, physical attitudes, and facial expressions. Most people signal their feelings and attitudes quite clearly, even while saying verbally something rather different.
6　Be ready to modify your approach.
7　If you seem to reach an impasse on one point and you do not seem to be getting anywhere, switch to another point; say 'Let's leave that one for the moment. How about . . . ?' When the less controversial point has been settled, the sticky one may look less sticky or else suggest a break for coffee, conference, referring back.
8　Have a list of points at issue and work through it systematically, ticking off points as they are dealt with and recapping periodically.
9　If you gain an important concession, think of something you can concede in turn. If on the other hand you have had to yield on some major point, use this as a lever to gain some *quid pro quo*.
10　The alternatives are not win or lose, as Gerry Nierenberg has pointed out: 'The creative negotiator is where there are no wars, no strikes, no lockouts. The old clichés of the playing field, I win, you lose, survival of the fittest, winner take all, don't apply to commercial negotiations in an advanced cultural system.'

[. . .]

NOTE

* This chapter has been adapted from excerpts from, Baily, P. J. H. (1987) *Purchasing & Supply Management (5th edition)*, chs 1 and 3, London, Chapman & Hall.

REFERENCES

Baily, P. (1983) *Purchasing Systems and Records*. Gower Publishing, Aldershot.

Buckner, H. (1967) *How British Industry Buys*. Hutchinson, London.

Croell, R. C. (1977) Measuring purchasing effectiveness. *Journal of Purchasing and Materials Management*, **13** (1), 3–4.

Kotler, P. and Balachandrian, V. (1975) Strategic remarketing, the preferred response to shortages and inflation. *Sloan Management Review*, August.

Kotler, P. and Levy, S. J. (1973) Buying is marketing too. *Journal of Marketing*, January.

Rowe, D. and Alexander, I. (1968) *Selling Industrial Products*, Hutchinson, London.

Webster, F. E. and Wind, Y. (1972) *Organizational Buying Behavior*, Prentice-Hall, Englewood Cliffs, New Jersey.

10

CONCEPT OF A MANUFACTURING SYSTEM*

John Parnaby

There is no single concept of a manufacturing system covering all industries in every detail. It is necessary to examine the fundamental properties and characteristics of a range of systems and to consider the way they are synthesized and operated before consolidating general conclusions. What is seen depends very much on the viewpoint and the narrowness of the focusing range. Nevertheless there is much to be gained from a fundamental study of all aspects of manufacturing systems and their interactions since there are opportunities for technology transfer between industries.

Manufacturing systems must be designed by taking into account both steady state and dynamic performance, whilst ensuring there is an adequate number of controllable variables to compensate the effects of uncontrolled disturbances. The technological process part of the manufacturing system is synthesised from interacting unit operating subsystems, and this itself is a subsystem of the overall business system. The business subsystem has a complex multivariable nature and for its effective control it is important that information flows and plans or set points are well defined to allow people to be effective controllers of the system.

System design and system control must be effectively integrated.

MANUFACTURING SYSTEM

In general terms, a manufacturing system is one in which raw materials are processed from one form into another, known as a product, gaining a higher or added value in the process. The output products from one manufacturing system may be the inputs to another. There is thus considerable interaction. Such systems incorporate particular product-dependent applications of science and technology via their processes and associated machinery and are usually complex. They directly involve many people who carry the process know-how and they interact in many complex ways with our social system and physical environment.

We live in a dynamic and competitive world where market competition is met at interfirm level and intercountry level. For a manufacturing industry to survive it must keep pace with change, and each and every firm must be efficient in achieving its objectives. Efficiency in terms of return on capital employed, or profit, has to be achieved these days in the face of increasingly complex interactions and constraints of a technical and sociological nature.

One representation of a manufacturing system, in an overall sense, is given in Figure 10.1 in input–output analysis form. This figure, whilst interesting, is not particularly useful other than to remind us that not all inputs to the system are controllable by management, and disturbances in these must be mitigated by manipulations in controllable inputs such as resources and plans.

Figure 10.1 gives the impression of manufacturing systems in general being a homogeneous group. However, this is not so for a number of reasons, not least of which is the differing natures of the products, as can be deduced from the list given in Table 10.1 of different manufacturing systems making up British manufacturing industry. Engineering companies and processing companies are represented in Table 10.1.

Certain features are common, for example:

1 A manufacturing system should be an integrated whole. It is composed of different subsystems, each of which interacts with the whole system. The system will have a number of objectives and the system must be operated in such a way as to optimize some weighted function of the objectives (Beishon and Peters, 1972).
2 The manufacturing system will be synthesized by selecting sets of energy consuming subsystems for raw materials processing from the typical list in Table 10.2 linking these together and operating or controlling the resulting system and its interactions with its environment.
3 To operate the system requires an administration information-flow system and decision-making processes.
4 The processes taking place in the unit operations and reactors must all be constrained to satisfy the laws of mass and energy conservation and of chemical combination.

However, there are many differences resulting from the various different combinations of subsystems met in each company as a result of product differences from company to company and also the differing interactions with the social and business environment. Each company in its way is a unique manufacturing system with its own set of problems, many of which also are unique in certain detailed aspects (Riggs, 1970).

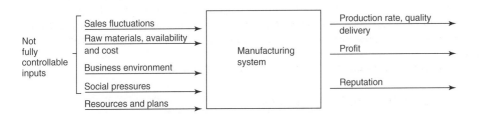

Figure 10.1 Overall view, input–output analysis

Table 10.1 Manufacturing industry

Food, drink, tobacco	Textiles
Chemicals and allied industries	Leather, leather goods and fur
Metal manufacture	Clothing and footwear
Engineering and electrical goods	Bricks, pottery, glass, cement, etc.
Shipbuilding and marine engineering	Timber, furniture, etc.
Vehicles	Paper, printing and publishing
Other metal goods	Others!

Table 10.2 Elemental subsystem building blocks

A: Unit operations – physical processes	B: Chemical processes
1. *Visco-elastic fluid flow* Pumping, mixing, casting, moulding, extrusion	1. Organic, inorganic reactions or combinations
2. *Heat transfer* (Possibly channelling heat to or from chemical reactions.) Annealing, melting, heating	2. Electrolysis
3. *Mass transfer* Gas absorption, stripping, leaching, absorption, ion exchange, conveying, solvent extraction, painting, coating, welding, plating	
4. *Separation* Filtration, sedimentation, elutriation, flocculation	
5. *Combined heat and mass transfer* Humidification, dehumidification, crystallization, drying, distillation	
6. *Cutting* Drilling, milling, shaping, sawing, planing, slicing, etc.	
7. *Elastic – plastic forming* Deep-drawing, vacuum forming, etc.	
8. *Assembly*	
9. *Inspection* Physical examination, chemical examination	

Again, there is a superficial apparent uniformity in that the block diagram in Figure 10.2 this time showing subsystems grouped on a functional (Lockyer, 1974) or departmental basis, appears to apply to all manufacturing companies. Clearly all will have a production function within which combinations of unit operations and reactions from Table 10.2 will be found. Clearly also the nature of the technology must affect the structure of the system, the way it is controlled and the types of staff employed, and one cannot really design and operate the system without an understanding of the technology.

In defining a manufacturing system, therefore, it is necessary to do so from a number of different viewpoints ranging from the overall macroscopic description of Figures 10.1 and 10.2 or Table 10.1, to a detailed microscopic analysis of the physical and chemical processes taking place and the static and dynamic interactions involved. It is natural when describing manufacturing systems to use as a language the process flow-block diagram to clarify the logic and help to correctly match inputs and outputs for the various subsystems. Typical examples of production process system flow-block diagrams are given in Figure 10.3 (Riggs, 1970; Lockyer, 1974; Vilbrandt and Dryden, 1959).

One essential basic requirement of all manufacturing systems, regardless of the types of production processes, machinery used and business environment, is that of long-term stable operation in the face of continually changing constraints and external disturbances. This creates a need for a supply of information to facilitate control decision making by

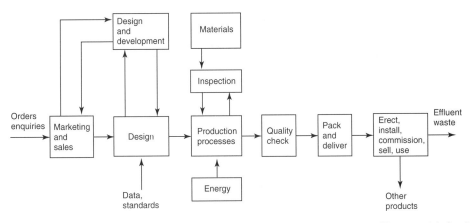

Figure 10.2 Equipment manufacturing company (arrows denote information and/or materials flow)

management and requires (Kochhar and Parnaby, 1977) the following three basic functions to be deliberately incorporated:

1 data acquisition and sorting function,
2 information flow function,
3 systems control function.

In order to further illustrate characteristics of manufacturing systems, it is necessary to next consider the interacting aspects of systems design and control.

DESIGN OF THE MANUFACTURING SYSTEM

Just as systems can, with great care and an experienced professional approach, be designed to be controllable, the converse is certainly also true if care is not taken. Every subsystem of the whole is required to process certain inputs and produce certain outputs. To obtain the desired outputs the correct inputs must be available. When all subsystems are put together the input and output interactions must be compatible (Rudd and Watson, 1968; Forrester, 1969).

Examples

1 The food manufacturing industry interacts with the agriculture system, with its time cycles of production, as well as with the chemical industry which supplies various additives such as colourings and flavours.
2 A man operating a machine tool must clearly have all the skills and knowledge of the product required to operate his machine whilst he must also have the broader skills required to allow him to fit harmoniously into the workshop social environment.
3 If a process reactor is supplied with liquid raw materials by a pump, then
   a the output variables of flow rate and pressure from the pump must always match the input variables required by the reactor to ensure the correct output rate of homogeneous, well-reacted product from the reactor;
   b the flow-rate/pressure characteristics of the pipeline connecting pump and reactor must correctly match the pump characteristics;
   c the pump input torque-speed characteristic must be carefully matched to the electric drive motor (Holmes, 1977).

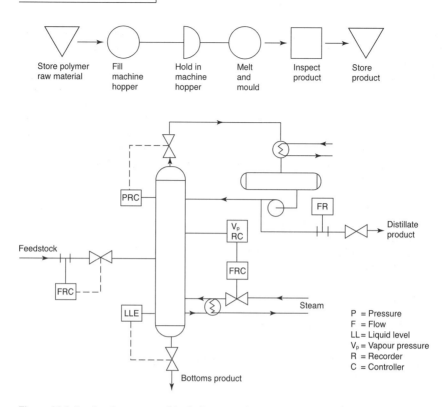

Figure 10.3 Production process block diagrams

Further consideration of the design of the simple production process system of example 3 above reveals the need for two stages in system design.

Steady-state design

Matching the elements of a system together based upon averaged input–output performance characteristics assumed to be constant at all times. This gives a figure for average overall performance.

Dynamic design

In example 3 above there are two largely uncontrollable variables which are likely to exhibit random changes and so continually alter system performance:

a   fluid properties: temperature, viscosity, density, reactivity, purity;
b   reactor environment: wind, rain, air temperature, internal clogging.

If the fluid properties vary, then the pump speed must change to compensate for flow-rate changes, so making demands for torque changes on the electric motor. If the reaction conditions change due to fluid property or flow-rate changes or environment changes then the reaction rates may be inhibited or increased and such possible changes must be examined.

The anticipation of the effects of dynamic changes in uncontrollable variables as well as in controllable variables at the system design stage is known as dynamic design and requires response times for the system elements to be known either empirically or theoretically.

As a consequence of dynamic or time-dependent changes in uncontrollable variables, it is necessary for the system to be provided with a means of control of system performance. This is a very fundamental property of real manufacturing systems which never operate under steady-state conditions (Forrester, 1969; Parnaby *et al.*, 1978). For the reactor-pump system it would be necessary to control production rate and product quality. This requires that data be continuously collected relating to these two variables prior to controlling changes by changing pump speed. Thus, five interrelated stages of manufacturing system design have been identified:

1 Subsystem input-output analysis working backwards from the product requirements.
2 Steady-state design using specifications from stage 1.
3 Dynamic design.
4 Specification of data-collection system required.
5 Control system design.

The above five stages are fundamental to the design of any part of the manufacturing system and are not specific only to the design of process plants. Example 4 illustrates this fact by reference to a different type of simplified production process system.

Example 4: Design and control of manufacturing system centred on a machine shop

Stage 1: Input–output analysis

Starting from a parts explosion for the product, the following typical variables and the types of subsystem for which inputs and outputs are necessary are defined:

types of machinery and assembly processes needed;
skills required of all personnel and personnel types needed;
product variables and associated tolerance limits.

Figure 10.4 gives some sample input–output descriptions for elements typically found in such a system.

Stage 2: Steady-state design

Here would be specified the number and types of departments, machines, staff and operators and steady-state operating levels based upon typically:

a an assumed average constant performance rate for each machine and person;
b an assumed average rate of flow of orders for the products;
c an assumed average estimated work content for each product;
d choice of operational rota systems for all sections.

Stage 3: Dynamic design

This would be based upon assessments of likely sources of variations in performance from the average steady-state values, e.g., machine breakdowns, operator absenteeism and

System element	Input variables necessary		Output variables required
1. Production Control Department	Knowledge of present and planned state of production process		Raw materials ordering schedule
	Detailed product designs		Allocation of work by time to work centres
	Order quantities	**1. PRODUCTION CONTROL DEPARTMENT**	Listing of production procedures
	Materials stock levels		Manpower utilization plan
	Finished stock levels		Machinery utilization plan
	Manpower availability		Performance checking procedure
	Any restrictions on time available		Estimated performance standards
2. Design Office	Desired customer equipment specification		Finished design arrangements
	Desired time scale		Detailed drawings for manufacture
	Adequate materials property data	**2. DESIGN OFFICE**	List of components and materials required
	Adequate technical reference files		Cost estimates
	Records of past jobs		List of standards met
	Access to a computer		
3. Sales Department	Knowledge of products in detail		Firm orders for production
	Knowledge of production plan and capability		Forecast of future orders
	Firm sales orders	**3. SALES DEPARTMENT**	Advice on product changes
	General business environment knowhow		Cost and profit advice
	Marketing strategies		Marketing strategy advice
	Customer feedback		
4. Machine Shop or Production Foreman	List of job quantities required		Short-term loading plan for production facilities
	Job sequence loading and route list		Manpower re-allocation
	Plant/machine capability, state and complement		Machine re-allocation
	Inventory levels	**4. MACHINE SHOP FOREMAN**	Interdepartment communication
	Detailed component and product drawings or specifications		General corrective actions
	Performance statistics to date		Operational data and process knowhow feedback
			Experienced guidance to others
			Regular reports
5. Payroll Computer Department	Categorized reference codes for all personnel		Payslip for each weekly staff employee
	Categorized hours worked by personnel		Payslip for each monthly staff employee
	Absenteeism, sickness, lateness data	**5. PAYROLL COMPUTER DEPARTMENT**	Summarized total weekly staff cost
	Holiday data		Summarized total monthly staff cost
	Bonus calculation data		Absenteeism, sickness, lateness summary
	Unit cost data per hour/week		Updated records
	Taxation, Nat. Ins. rules		Taxation, Nat. Ins., etc. summary update

Figure 10.4 Examples of input–output analysis

performance variation, changes in raw materials processability characteristics, product changes, sales-level variation, changes in legislation, activities of competitors, etc. End-products of this stage would include sizing of interstage buffer inventories, stock or order policies, maintenance plans, sizes of data sampling time intervals to suit the dynamic response of each subsystem, assembly plans, policy for overtime working and work subcontracting.

Stage 4: Data collection system design

It would be necessary to specify which variables were to be frequently sampled and the time intervals for sampling, suited to the particular requirements of each subsystem for efficient control. Thus, information relating to the following variables might typically be collected at regular intervals:

- level of work in progress in each subsystem;
- state of each machine, i.e., working/not working;
- queue levels in each subsystem;
- general stock levels;
- level of scrapped work;
- state of completion of each product ordered;
- manpower availability;
- level of sales.

In other words detailed information relating to the states of all manpower, machinery and materials involved in the production process as well as for design offices and other areas would be collected.

Stage 5: Control system design

This would involve the careful definition of procedures for providing and changing control set points or plans, such as:

a Authorized work schedules, i.e., list of total waiting work required to meet sales/forecasts in the various categories, e.g., drilling, milling, grinding, welding, assembly, painting, etc., in hours of estimated operation to match customer orders. A coded list of operations required in sequence would also be provided for each component part.

b Loading schedules: detailed route plans showing consecutive machine operations for each component and detailed hourly, daily, weekly or monthly plans showing the actual jobs associated with each order allocated to machines or operators taking into account the estimated time needed for each operation and the length of each working day.

c Materials schedules showing the detailed raw materials and bought-in, component, sub-assembly lists required for each order, together with a time-scale plan for the ordering of supplies, allowing for delivery of materials to detailed time schedule as required by the loading schedule.

d Inspection schedules: inspection points, frequency and quantity of samples required for efficient product quality control.

e Cost schedules: unit-cost standards for each operation carried out, together with procedures for warning when departures from planned component costs are taking place.

f Delivery schedules: plans showing when each customer order is estimated to be completed if the schedules in *a* to *e* are closely followed.

The services *a* to *f* must be provided by a department or subsystem having a responsibility for production control within the manufacturing system. Clearly there is considerable scope for using a computer to assist with the detailed information flows required for control.

CONTROL OF THE MANUFACTURING SYSTEM

The dynamic processes involved in a manufacturing system must be ordered and controlled if they are to efficiently meet the system objectives. At the same time they must be adaptive, i.e., able to change their structures and characteristics, in order to survive. Their adaptive nature comes from the dominant involvement of people in the control procedures and decision-making strategies at all levels. Manufacturing systems involve many people and exist to serve people, and clear recognition of this fundamental point is essential to good control. Management at all levels clearly has to see it has a controller function and must ensure it has adequate information flow systems, computers, etc. to facilitate control (Hammond and Oh, 1973; Alford, 1973).

As manufacturing systems are so complex in general, it is not possible for a control theory approach to be used for continuous real-time overall optimization. Instead a theoretically based heuristic procedure is necessary where major control functions are applied to maintain overall control discontinuously (Hammond and Oh, 1973; Alford, 1973).

For example, in the production control layer, supervisors maintain continuous real-time control of production (Hollwey *et al.*, 1978) by reference to sales, in parallel with a cost control layer which operates with a different time scale and different sampling time intervals but nevertheless in real time so far as effective control of costs is required. There is regular routine flow of information between these two layers but, in addition, at irregular intervals the cost control system interacts strongly with the control set points for production control in an overriding way owing to emergencies, effects of cost inflation on standard cost data, etc. Similarly, there may nowadays be an energy control system layer which only interacts strongly with production when energy usage or cost set points require major changes. Furthermore, sudden market changes can take priority and cause overruling of routine production control systems.

Within the production system itself, for similar reasons of complexity, one can often identify several levels of control which have tended to operate in a pseudo-independent way (Hammond and Oh, 1973; Alford, 1973). However, the increasing distributed use of linked mini-computers and micro-processors promises the opportunity during the next decade of a better overall integrated form of control, whilst at the same time allowing individual managers to have adaptively controllable units more effectively under their control (Parnaby, 1979).

Figure 10.5 shows schematically the levels of control typically found in a production subsystem and indicates how the following two areas of control have to integrate in practice:

process control – automated control of technological processes to manual set points with overall managerial supervision;
production control – control by people, based on information flow systems involving computers, of processes involving people and machines.

In discrete manufacturing, such as machine tool or motor car manufacture, the production control system will be dominant owing to high product complexity and number of items. In a processing industry such as chemicals manufacturing, process control systems will be dominant (Parnaby and Billington, 1976; Parnaby, 1977).

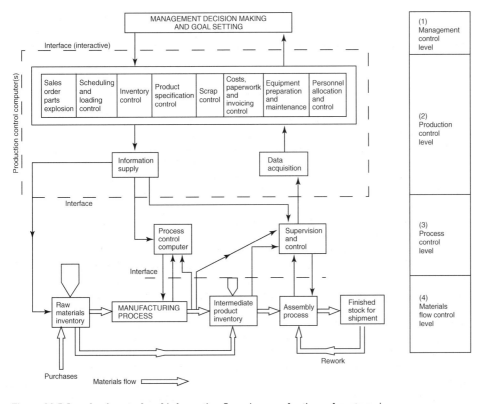

Figure 10.5 Levels of control and information flows in a production subsystem

In addition to ensuring that control of individual layers of the manufacturing systems, such as the production subsystem, is satisfactory, it is necessary that overall control of the manufacturing system is maintained in the face of market and other environmental disturbances. Figure 10.6 illustrates high-level overall feedforward control of the total manufacturing system based upon predictions of future requirements. Such a form of control is happening now in all manufacturing systems even if in some the forecasting roles of elements A and B and the models of element C (Kochhar *et al.*, 1978) are simply intuitive ideas in the minds of managers, or if the marketing strategy involves merely the spreading of rumours over a pint of beer in the pub on a Friday night. However, an awareness of the implications of Figure 10.6 may help to improve such rudimentary forms of control. Figure 10.7 shows a form of on-line real-time production control system desirable to facilitate feedforward control. Note that each VDU user in Figure 10.7 sees a different system and a different control problem. Each must have information available at time intervals suited to the nature and dynamic response of the particular control function he carries out to ensure truly on-line real-time control as in process control.

CONCLUSIONS

There is no clear concept of a manufacturing system acceptable to everyone. Much depends upon the viewpoint, the nature of the industry and the type of product. However, there are certain properties and characteristics which may be regarded as somewhat fundamental.

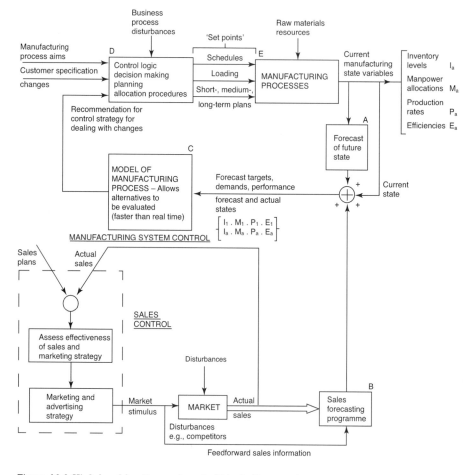

Figure 10.6 High-level feedforward control block diagram

One of these is a clear need for good control systems to counteract the many external disturbances interacting with manufacturing systems. Control has, of course, clearly to recognize the many constraints, including legislation. In manufacturing systems the basic overall structural and performance logic can easily be obscured by a mass of paperwork and detail as well as by stultifying administrative systems. It must be clearly recognized that such systems are dynamic and must be adaptive to survive.

There is the basic dilemma of ensuring that the overall system operational and control philosophy and objectives are clear, whilst paying sufficient attention to detail at all levels, which creates a major demand for leadership from managers and engineers. Effective leadership requires, amongst other things, a sound education in fundamentals relative to manufacturing systems design and control. [. . .] Adequately broadly trained engineers are an essential ingredient of any recipe for improving the performance of the British manufacturing system.

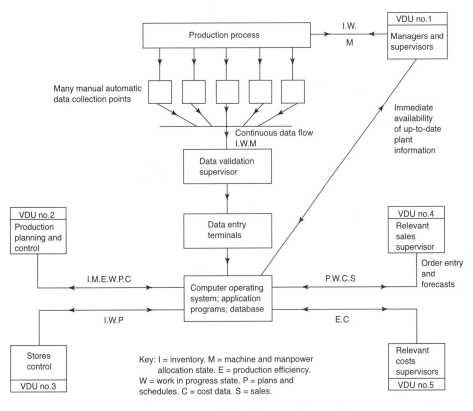

Figure 10.7 **Elements of an on-line real-time production control system**

NOTE

* This chapter has been adapted from, Parnaby, J. (1979) "Concept of a manufacturing system", *Int. J. Production Research* **17**, 2.

REFERENCES

Alford, C. A. (1973) "Design aspects of computer control in discrete manufacturing", *I.E.E. Trans. Manuf. Tech.* **1**, 26.

Beishon, J. and Peters, G. (eds.) (1972) *Systems Behaviour*, Harper and Row, London, for the Open University.

Forrester, J. W. (1969) *Industrial Dynamics*, MIT Press, Cambridge, Mass.

Hammond, J. L. and Oh, S. J. (1973) "Evolution of systems approaches to computer control in discrete manufacturing, *I.E.E. Trans. Manuf. Tech.* **1**, 4.

Hollwey. M. W. M., Kochhar, A. K., Parnaby, J. and Ephraim, O. M. (1978) "Using a real time minicomputer for production control", *J. Inst. Prod. Engrs.* **55**, 37.

Holmes, R. (1977) *The Characteristics of Mechanical Engineering Systems*, Pergamon Press, London.

Kochhar, A. K. and Parnaby, J. (1977) "The choice of computer systems for real-time production control", *J. Inst. Prod. Engrs.* **56**, 29.

Kochhar, A. K. *et al.* (1978) "Comparison of stochastic identification techniques for dynamic modelling of plastics extrusion processes", *Proc. I. Mech. E.* **192**, 299.

Lockyer, K. G. (1974) *Factory and Production Management*, Pitman, London.

Parnaby, J. (1977) "The design and control of homogenising systems for minerals processing", *Trans. Inst. Chem. Engrs.* **55**, 104.

Parnaby, J. (1979) *Product manufacturing technology utilising minicomputers and microcomputers*, Proceedings of the Jubilee Conference (Rubber and Plastic Research Association, Shrewsbury).

Parnaby, J., Battye, E. A. A., Hassan, C. P. and Hadwell, C. P. (1978) "Computer controlled injection moulding and extrusion", *Plastics and Rubber: Processing* 3, 89.

Parnaby, J. and Billington, D. (1976) "Computer modelling and control of manufacturing systems – with particular reference to the tailoring industry", *Trans. Instn. Elect. Engrs.* **123**, 835.

Riggs, J. L. (1970) *Production Systems*, Wiley, New York.

Rudd, D. F. and Watson, C. C. (1968) *Strategy of Process Engineering*, Wiley, New York.

Vilbrandt, F. C. and Dryden, C. E. (1959) *Chemical Engineering Plant Design*, McGraw-Hill, New York.

11

LOGISTICS AND COMPETITIVE STRATEGY*

Martin Christopher

In the early part of 1991 the world was given a dramatic example of the importance of logistics. As a precursor to the Gulf War it had been necessary for the United States and its allies to move huge amounts of material great distances in what were thought to be impossibly short time-frames. Half a million people and over half a million tonnes of material and supplies were airlifted 12,000 kilometres with a further 2.3 million tonnes of equipment moved by sea – all of this achieved in a matter of months.

Throughout the history of mankind wars have been won and lost through logistics strengths and capabilities – or the lack of them. It has been argued that the defeat of the British in the American War of Independence can largely be attributed to logistics failure. The British Army in America depended almost entirely upon Britain for supplies. At the height of the war there were 12,000 troops overseas and for the most part they had not only to be equipped, but fed from Britain. For the first six years of the war the administration of these vital supplies was totally inadequate, affecting the course of operations and the morale of the troops. An organization capable of supplying the army was not developed until 1781 and by then it was too late.[1]

In the Second World War logistics also played a major role. The Allied Forces' invasion of Europe was a highly skilled exercise in logistics, as was the defeat of Rommel in the desert. Rommel himself once said that '. . . before the fighting proper, the battle is won or lost by quartermasters'.

However whilst the Generals and Field Marshals from the earliest times have understood the critical role of logistics, strangely it is only in the recent past that business organizations have come to recognize the vital impact that logistics management can have in the achievement of competitive advantage. Partly this lack of recognition springs from the relatively low level of understanding of the benefits of integrated logistics. Whilst Arch Shaw, writing in 1915 pointed out that:

> The relations between the activities of demand creation and physical supply . . . illustrate the existence of the two principles of interdependence and balance. Failure to co-ordinate any one of these activities with its group-fellows and also with those in the other group,

or undue emphasis or outlay put upon any one of these activities, is certain to upset the equilibrium of forces which means efficient distribution.

... The physical distribution of the goods is a problem distinct from the creation of demand ... Not a few worthy failures in distribution campaigns have been due to such a lack of co-ordination between demand creation and physical supply ... Instead of being a subsequent problem, this question of supply must be met and answered before the work of distribution begins.[2]

It has taken a further 70 years or so for the basic principles of logistics management to be clearly defined.

What is logistics management in the sense that it is understood today? There are many ways of defining logistics but the underlying concept might be defined as:

Logistics is the process of strategically managing the procurement, movement and storage of materials, parts and finished inventory (and the related information flows) through the organization and its marketing channels in such a way that current and future profitability are maximized through the cost-effective fulfilment of orders.

[. . .]

COMPETITIVE ADVANTAGE

Effective logistics management can provide a major source of competitive advantage – in other words a position of enduring superiority over competitors in terms of customer preference may be achieved through logistics.

The bases for success in the market place are numerous, but a simple model is based around the triangular linkage of the company, its customers and its competitors – the 'Three Cs'. The 'Three Cs' in question are: the customer, the competition and the company. Figure 11.1 illustrates the three-way relationship.

The source of competitive advantage is found firstly in the ability of the organization to differentiate itself, in the eyes of the customer, from its competition and secondly by operating at a lower cost and hence at greater profit.

Seeking a sustainable and defensible competitive advantage has become the concern of every manager who is alert to the realities of the market place. It is no longer acceptable to assume that good products will sell themselves, neither is it advisable to imagine that success today will carry forward into tomorrow.

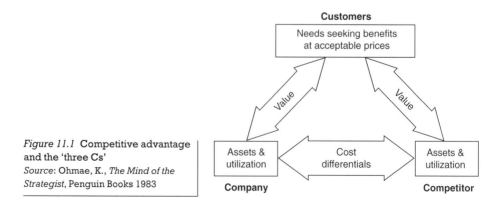

Figure 11.1 Competitive advantage and the 'three Cs'
Source: Ohmae, K., *The Mind of the Strategist*, Penguin Books 1983

Let us consider the bases of success in any competitive context. At its most elemental, commercial success derives either from a cost advantage or a value advantage or, ideally, both. It is as simple as that – the most profitable competitor in any industry sector tends to be the lowest cost producer or the supplier providing a product with the greatest perceived differentiated values. To be successful in the automobile industry, for example, you either have to be a Nissan (i.e. a cost advantage) or a BMW (i.e. a value advantage).

Put very simply, successful companies either have a productivity advantage or they have a 'value' advantage or a combination of the two. The productivity advantage gives a lower cost profile and the value advantage gives the product or offering a differential 'plus' over competitive offerings.

Let us briefly examine these two vectors of strategic direction.

Productivity advantage

In many industries there will be typically one competitor who will be the low cost producer and, more often than not, that competitor will have the greatest sales volume in the sector. There is substantial evidence to suggest that 'big is beautiful' when it comes to cost advantage. This is partly due to economies of scale which enable fixed costs to be spread over a greater volume but more particularly to the impact of the 'experience curve'.

The experience curve is a phenomenon which has its roots in the earlier notion of the 'learning curve'. Researchers discovered during the last war that it was possible to identify and predict improvements in the rate of output of workers as they became more skilled in the processes and tasks on which they were working. Subsequent work by Bruce Henderson, founder of the Boston Consulting Group, extended this concept by demonstrating that *all* costs, not just production costs, would decline at a given rate as volume increased. In fact, to be precise, the relationship that the experience curve describes is between *real* unit costs and *cumulative* volume. Further it is generally recognized that this cost decline applies only to 'value added', i.e. costs other than bought in supplies.

Traditionally it has been suggested that the main route to cost reduction was by gaining greater sales volume and there can be no doubt about the close linkage between relative market share and relative costs. However it must also be recognized that logistics management can provide a multitude of ways to increase efficiency and productivity and hence contribute significantly to reduced unit costs. [. . .]

Value advantage

It has long been an axiom in marketing that 'customers don't buy products, they buy benefits'. Put another way the product is purchased not for itself but for the promise of what

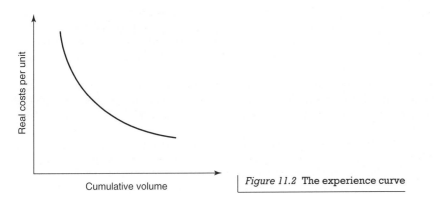

Figure 11.2 **The experience curve**

it will 'deliver'. These benefits may be intangible, i.e. they relate not to specific product features but rather to such things as image or reputation. Alternatively the delivered offering may be seen to out-perform its rivals in some functional aspect.

Unless the product or service we offer can be distinguished in some way from its competitors there is a strong likelihood that the market place will view it as a 'commodity' and so the sale will tend to go to the cheapest supplier. Hence the importance of seeking to add additional values to our offering to mark it out from the competition.

What are the means by which such value differentiation may be gained? Essentially the development of a strategy based upon added values will normally require a more segmented approach to the market. When a company scrutinises markets closely it frequently finds that there are distinct 'value segments'. In other words different groups of customers within the total market attach different importance to different benefits. The importance of such benefit segmentation lies in the fact that often there are substantial opportunities for creating differentiated appeals for specific segments. Take the motor car as an example. A model such as the Ford Sierra is not only positioned in the middle range of European cars but within that broad category specific versions are aimed at defined segments. Thus we find the basic, small engine, two-door model at one end of the spectrum and the four-wheel-drive, high performance version at the other extreme. In between are a whole variety of options each of which seeks to satisfy the needs of quite different 'benefit segments'. Adding value through differentiation is a powerful means of achieving a defensible advantage in the market.

Equally powerful as a means of adding value is *service*. Increasingly we are finding that markets are becoming more service sensitive and this of course poses particular challenges for logistics management. There is a trend in many markets towards a decline in the strength of the 'brand' and a consequent move towards 'commodity' market status. Quite simply this means it is becoming progressively more difficult to compete purely on the basis of brand or corporate image. Additionally, there is increasingly a convergence of technology within product categories which means that it is no longer possible to compete effectively on the basis of *product* differences. Thus the need to seek differentiation through means other than technology. A number of companies have responded to this by focusing upon service as a means of gaining a competitive edge. Service in this context relates to the process of developing *relationships* with customers through the provision of an augmented offer. This augmentation can take many forms including delivery service, after-sales services, financial packages, technical support and so forth.

In practice what we find is that the successful companies will often seek to achieve a position based upon *both* a productivity advantage *and* a value advantage. A useful way of examining the available options is to present them as a simple matrix. (See Figure 11.3.) Let us consider these options in turn.

For companies who find themselves in the bottom left hand corner of our matrix (Figure 11.3) the world is an uncomfortable place. Their products are indistinguishable from their competitors' offerings and they have no cost advantage. These are typical commodity market situations and ultimately the only strategy is either to move to the right on the matrix, i.e. to cost leadership, or upwards into a 'niche'. Often the cost leadership route is simply not available. This particularly will be the case in a mature market where substantial market share gains are difficult to achieve. New technology may sometimes provide a window of opportunity for cost reduction but in such situations the same technology is often available to competitors.

Cost leadership, if it is to form the basis of a viable long-term marketing strategy, should essentially be gained early in the market life-cycle. This is why market share is considered to be so important in many industries. The 'experience curve' concept, briefly described earlier, demonstrates the value of early market share gains – the higher your share relative

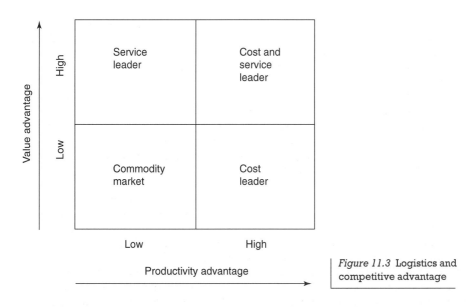

Figure 11.3 Logistics and competitive advantage

to your competitors the lower your costs should be. This cost advantage can be used strategically to assume a position of price leader and, if appropriate, to make it impossible for higher cost competitors to survive. Alternatively, price may be maintained enabling above average profit to be earned which potentially is available to further develop the position of the product in the market.

The other way out of the 'commodity' quadrant of our matrix is to seek a 'niche' or segment where it is possible to meet the needs of the customers through offering additional values. Sometimes it may not be through tangible product features that this value-added is generated, but as we have noted, opportunities may often exist for adding value through service. For example, a steel stockholder who finds himself in the commodity quadrant may seek to move up to the niche quadrant by offering daily deliveries from stock, by providing additional 'finishing' services for his basic products or by focusing upon the provision of a range of special steels for specific segments.

What does seem to be an established rule is that there is no middle ground between cost leadership and niche marketing. Being caught in the middle i.e. neither a cost leader nor a niche-based provider of added values is generally bad news.

Finally, perhaps the most defensible position in the matrix is the top right hand corner, Companies who occupy that position have products that are distinctive in the values they offer *and* are also cost competitive. Many Japanese products, particularly in consumer markets, arguably have achieved this position. Clearly it is a position of some strength, occupying 'high ground' which is extremely difficult for competitors to attack. Figure 11.4 clearly presents the strategic challenge to logistics: it is to seek out strategies that will take the business away from the 'commodity' end of the market towards a securer position of strength based upon differentiation and cost advantage.

GAINING COMPETITIVE ADVANTAGE THROUGH LOGISTICS

Of the many changes that have taken place in management thinking over the last 10 years or so perhaps the most significant has been the emphasis placed upon the search for strategies that will provide superior value in the eyes of the customer. To a large extent the credit for this must go to Michael Porter, the Harvard Business School Professor, who

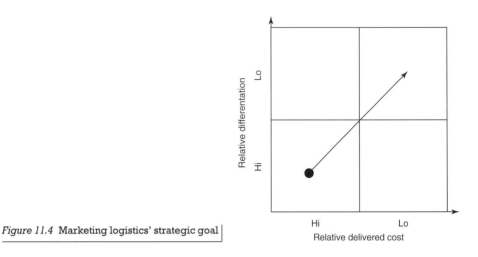

Figure 11.4 Marketing logistics' strategic goal

through his research and writing[3,4] has alerted managers and strategists to the central importance of competitive relativities in achieving success in the market place.

One concept in particular that Michael Porter has brought to a wider audience is the 'value chain':

> Competitive advantage cannot be understood by looking at a firm as a whole. It stems from the many discrete activities a firm performs in designing, producing, marketing, delivering, and supporting its product. Each of these activities can contribute to a firm's relative cost position and create a basis for differentiation . . . The value chain disaggregates a firm into its strategically relevant activities in order to understand the behaviour of costs and the existing and potential sources of differentiation. A firm gains competitive advantage by performing these strategically important activities more cheaply or better than its competitors.[4]

Value chain activities, shown in Figure 11.5 can be categorized into two types – primary activities (inbound logistics, operations, outbound logistics, marketing and sales, and service) and support activities (infrastructure, human resource management, technology

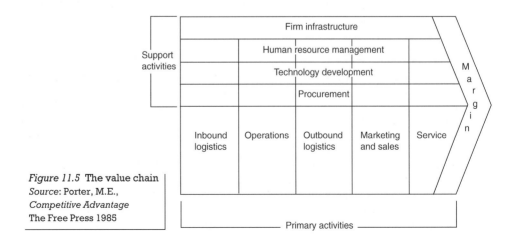

Figure 11.5 **The value chain**
Source: Porter, M.E.,
Competitive Advantage
The Free Press 1985

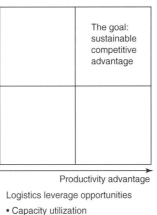

Value advantage

Logistics leverage opportunities

• Tailored service
• Distribution channel strategy
• Customer relations etc.

The goal: sustainable competitive advantage

Productivity advantage

Logistics leverage opportunities

• Capacity utilization
• Asset turn
• Co-makership/schedule integration etc.

Figure 11.6 Gaining competitive advantage through logistics

development and procurement). These support activities are integrating functions that cut across the various primary activities within the firm. Competitive advantage grows out of the way in which firms organize and perform these discrete activities within the value chain. To gain competitive advantage over its rivals, a firm must promote value to its customers through performing activities more efficiently than its competitors or by performing activities in a unique way that creates greater buyer value.

Logistics management, it can be argued, has the potential to assist the organization in the achievement of both a cost/productivity advantage and a value advantage. As Figure 11.6 suggests, in the first instance there are a number of important ways in which productivity can be enhanced through logistics. Whilst these possibilities for leverage will be discussed in detail later in the book, suffice it to say that the opportunities for better capacity utilization, inventory reduction and closer integration with suppliers at a planning level, are considerable. Equally the prospects for gaining a value advantage in the market place through superior customer service should not be underestimated. It will be argued later that the way we service the customer has become a vital means of differentiation.

To summarize, those organizations that will be the leaders in the markets of the future will be those that have sought and achieved the twin peaks of excellence: they have gained both cost leadership *and* service leadership.

THE MISSION OF LOGISTICS MANAGEMENT

It will be apparent from the previous comments that the mission of logistics management is to plan and co-ordinate all those activities necessary to achieve desired levels of delivered service and quality at lowest possible cost. Logistics must therefore be seen as the link between the market place and the operating activity of the business. The scope of logistics spans the organization, from the management of raw materials through to the delivery of the final product. Figure 11.7 illustrates this total systems concept.

Logistics management, from this total systems viewpoint, is the means whereby the needs of customers are satisfied through the co-ordination of the materials and information flows that extend from the market place, through the firm and its operations and beyond that to suppliers. To achieve this company-wide integration clearly requires a quite different orientation than that typically encountered in the conventional organization.

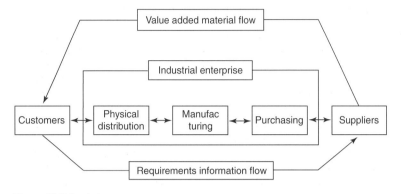
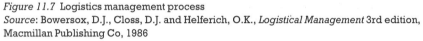

Figure 11.7 Logistics management process
Source: Bowersox, D.J., Closs, D.J. and Helferich, O.K., *Logistical Management* 3rd edition, Macmillan Publishing Co, 1986

For example, for many years marketing and manufacturing have been seen as largely separate activities within the organization. At best they have coexisted, at worst there has been open warfare. Manufacturing priorities and objectives have typically been focused on operating efficiency, achieved through long production runs, minimized set-ups and change-overs and product standardization. On the other hand marketing has sought to achieve competitive advantage through variety, high service levels and frequent product changes.

In today's more turbulent environment there is no longer any possibility of manufacturing and marketing acting independently of each other. The internecine disputes between the 'barons' of production and marketing are clearly counter-productive to the achievement of overall corporate goals.

It is no coincidence that in recent years both marketing and manufacturing have become the focus of renewed attention. Marketing as a concept and a philosophy of customer orientation now enjoys a wider acceptance than ever in the western world. It is now generally accepted that the need to understand and meet customer requirements is a prerequisite for survival. At the same time, in the search for improved cost competitiveness, manufacturing management has been the subject of a massive renaissance. The last decade has seen the rapid introduction of flexible manufacturing systems (FMS), of new approaches to inventory based on materials requirements planning (MRP) and just-in-time (JIT) methods and, perhaps most important of all, a sustained emphasis on quality.

As we have noted, success in the market place can only come through cost leadership or product differentiation or a combination of the two. Manufacturing and marketing between them hold the key to the achievement of these twin goals. To become a cost leader requires not only low cost production but also efficient marketing and distribution systems. Thus marketing and manufacturing strategies that work together to achieve low cost, volume-based positions can provide a major source of competitive advantage. Similarly, manufacturing strategies that can support differentiated marketing through the provision of unique customer values can also provide the basis for competitive success. To combine both cost leadership and product differentiation through parallel manufacturing and marketing strategies should be the ultimate goal of any organization that is intent upon sustained, long-term profitability.

Equally there is a crucial requirement to extend the logic of integration outside the boundaries of the firm to include suppliers and customers. This is the concept of *supply chain management*.

THE SUPPLY CHAIN AND COMPETITIVE PERFORMANCE

Traditionally most organizations have viewed themselves as entities that exist independently from others and indeed need to compete with them in order to survive. There is almost a Darwinian ethic of the 'survival of the fittest' driving much of corporate strategy. However such a philosophy can be self-defeating if it leads to an unwillingness to co-operate in order to compete. Behind this seemingly paradoxical concept is the idea of supply chain integration.

The supply chain is the network of organizations that are involved, through upstream and downstream linkages, in the different processes and activities that produce value in the form of products and services in the hands of the ultimate consumer. Thus for example a shirt manufacturer is a part of a supply chain that extends upstream through the weavers of fabrics to the manufacturers of fibres, and downstream through distributors and retailers to the final consumer. Each of these organizations in the chain are dependent upon each other by definition and yet paradoxically by tradition do not closely co-operate with each other.

Supply chain management is not the same as 'vertical integration'. Vertical integration normally implies ownership of upstream suppliers and downstream customers. This was once thought to be a desirable strategy but increasingly organizations are now focusing on their 'core business' – in other words the things they do really well and where they have a differential advantage. Everything else is 'out-sourced' – in other words it is procured outside the firm. So, for example, companies that perhaps once made their own components now only assemble the finished product, e.g. automobile manufacturers. Other companies may also subcontract the manufacturing as well, e.g. Amstrad in computers and word-processors. Many companies of course use third parties for distribution and logistics services. A typical example of this new type of business organization is provided by Apple Computers where 93 per cent of the cost of sales of a typical Apple computer is purchased content.

Clearly this trend has many implications for logistics management, not the least being the challenge of integrating and co-ordinating the flow of materials from a multitude of suppliers, often off-shore, and similarly managing the distribution of the finished product by way of multiple intermediaries.

In the past it was often the case that relationships with suppliers and downstream customers (such as distributors or retailers) were adversarial rather than co-operative. It is still the case today that companies will seek to achieve cost reductions or profit improvement at the expense of their supply chain partners. Companies such as these do not realize that simply transferring costs upstream or downstream does not make them any more competitive. The reason for this is that ultimately all costs will make their way to the final market place to be reflected in the price paid by the end user. The leading-edge companies recognize the fallacy of this conventional approach and instead seek to make the supply chain as a whole more competitive through the value it adds and the costs that it reduces *overall*. They have realized that the real competition is not company against company but rather supply chain against supply chain.

It must be recognized that the concept of supply chain management whilst relatively new, is in fact no more than an extension of the logic of logistics. Logistics management is primarily concerned with optimizing flows within the organization whilst supply chain management recognizes that internal integration by itself is not sufficient. Figure 11.9 suggests that there is in effect an evolution of integration from the stage I position of complete functional independence where each business function such as production or purchasing does their own thing in complete isolation from the business functions. An example would be where production seeks to optimize its unit costs of manufacture by long production runs without regard for the buildup of finished goods inventory and

Fundamentals of supply chain management

Supply chain management differs significantly from classic materials and manufacturing control in four respects. First, it views the supply chain as a single entity rather than relegating fragmented responsibility for various segments in the supply chain to functional areas such as purchasing, manufacturing, distribution, and sales (see diagram below). The second distinctive feature of supply chain management flows directly from the first: It calls for – and in the end depends upon – strategic decision making. 'Supply' is a shared objective of practically every function in the chain and is of particular strategic significance because of its impact on overall costs and market share. Third, supply chain management provides a different perspective on inventories which are used as a balancing mechanism of last, not first, resort. Finally, supply chain management requires a new approach to systems: integration, not simply interface, is the key.

All of these features and all of the challenges of the business environment that lie behind the move towards supply chain management point in one direction: to the top. Only top management can ensure that conflicting functional objectives along the supply chain are reconciled and balanced: that inventories assume their proper role as a mechanism for dealing with inevitable residual imbalances; and finally, that an integrated systems strategy that reduces the level of business vulnerability is developed and implemented. Logistics and materials managers will continue to play important roles, but only top management can be expected to have the perspective to recognize the significance of supply chain management, and only top management can provide the impetus for adopting this new approach.

The scope of supply chain management

Supply Chain Management covers the flow of goods from supplier through manufacturing and distribution chains to the end user.

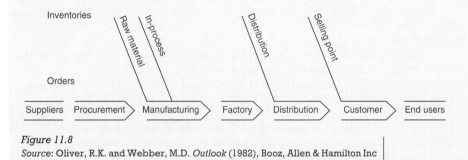

Figure 11.8
Source: Oliver, R.K. and Webber, M.D. *Outlook* (1982), Booz, Allen & Hamilton Inc

heedless of the impact it will have on the need for warehousing space and the impact on working capital.

Stage 2 companies have recognized the need for at least a limited degree of integration between adjacent functions, e.g. distribution and inventory management or purchasing and materials control. The natural next step to stage 3 requires the establishment and implementation of an 'end-to-end' planning framework that will be fully described later in this book.

Finally, stage 4 sees the company as part of a pipeline that achieves optimal value added in terms of each customer's requirements whilst maximising total supply chain profit.

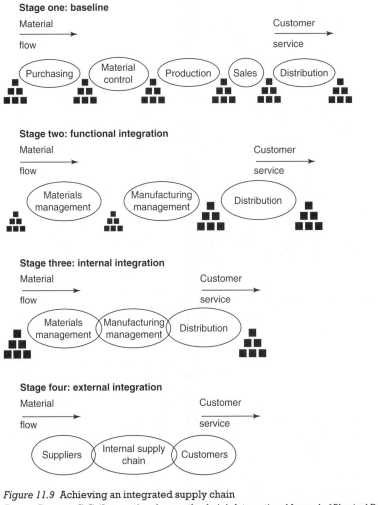

Figure 11.9 Achieving an integrated supply chain
Source: Stevens, G.C. 'Integrating the supply chain', *International Journal of Physical Distribution and Materials Management*, Vol. 19, No. 8, 1989

THE CHANGING LOGISTICS ENVIRONMENT

As the competitive content of business continues to change, bringing with it new complexities and concerns for management generally, it also has to be recognized that the impact on logistics of environmental change can be considerable. Indeed, of the many strategic issues that confront the business organization today, perhaps the most challenging, are in the area of logistics.

[. . .]

- The customer service explosion
- Time compression
- Globalization of industry
- Organizational integration

The customer service explosion

So much has been written and talked about service, quality and excellence that there is no escaping the fact that the customer in today's market place is more demanding, not just of product quality, but also of service.

As more and more markets become in effect 'commodity' markets, where the customer perceives little technical difference between competing offers, the need is for the creation of differential advantage through *added value*. Increasingly a prime source of this added value is through customer service.

Customer service may be defined as the consistent provision of time and place utility. In other words products don't have value until they are in the hands of the customer at the time and place required. There are clearly many facets of customer service, ranging from on-time delivery through to after-sales support. Essentially the role of customer service should be to enhance 'value-in-use', meaning that the product becomes worth more in the eyes of the customer because service has added value to the core product. In this way significant differentiation of the total offer (that is the core product plus the service package) can be achieved.

Those companies that have achieved recognition for service excellence, and thus have been able to establish a differential advantage over their competition are typically those companies where logistics management is a high priority. Companies like Rank Xerox, BMW, Benetton and IBM are typical of such organizations. The achievement of competitive advantage through service comes not from slogans or expensive so-called customer care programmes, but rather from a combination of a carefully thought out *strategy* for service, the development of appropriate *delivery systems* and *commitment* from people, from the Chief Executive down.

The attainment of service excellence in this broad sense can only be achieved through a closely integrated logistics strategy. In reality, the ability to become a world class supplier depends as much upon the effectiveness of one's operating systems as it does upon the presentation of the product, the creation of images and the influencing of consumer perceptions. In other words, the success of McDonald's, British Airways, or any of the other frequently-cited paragons of service excellence, is not due to their choice of advertising agency, but rather to their recognition that the logistics of service delivery on a consistent basis is the crucial source of differential advantage.

Time compression

One of the most visible features of recent years has been the way in which time has become a critical issue in management. Product life cycles are shorter than ever, industrial customers and distributors require just-in-time deliveries, and end-users are ever more willing to accept a substitute product if their first choice is not instantly available.

In the case of new product introduction there are many implications for management resulting from this reduction of the time 'window' in which profits may be made. Many commentators have focused upon the need to seek out novel forms of managing the new product development process; venture teams along the lines pioneered by DuPont and 3M being one such approach. Others have highlighted the need to improve the quality of their feedback from the market place and to link this more directly into the firm's R&D effort.

All of these initiatives are indeed necessary if the business is to stay alive. However, amidst all the concern with the process of creating and managing innovation, there is one issue which perhaps is only now being given the attention it demands. That issue is the problem of extended logistics lead-times.

The concept of logistics lead-time is simple: How long does it take to convert an order into cash? Whilst management has long recognized the competitive impact of shorter order cycles, this is only a part of the total process whereby working capital and resources are committed to an order.

From the moment when decisions are taken on the sourcing and procurement of materials and components through the manufacturing subassembly process to the final distribution and after-market support, there are a myriad of complex activities that must be managed if markets are to be gained and retained. This is the true scope of logistics lead-time management.

As we have noted, one of the basic functions of logistics is the provision of 'availability'. However, in practice, what is so often the case is that the integration of marketing and manufacturing planning that is necessary to achieve this competitive requirement is lacking. Further problems are caused by limited co-ordination of supply decisions with the changing requirements of the market place and the restricted visibility that purchasing and manufacturing have of final demand, because of extended supply and distribution 'pipelines'.

To overcome these problems and to establish enduring competitive advantage by ensuring timely response to volatile demand a new and fundamentally different approach to the management of lead-times is required.

Globalization of industry

The third of the strategic issues that provide a challenge for logistics management is the trend towards globalization.

A global company is more than a multinational company. In the global business materials and components are sourced world-wide, manufactured off-shore and sold in many different countries perhaps with local customization.

[. . .]

For global companies like Digital, Philips and Caterpillar, the management of the logistics process has become an issue of central concern. The difference between profit and loss on an individual product can hinge upon the extent to which the global pipeline can be optimized, because the flows of goods and materials are so great. The global company seeks to achieve competitive advantage by identifying world markets for its products and then to develop a manufacturing and logistics strategy to support its marketing strategy. So a company like Caterpillar, for example, has dispersed assembly operations to key overseas markets and uses global logistics channels to supply parts to off-shore assembly plants and after-markets. Where appropriate, Caterpillar will use third party companies to manage distribution and even final finishing. So for example in the U.S. a third party company, Leaseway Transportation, in addition to providing parts inspection and warehousing actually attaches options to fork lift trucks. Wheels, counterweights, forks and masts are installed as specified by Caterpillar. Thus local market needs can be catered for from a standardized production process.

Even in a geographically compact area like Europe we find that there is still a significant need for local customization. A frequently cited example is the different preferences for washing machines. The French prefer top-loading machines, the British go for front-loaders, the Germans prefer high-speed spins, the Italians prefer a lower speed! In addition there are differences in electrical standards and differences in distribution channels. In the UK most washing machines are sold through national chains specializing in white goods. In Italy, white goods are sold through a profusion of small retailers and customers bargain over price.

The challenge to a global company like Whirlpool therefore is how to achieve the cost advantage of standardization whilst still catering for the local demand for variety. Whirlpool is responding to that challenge by seeking to standardize on parts, components and modules and then through flexible manufacturing and logistics to provide the specific products demanded by each market.

Organizational integration

Whilst the theoretical logic of taking a systems view of the business might be apparent, the reality of practical implementation is something else. The classical business organization is based upon strict functional divisions and hierarchies. It is difficult to achieve a closely integrated, customer focused materials flow whilst the traditional territorial boundaries are jealously guarded by entrenched management with its outmoded priorities.

In these conventional organizations, *materials managers* manage materials, whilst *production managers* manage production and *marketing managers* manage marketing. Yet these functions are components of a system that needs some overall plan or guidance to fit together. Managing the organization under the traditional model is just like trying to complete a complex jigsaw puzzle without having the picture on the box cover in front of you.

The challenges that face the business organization in today's environment are quite different from those of the past. To achieve a position of sustainable competitive advantage, tomorrow's organization will be faced with the need to dispense with outmoded labels like marketing manager, manufacturing manager or purchasing manager. Instead we will need broad-based integrators who are oriented towards the achievement of market place success based upon managing systems and people that deliver service. Generalists rather than narrow specialists will increasingly be required to integrate materials management with operations management and delivery. Knowledge of systems theory and behaviour will become a prerequisite for this new type manager. As important will be the orientation of these managers: they will be market-orientated with a sharp focus upon customer service as the primary source of competitive advantage.

THE CHALLENGE OF LOGISTICS MANAGEMENT

One of the most significant business trends of the late 20th century has been the emergence of logistics as an integrative concept spanning the entire supply chain from raw material through to the point of consumption. The underlying philosophy behind the logistics concept is that of planning and co-ordinating the materials flow from source to user as an integrated system rather than, as is so often the case, managing the goods flow as a series of independent activities. Thus under a logistics management regime the goal is to link the market place, the distribution network, the manufacturing process and the procurement activity, in such a way that customers are serviced at higher levels and yet at lower cost. In other words to achieve the goal of competitive advantage through both cost reduction and service enhancement.

Can such a situation really be achieved in practice?

When Nissan began manufacturing cars in Britain in the late 1980s it was estimated that each car would be produced for about £600 less than it cost a British manufacturer to make an equivalent model. Industrial experts suggested that the reason for this Japanese cost advantage was not cheaper labour costs but superior logistics management. Nissan manage the total material flow, from component source to final car, as a single system. As a result their inventory of materials, work in progress, goods in transit and finished goods is kept to a minimum; throughput times are reduced; transport costs are lower – yet their ability to service the end market is not diminished.

We have already commented that product life-cycles are getting shorter. What we have witnessed in many markets is the effect of changes in technology and consumer demand combining to produce more volatile markets where a product can be obsolete almost as soon as it reaches the market. There are many current examples of shortening life-cycles but perhaps the personal computer symbolizes them all. In this particular case we have seen rapid developments in technology which have firstly created markets where none existed before and then almost as quickly have rendered themselves obsolete as the next generation of product is announced.

Such shortening life-cycles create substantial problem for logistics management. In particular, shorter life-cycles demand shorter lead-times – indeed our definition of lead-time may well need to change. Lead-times are traditionally defined as the elapsed period from receipt of customer order to delivery. However, in today's environment there is a wider perspective that needs to be taken. The real lead-time is the time taken from the drawing board, through procurement, manufacture and assembly to the end market. This is the concept of *strategic lead-time* and the management of this time span is the key to success in managing logistics operations.

There are already situations arising where the life-cycle is shorter than the strategic lead-time. In other words the life of a product on the market is less than the time it takes to design, procure, manufacture and distribute that same product! The implications of this are considerable both for planning and operations. In a global context the problem is exacerbated by the longer transportation times involved.

Ultimately, therefore, the means of achieving success in such markets is to accelerate movement through the supply chain and to make the entire logistics system far more flexible and thus responsive to these fast-changing markets.

Whilst there are many implications of these pressures for the way we manage logistics there are three key issues [. . .].

Cutting short the pipeline

Many companies have not paid proper attention to the length of the pipeline from suppliers through to customers, particularly with regard to transit times and intermediate stock holding. The presence of inventory in the supply chain, whether components, subassemblies, work-in-progress or finished goods inevitably adds to the total pipeline length. In the past the case for this inventory has been based upon the principle of 'protection', i.e. the desire to protect production, distribution or marketing against upstream or downstream fluctuations in supply or demand. Such a motivation however should be considered unwise since it only serves to reduce flexibility. Instead the emphasis must be upon the adoption of 'just-in-time' principles in delivery and manufacture to 'fast track' products to the market place. Similarly closer co-operation with suppliers, who also will be substantially fewer in number as a result of a move towards increased single-sourcing, must be the norm. Treating suppliers as partners rather than adversaries means that even greater responsiveness to changed market needs can be achieved.

Improve pipeline visibility

Poor co-ordination in the supply chain will result in a lack of visibility in the logistics pipeline. Traditional functional divisions in the organization ensure that all we ever see is our own particular section of that pipeline. Bottlenecks and excess inventories are not easily identified and thus smooth and efficient movement through the pipeline is impeded.

The priority here has to be the removal of the organizational barriers that lie at the root of the problem. Typically the companies that lack pipeline visibility, and thus control over what happens in the pipeline, are also those that have conventional, functionally-oriented organization structures. 'Territory' is jealously guarded and little information is shared. On the other hand the pace-setting global corporations have discarded these organizational strait-jackets for structures which are market-focussed. They are also characterized by the quality of their information systems – they can identify, in a real-time setting, the current status of each stage in the supply chain.

Manage logistics as a system

Because today's company tends by its very nature to operate in a context of an extended supply chain, it has been forced to confront the issue of integrated logistics management. In this scenario the needs of the market place must be matched with the organization's production capability, against the overriding objective of meeting service requirements whilst keeping costs to a minimum. The achievement of this complex balancing act can only come about through a process of management which recognizes the interrelationships and the interconnections of the chain of events that link the supply market with the customer. In a sense the globalization of industry has brought the logistics management concept to centre stage. The essence of logistics is that it seeks to manage the materials flow from source to user. Logistics management demands that all those activities which link the supply market to the demand market be viewed as an interconnected system – the point being that a decision taken in one part of that system will impact throughout the entire system. Now the emphasis has switched from a narrow *functional* orientation to the wider view of the value chain, in other words management has come to recognize that the primary purpose of business is to serve markets by adding value. The management of that added value, it is argued, is best accomplished by focussing upon the materials flow rather than upon traditional notions of functional or departmental efficiency.

To conclude, the pressures and imperatives of doing business on a global scale [. . .] are inevitably leading to a recognition of the central role of logistics. Our definition of logistics has been broad, but in essence it reflects a concern with the need to gain a competitive advantage in markets that are subject to rapid change. The prizes in today's markets go only to those companies which are capable of providing added value in ever-shortening time scales.

NOTE

* This chapter has been adapted from excerpts from, Christopher, M., *Logistics & Supply Chain Management*, ch.1 , London, FT-Pitman, 1992.

REFERENCES

1 Bowler, R.A., *Logistics and the Failure of the British Army in America* 1775–1783, Princeton University Press, 1975.
2 Shaw, A.W., *Some Problems in Market Distribution*, Harvard University Press, 1915.
3 Porter, M.E., *Competitive Strategy*, The Free Press, 1980.
4 Porter, M.E., *Competitive Advantage*, The Free Press, 1985.

12

REVERSE LOGISTICS*

Richard A. Lancioni

The state of the world energy situation has stabilized since 1980. Crude oil supplies have stabilized, and the oil-consuming countries have reached a consensus that efficiency is an essential ingredient in all aspects of transportation and distribution. With this realization has come a new dilemma in the environmental movement – how to handle the huge amounts of solid waste that is generated from industrial and consumer consumption systems and what is the most efficient way of transporting and handling it.

Also, the increase in the number of laws requiring that firms recall products that are defective has resulted in the realization that companies must now begin to develop reverse distribution systems to handle the flow of recycled and defective products. Product recalls are no longer in the realm of theoretical possibilities: it is a regular fact of business life among manufacturers of both industrial and consumer products. Machine tools, automobiles, television sets, appliances, cosmetics, clothes – no product is immune and the list is virtually endless. The actual value of product units recalled and solid recycled waste needed to be transported runs into billions of dollars. Moreover, the prognostication from the evidence so far is that the trend will continue principally for the following reasons:

1 fast-changing technology necessitating frequent changes in product design;
2 new laws being enacted worldwide, requiring the recall of defective products and the recycling of solid waste.

Despite the gravity of the problem, most logisticians in both large and small companies have been lax in developing systematic plans to recall defective products and recycle solid wastes. Their reactions when faced with recall decisions or recycling decisions have been shortsighted. What is needed is for the logistician to take a strategic view of product recall and develop a plan of action to deal with the issue.

THE CONCEPT OF BACKWARD DISTRIBUTION

In designing a total system of distribution logisticians have traditionally examined the distribution process starting with the producer and the flow of goods from the producer to the consumer.

However, today, for a variety of reasons other than just defective products, logisticians should start thinking of reverse distribution systems – that is, consumer to producer – and the economics and efficiency of building good reverse distribution systems. For example, recycling of wastes is now a major goal of many ecologists, environmentalists and conservationists. One of the major obstacles in the recycling process is the lack of an orderly reverse distribution system and the enormous cost of collection and transportation. The American Paper Institute reckons that a major portion of the cost of recycling paper (90 per cent) is the cost of distribution.[1] The Glass and Aluminium industry also constantly evaluates the economics of reverse physical distribution and searches for efficient methods of reverse distribution systems.[2]

The crucial area where the concept of reverse physical distribution applies is, of course, the product recall area. It is logical that product recall be treated as a reverse distribution problem because here, too, as in the cases cited above, the traditional physical flow of products is reversed. While conceptually it may sound easy, logisticians should be fore-warned about underestimating the difficulty of reversing the distribution process. This is because, for most companies and products, the distribution system has evolved gradually over time, rather than as a result of some systematic planning. And to devise a reverse distribution process for a company or a product, where in many cases no systematic forward distribution plan exists, is indeed difficult.[3] Further, many products pass into the hands of retailers and consumers without any record of the identity of the product or the purchaser. Locating these products and sending back and upward into the hands of the manufacturer is a very costly process. For example, one can hardly underestimate the problem and cost involved in locating and recalling thousands of cases of soup from many distribution centres, hundreds of supermarkets and thousands of small grocery stores. Very few studies have been carried out on improving the economics and efficiency of the reverse distribution problem.

URGENCY, SCOPE AND EFFECTIVENESS OF THE RECALL PROCESS

Products could be recalled by a company for a variety of reasons. They could, for example, be recalled because of poor packaging, improper labelling or improper distribution methods resulting in loss of temperature control, contamination and the like. The urgency of a recall depends on certain factors, the most important of which of course is the seriousness of the product hazard. In this connection, generally three classes of recalls can be cited.[4]

- *Class I* Products in this class are recalled because they are declared to be imminently hazardous by the Food and Drug Administration or Consumer Product Safety Commission, and as such pose an immediate danger of death or serious injury to the consumers of the product. In such cases, the products involved have to be recalled in the shortest possible time. Efforts are made to trace each and every item (100 per cent recall) in the distribution system. Bon Vivant soups with the deadly botulism toxin exemplifies this class of products. For logisticians this class of recall presents the greatest problems.
- *Class II* Products in this class, while not imminently hazardous, might still be of a dangerous nature and have the potential to cause injury and possibly be life-threatening as well. Tris-treated clothes and other such products would exemplify this class of recall. Such products also have to be cleared as quickly as possible, but the time urgency is of a slightly lesser order.
- *Class III* Products in this class are recalled for a variety of reasons. Some of them may be recalled because of some conscious or unconscious violation of federal regulations.

Mislabelled, misbranded products come into this category. They may have only a remote chance of threatening life or limb and yet they have to be recalled. Recalls of a 'defensive type' involving quality failures would also fall into this class. Many companies, especially the automobile companies, take a conservative posture and recall products voluntarily even though there are no complaints. Their reasoning in such cases is that it is better to be safe than sorry. For logisticians this class of recall is relatively easier to carry out.

The scope of the recall process depends on the nature of the product and the level of penetration in the distribution system. Industrial products with direct or short channels of distribution are easier to recall than consumer products with longer or indirect channels of distribution. Other variables that affect the recall process are: fewer units manufactured, fewer units in consumers' hands and longer product life. The scope and effectiveness of the recall process also depends upon certain other factors. For example, the ability to locate and notify consumers directly, requiring no initiative from consumers, and replacing or repairing the product at their homes increases the effectiveness of the recall.[5] Likewise decisions to limit the recall and correct the problem by methods other than recall also affect the scope and effectiveness of the recall process.

The challenge, however, exists for a logistician to design a reverse system of distribution and to get it to work at a desired performance level at the lowest possible total cost.

LOCATING THE PRODUCT

Since locating a product in a distribution system is the primary step in a recall process, the first task for a logistician would be to see if a product can be located anywhere within the existing distribution system with ease. Three distinct levels of difficulty associated with the penetration of the product in the system can be isolated.[6] At the first level the product is still under the control of the manufacturer in company-controlled warehouses or primary distributor-controlled warehouses. At this level locating the product and recovering and recalling the product is a simple matter of stock recovery for a logistician. At the second level the product would have to be located and withdrawn from the middlemen involved in the distribution of the product, namely wholesalers and retailers. The recall in this case becomes slightly more difficult. At the third level the product is in the hands of consumers. Locating and recovering products at this level is the most difficult of all. Needless to add that the movement of the product into each successive level not only complicates the recall for the logistician but adds to the cost of the operation as well.

MECHANISM FOR LOCATING PRODUCTS IN THE CHANNEL

Locating durable products with a direct distribution link, that is manufacturer to consumer – is perhaps the easiest of all. For many products, especially industrial products, a direct forward or backward link can be established for repair, replacement or refund of the product through bills, invoices or other such devices. In the case of most consumer durable products, a logistician can locate these products through a good warranty card system. A computerized warranty card can be precoded with all the critical information necessary for tracking the product in the distribution system. The kinds of information that can be coded are: product description, manufacturing plans, lot, batch number and dates with quantities manufactured, forward order number, shipping dates, rail or truck number, geographic areas of distribution, scheduled arrival dates, shelf life and estimated rate of use. Customer name and address obtained after the sale can then be coded into the card and stored for fast retrieval whenever necessary. Warranty cards are, however, not always returned by

LIBRARY
BISHOP BURTON COLLEGE
BEVERLEY HU17 8QG

consumers and this is a weak link in the system. The reasons for warranty cards not being returned are that:

a) they are perceived as information-gathering devices, with the name and addresses being used for unsolicited mailings later on; and

b) other documentary evidence like receipts and cheques can be used to show proof of purchase, should the need to repair or return the product occur later on.

However the return of warranty cards can be improved by:

a) designing them attractively and stressing boldly in front the importance of returning them for tracing ownerships in the case of a recall;

b) providing postage-paid warranty cards; and

c) negotiating contractual agreements with retailers wherein they agree to retain records of the identity of the owner of warranty cards.

Such methods have achieved a fair amount of success in many cases. Locating consumers and notifying them directly are prime factors in a recall success.

In the case of consumer non-durables, the problem of location is relatively more difficult because the distribution system is much more complex and indirect. First, a product is likely to be produced in several geographically dispersed manufacturing locations and follow many different routes in reaching an ultimate destination. There may be multiple primary distributors, intermediate sellers and retail organizations made up of hundreds of independent units. The product is therefore likely to rest in public warehouses, cooperative warehouses, distribution centres and a variety of other such places before reaching its ultimate destination. Record-keeping is therefore of vital importance. Good systems provide adequate information about the products' manufacturing locations and, in addition, also provide computerized tear-off or tag cards to show each critical move of a product within the distribution system up to the last transfer point before being sold to a consumer. Most logistics departments maintain a tracing section to locate a product in the distribution system. In conjunction with a carrier they provide a 'pro' number which allows rapid location to transfer points and destinations. Once the logistician traces the product to the last retailing point he can get the retailers to take the defective product off the shelves and hold for further instructions. However, if the product has been sold to consumers a media blitz in the vicinity of the stores that sold the defective product, requesting the return of the product, is the best method of locating it. The recall advertisement should also be displayed prominently in all the stores.

RETRIEVAL OF PRODUCTS

After the product is located, logisticians can coordinate the process of retrieving the product in the field either through:

a) the company's field salesforce;

b) the retailer or other middlemen;

c) outside collection specialists.

This new breed of specialists, specialising in recall, not only help locate suspect products with their own field representatives, but also monitor and audit the whole process as well. However in many cases the manufacturers and their logistics staff take direct control of the recall, isolating all others in the process.

Effective retrievals require that:

- the customer be motivated to return defective products for repair, replacement or refund; and
- good relationships be established among carriers and other participants in the distribution process such as channel members.

The biggest obstacle in recalling products however is the consumer. The experience of many firms indicate that consumers are unwilling or lax in returning hazardous products even if notified, especially if the product cost less than 20 or 30 dollars. Motivating consumers to return such products is a difficult task. Financial incentives and education of consumers through instruction manuals including warnings that buyers may be liable in civil contributor negligence if they fail to return the hazardous products has been suggested as an answer.[7] Legislation, forcing consumers to return recalled products has also been suggested, although such legislation is unlikely. Even if enacted, such legislation would not change the situation drastically.

Retailers, carriers and others involved in the distribution process must be willing to cooperate with the manufacturers if the reverse distribution process is to work properly. More often than not, members of the distribution process are not prepared to cope with the problems and responsibilities of reverse distribution because they do not receive specific guidelines from the logisticians in terms of quality or quantity. The failure of logisticians to reimburse the distribution members for certain out-of-pocket expenses involved in the recall of hazardous products is also a contributory factor. The problems associated with the recall of Tris-treated sleepwear for children exemplifies the above mentioned points clearly. Thousands of garments are piled up at retailers' warehouses with no instruction whatsoever. This lack of communication can be a major source of conflict for participants in the distribution process if not handled properly.

REVERSE DISTRIBUTION AS A PART OF LOGISTICS STRATEGY

From the company viewpoint, the reverse distribution process for product recall should be treated as an integral part of logistics strategy. The success of a firms' recall will to a large extent be contingent upon prior planning and the clear assignment of responsibilities. Accordingly, the concern of logistics managers must be to determine in advance what, if any, modifications are needed in the existing distribution system to handle recalls. Management of the logistics aspects of the reverse distribution system should be assigned to a senior coordinator who will be responsible for interfacing and preplanning with all the other departments involved. All subsystems within the logistics network should be tested to see if they perform easily in reverse in an emergency. Logisticians should also take care to look at existing systems in companies that have had some experience in this area, before modifying their internal distribution system for recall purposes. Some automobile, aluminium and food companies have developed good reverse distribution systems. All possible alternatives should be studied.

FACILITY NETWORK

The existing geographical distribution of manufacturing locations, warehouses, retail outlets and all other such facilities utilized by the company for the physical flow of goods should be pinpointed. In the event of a recall it is essential that production and flow data be traced back to certain specific locations in the total facilities network. Also, logisticians must be able to determine at short notice the number of defective products anywhere in the distribution system, be they in company warehouses or public warehouses. Establishing inventory and identifying locations in a hurry, especially where brokers, drop shipments or transhipments are involved can be complicated. In a recall, it is a primary function whose importance cannot be overstated.

COMMUNICATIONS AND ORDER PROCESSING

The order processing systems and procedures should be reviewed. In fact, a review of all the communications system should be undertaken. Invoice handling and warranty card administration should be checked with special care. In a recall they perform a vital function. A good communications system will allow the logisticians substantially to reduce the time and manpower required for a recall and limit geographical area of involvement.

TRANSPORTATION AND TRAFFIC MANAGEMENT

Transportation and traffic management system should be reviewed with special emphasis on pinpointing shipping dates, orders, destinations and vehicle identifications, and stoppage of further movement. Documentation of product movement is crucial for the reverse distribution process. Carriers in a recall must receive clear instructions about pick-up and return procedures. Carriers must be evaluated for speed, capability, availability and dependability. Collection points for the return of the products should be designed along with instructions for their disposal or salvage if possible. Policies for returned merchandise and arrangements for replacements should also be made.

LOGISTICS COSTING

An accounting and cost review of expenditures for the performance of activities involved in recall must also be made. Table 12.1 gives some of the cost elements involved in a recall.[8]

The costs of recall and reverse distribution are two or three times higher than the costs of forward distribution because of the small quantities involved and the urgency of the problem.

A reverse distribution model

The stages in a reverse distribution system are shown in Figure 12.1 and end at the production source. What is required is that a firm views the system in the same way that it operates its outbound or forward distribution system and that these activities be integrated with the reverse distribution tasks that may arise at different times. A reverse distribution system, like a forward or outbound system, has multi-level inventory retrieval activities, transportation gap problems, a requirement for communications and other processing, the need for materials handling, and storage. Each activity involves the same type of management decisions involved in outbound product distribution. Figure 12.2 presents recall distribution decision model detailing the system objectives in each decision area and the overall system objectives.

As shown in Figure 12.2 the objective of each logistics area in handling the product recall are focused in speeding up withdrawal of the product(s) from the marketplace at a reduced cost. In the transportation area, the distribution manager has the task of the selection of the proper mode of transport for return of the goods, while at the same time ensuring that the return haul is utilized to the fullest extent. [. . .] The warehousing of returned goods must be combined with the routine storage of products destined for final consumption. Here, the

Table 12.1 Cost elements involved in a product recall

Communication Costs

Registered and certified mail
Return receipts
Employee visits
Telephone, telegrams
Messenger service

Documentation Costs

Filing of receipts of notices for recall
Estimates for disposition and replacement
Plans of item recalled
Plans for replacement item
Instructions for replacement/repair
Authorisations for work to be performed
Receipts for items replaced/repaired

Replacement Costs
Manufacture and installation
Label
Instructions
Shipping, packing and warehousing
Testing and retesting
Identification of product
Identification of carton
Identification of shipping carton
Temporary personnel
Invoicing
Overtime of employees

Disposition Costs
Locating all items
Inventory of items
Removal from customer's property
Packaging and unpacking
Labelling
Shipping
Inspection
Repair or replace
Discard or salvage
Instruction pamphlet
Refunding
Allowances for time used
Repurchase of item
Compensation for loss of use
Warehousing – storage

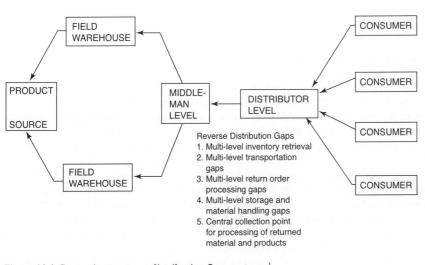

Figure 12.1 Stages in a reverse distribution flow system

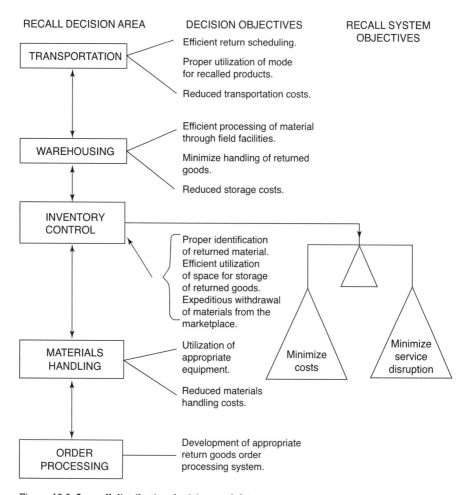

RECALL DECISION AREA

TRANSPORTATION

WAREHOUSING

INVENTORY CONTROL

MATERIALS HANDLING

ORDER PROCESSING

DECISION OBJECTIVES

Efficient return scheduling.

Proper utilization of mode for recalled products.

Reduced transportation costs.

Efficient processing of material through field facilities.

Minimize handling of returned goods.

Reduced storage costs.

Proper identification of returned material. Efficient utilization of space for storage of returned goods. Expeditious withdrawal of materials from the marketplace.

Utilization of appropriate equipment.

Reduced materials handling costs.

Development of appropriate return goods order processing system.

RECALL SYSTEM OBJECTIVES

Minimize costs

Minimize service disruption

Figure 12.2 **A recall distribution decision model**

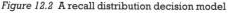

space allotted to returned goods should be kept at a minimum and the handling and repackaging time also reduced. The reverse distribution flow of goods through field warehouses will be small, and internal efficiencies can only be maintained if this flow is integrated into the normal operational routine of the system.

The inventory of returned goods should be integrated into the same master inventory system utilized to handle the outbound products. Here, special product codes should be assigned to the returned flow items to identify and segregate them from the normal inventory items. The expeditious removal of the product from the marketplace and possible salvaging, reprocessing or refabrication of the returned goods into new inventory which can later be remarketed, are necessary tasks. In one consumer products firm where the problem of reverse distribution has arisen numerous times in the past, the company has established a returned goods inventory group that traces, locates, handles the removal of the good from the marketplace, and explores ways of reprocessing the product for possible resale.

As Figure 12.2 shows the materials handling component of a distribution recall system stresses the objectives of proper equipment utilization and reduced costs. Since materials handling is an activity which occurs throughout a logistics system, distribution costs can be minimized if this activity is properly handled. For example, the stacking of returned goods, while at the same time retrieving outbound products, is an activity that could occur in every level of the distribution system (Figure 12.1). Materials handling costs could also be reduced, if the returned goods are loaded on vehicles normally scheduled to make return trips to a central warehousing facility. Truck or car utilization will be improved and transportation costs lowered.

The final activity important in a recall distribution system is order processing. Proper documentation of the returned merchandise is important to expedite its handling and inventory processing. In effect, a return product document system is necessary. This was implemented in one major US automobile firm, where cars that were recalled were assigned an identifying code and a document set. The documents included a recall activity report; *a maintenance completion form* which detailed the repairs performed on the vehicle; *a dealer assigned form* indicating the dealership where the repairs were made; and *a warranty completion form* detailing the owner's name, warranty coverage, and manufacturer's liability. Each of these documents was computer-generated, and an accurate record was kept of all vehicles involved in a recall.

The distribution activities involved in the returned product flow are integrated and are interdependent. The efficient performance of each activity depends upon the other. The overall system objectives in the recall distribution process are cost minimization and minimal service disruption. If these objectives can be achieved in each reverse logistics situation, then the task that is becoming more frequent in the marketplace will be easier for firms to perform.

CONCLUSION

Reverse logistics systems will be important in the future. The need to understand how such systems can be adapted to a company's operation are important if a firm is to deal effectively with the challenge of product recall and waste disposal [. . .].

NOTE

* This chapter has been adapted from, Lancioni, R. A., "Reverse Logistics", in The Gower Handbook of Logistics & Distribution Management (4th edn). Ed. J. Gattorna, Aldershot, Gower, 1900, ch. 28.

REFERENCES

1 Margulies, W. P., "Steel and Paper Industries Look to Recycling as an Answer to Pollution", Advertising Age, Vol. 41, October 19, 1970, p.63.
2 Margulies, W. P. "Glass, Paper Makers Tackle our Package Pollution Woes," Advertising Age, Vol 41, September 1970, p. 43.
3 James, D. E., "Distribution Channel Consideration," in Managing Product Recalls, Ed. E. P. McGuire, New York, The Conference Board, 1974, pp. 77–81.
4 Healand, J., "Product Recall Problems and Options-Non Durable Products", in Managing Product Recalls. Ed. E. P. McGuire, New York, The Conference Board, 1974, pp. 57–65.
5 Product Safety Letter, Washington DC, 17 January 1977, p. 1.
6 Ibid, citation 4 above.
7 McGuire, E. P., "What is Ahead in Product Safety?", The Conference Board Record, August 1976, pp. 33–34.
8 Hammer, W., "Handbook of System and Product Safety". Englewood Cliffs, NJ. Prentice Hall, 1972, p. 7.

SECTION 5: BUSINESS PROCESS MANAGEMENT

INTRODUCTION

This section examines the way in which firms organise themselves in order to undertake their business activities. During the 1990s, there was considerable interest, from both practitioners and academics, in the application of a business process perspective to the management of organisations. To overcome the problems associated with the traditional (i.e. functional) structures many organisations have attempted to improve organisational performance by aligning organisational structures with business processes. This approach to reorganisation based on business processes is usually referred to as Business Process Re-engineering. BPR has had a major impact on organisations in recent years.

In chapter 13, Hammer, who with co-author Champny, did most to popularise the concept of BPR in the early 1990s, argues that organisations can be managed more effectively by organising their activities around their business processes. Since the industrial revolution, business organisations have based their structures on tasks, grouping together workers carrying out similar work, creating the departments, like accounting, marketing, production and so on, that most of us are familiar with. Hammer argues that such traditional, functionally based, task-centred organisations tend to create problems of inefficiencies, inaccuracies and inflexibilities, arising from the fragmentary nature of each task. The process view, on the other hand, takes a systemic view of work by linking together the various tasks that make a complete business process.

The key issue is that a process must start from the customer. The organisation needs to conceive of itself as a series of processes that deliver added value to customers. This sounds simple enough. However, such organisational arrangements inevitably cut across the existing departments with their vested interests and power bases. Hammer notes that the process perspective requires that everyone involved be directed towards a common goal. The concept of a common goal, presumably determined by senior management, to which everyone is committed, is a central assumption of the systems view of organisations. This is somewhat simplistic, and may not accord with organisational reality. Hammer seems to regard anyone who fails to pursue this common goal as some kind of deviant, whose behaviour can be wished or even ordered away. However in reality the change to a process-centred organisation seems likely to be difficult to achieve.

Chapter 14, by Shapiro *et al.* describes a business process, that must be undertaken by all organisations; that of fulfilling a customer's order. It provides a useful illustration of the potential problems of managing business activities in traditionally structured organisations, by following a typical order through a functionally structured organisation. Problems usually occur due to the order falling between the cracks between the various departments that deal with different stages of the process. In most cases the problems arise from a failure to take a process perspective and from political problems between departments. Taking a process perspective forces the organisation to become customer focused, highlighting the fact that an order is a surrogate for the customer. As the authors put it, 'Every time the order is handled, the customer is handled. Every time the order sits unattended, the customer sits unattended'. Echoing the Hammer chapter, they note that in most organisations there is lack of awareness of process, with each department ignorant of what happens in other departments. Different departments use their own criteria for prioritising orders, resulting in dysfunctional behaviour when viewed from the perspective of the organisation as a whole, with each department pursuing its own rather than the organisation's objectives. Also like Hammer, Shapiro *et al.* stress the importance of achieving a systemic view, a process-centred perspective of organisational activity, to break down departmental barriers and focus on the customer. However, unlike Hammer, they recognise the need to manage the politics that are inevitable within any organisation.

Chapter 15, by Childe *et al.*, seeks to provide some clarity to the often confusing terminology associated with BPR. It outlines the key issues facing organisations seeking to adopt a process orientation, and presents frameworks for identifying business processes and classifying different types of Business Process Re-engineering. Childe *et al.*'s chapter is analytical in nature and hence in marked contrast to the previous two chapters. They are essentially prescriptive, advocating as they do the need for organisations to manage their activities based on their business processes. The type of frameworks presented in the chapter can facilitate the type of thorough critical analysis that is often sadly missing in the BPR debate.

The final chapter, chapter 16, – by Holtham, presents a critique of the BPR phenomena. Business Process Re-engineering has had a significant impact over the last decade, yet it is a term that has been abused as much as it has been used. Holtham argues that BPR does have some core concepts that are valuable, but these need to be considered independently from its often evangelical promotion. He highlights some of its weaknesses that might explain why between 50 and 70 per cent of re-engineering projects are considered to have failed. Whereas BPR has been presented as a universal panacea, especially by those who have a material interest in its adoption (e.g. management consultants) some organisations may not need BPR. Business processes are bound to cut across the departmental boundaries that exist in functionally structured organisations, and as Holtham puts it, 'when the verbiage and hype are stripped away', most organisations have functionally based structures. However, much of what has happened in practice in the name of BPR has been little more than restructuring within this paradigm, rather than moving to organisational arrangements which facilitate the type of cross-functional co-operation required by a true process-orientation. BPR is about changing business processes. This may or may not call for changes in organisational structure. Holtham claims that the most significant improvements in performance resulting from BPR have occurred where existing previous performance was weak or disastrous, and where a new chief executive was able to force through the required changes. This is not likely to be the case for most organisations, where, echoing the point about organisational politics made in Shapiro *et al.*'s chapter, not all employees will welcome BPR. This may be because of self-interest or because they believe BPR will act to the detriment of the organisation as a whole. Organisations are not necessarily the unitary entities in which all members are committed to the goals set by its senior managers, as assumed by systems theory.

The most valuable element of BPR is its requirement to think about an organisation in terms of its business processes. To be successful, any organisation is likely to have to satisfy its customers. Taking the process-orientation that is at the heart of BPR, should force an organisation to concentrate on those processes which deliver maximum value to customers at minimum cost.

13

THE TRIUMPH OF PROCESS*

Michael Hammer

Revolutions often begin with the intention of only improving the systems they eventually bring down. The American, French, and Russian revolutions all started as efforts to ameliorate the rule of a monarch, not to end it. Reform turns into revolt when the old system proves too rigid to adapt. So, too, the revolution that has destroyed the traditional corporation began with efforts to improve it.

For some twenty years managers of large American corporations have been engaged in a relentless effort to improve the performance of their businesses. Pressured by suddenly powerful international (especially Japanese) competition and ever more demanding customers, companies embarked on crusades to lower costs, improve productivity, increase flexibility, shrink cycle times, and enhance quality and service. Companies rigorously analyzed their operations, dutifully installed the newest technological advances, applied the latest management and motivational techniques, and sent their people through all the fashionable training programs – but to little avail. No matter how hard they tried, how assiduously they applied the techniques and tools in the management kit bag, performance barely budged.

The problems motivating managers to make these efforts were not minor. The operating performance of established corporations was grossly unsatisfactory, especially when compared with that of aggressive international competitors or hungry start-ups. Some cases in point:

- Aetna Life & Casualty typically took twenty-eight days to process applications for homeowner's insurance, only twenty-six minutes of which represented real productive work.
- When buying anything through their purchasing organization, even small stationery items costing less than $10, Chrysler incurred internal expenses of $300 in reviews, sign-offs, and approvals.
- It took Texas Instruments' Semiconductor Group 180 days to fill an order for an integrated circuit while a competitor could often do it in thirty days.
- GTE's customer service unit was able to resolve customer problems on the first call less than 2 percent of the time.
- Pepsi discovered that 44 percent of the invoices that it sent retailers contained errors, leading to enormous reconciliation costs and endless squabbles with customers.

This list could be extended indefinitely. The inefficiencies, inaccuracies, and inflexibilities of corporate performance were prodigious. This was not a new phenomenon; it was just that by 1980 these problems were starting to matter. When customers had little choice and all competitors were equally bad, there was little incentive for a company to try to do better. But when sophisticated customers began deserting major companies in droves, these problems rocketed to the top of the business agenda. The persistence of performance problems in the face of intense efforts to resolve them drove corporate leaders to distraction.

After a while, understanding gradually dawned on American managers: They were getting nowhere because they were applying task solutions to process problems.

The difference between task and process is the difference between part and whole. A task is a unit of work, a business activity normally performed by one person. A process, in contrast, is a related group of tasks that together create a result of value to a customer. Order fulfillment, for instance, is a process that produces value in the form of delivered goods for customers. It is comprised of a great many tasks: receiving the order from the customer, entering it into a computer, checking the customer's credit, scheduling production, allocating inventory, selecting a shipping method, picking and packing the goods, loading and sending them on their way. None of these tasks by itself creates value for the customer. You can't ship until it's been loaded, you can't pack until it's been picked. A credit check by itself is simply an exercise in financial analysis. Only when they are all put together do the individual work activities create value.

The problems that afflict modern organizations are not task problems. They are process problems. The reason we are slow to deliver results is not that our people are performing their individual tasks slowly and inefficiently; fifty years of time-and-motion studies and automation have seen to that. We are slow because some of our people are performing tasks that need not be done at all to achieve the desired result and because we encounter agonizing delays in getting the work from the person who does one task to the person who does the next one. Our results are not full of errors because people perform their tasks inaccurately, but because people misunderstand their supervisor's instructions and so do the wrong things, or because they misinterpret information coming from co-workers. We are inflexible not because individuals are locked into fixed ways of operating, but because no one has an understanding of how individual tasks combine to create a result, an understanding absolutely necessary for changing how the results are created. We do not provide unsatisfactory service because our employees are hostile to customers, but because no employee has the information and the perspective needed to explain to customers the status of the process whose results they await. We suffer from high costs not because our individual tasks are expensive, but because we employ many people to ensure that the results of individual tasks are combined into a form that can be delivered to customers. In short, our problems lie not in the performance of individual tasks and activities, the units of work, but in the processes, how the units fit together into a whole. For decades, organizations had been beating the hell out of task problems but hadn't laid a glove on the processes.

It wasn't surprising that it took managers a long time to recognize their mistake. Processes, after all, were not even on the business radar screen. Though processes were central to their businesses, most managers were unaware of them, never thought about them, never measured them, and never considered improving them. The reason for this is that our organizational structures for the last two hundred years have been based on tasks. The fundamental building block of the corporation was the functional department, essentially a group of people all performing a common task. Tasks were measured and improved, the people performing them were trained and developed, managers were assigned to oversee departments or groups of departments, and all the while the processes were spinning out of control.

Slowly and even reluctantly, American corporations began in the 1980s to adopt new methods of business improvement that focused on processes. The two best known and most successful were total quality management (TQM) and reengineering. Through a long period of intensive application of these techniques, American businesses made enormous headway in overcoming their process problems. Unnecessary tasks were eliminated, tasks were combined or reordered, information was shared among all the people involved in a process, and so on. As a result, order of magnitude improvements were realized in speed, accuracy, flexibility, quality, service, and cost, all by at last attending to processes. The application of process-oriented business improvement programs played a major role in the competitive resurgence of American companies and the revitalization of the American economy in the 1990s.

So far, so good. But to paraphrase an infamous statement from the Vietnam era, process-centered improvement techniques saved companies by destroying them. By bringing processes to the fore, the very foundations of the traditional organization were undermined. A disregard for processes had been built into the structure and culture of industrial era corporations. The premise on which modern organizations were founded, Adam Smith's idea of the specialization of labor, was in fact a rejection of process. It argued that success was based on fragmenting processes into simple tasks and then resolutely focusing on these tasks. By attending to processes instead, the new improvement efforts created stresses that could not be papered over.

Who would have control over the newly recognized and appreciated processes? Consisting as they did of diverse tasks, processes crossed existing organizational boundaries and thereby imperiled the protected domains of functional managers. The new ways of working did not fit into the classical organization. They often entailed the use of teams, groups of individuals with various skills drawn from different functional areas. But such teams had no place in the old organizational chart. Whose responsibility would they be? The new processes often called for empowered frontline individuals who would be provided with information and expected to make their own decisions. This was heresy in organizations where workers were considered too simple to make decisions and where the need for supervisory control was considered a law of nature. In short, it quickly became clear that the new ways of working that marvelously improved performance were incompatible with existing organizations: their structure, personnel, management styles, cultures, reward and measurement systems, and the like.

There were only two options: Abandon the new processes that had saved the company or adapt the company to the new ways of working. The choice was clear, albeit difficult and, to some, unwelcome. The death knell was ringing for the traditional corporation. In its place would arise a new kind of enterprise, one in which processes play a central role in the operation and management of the enterprise: the process-centered organization.

No company adopted process centering as an end in itself, or because managers thought it would be interesting, exciting, or fashionable. Companies did it because they had no choice, because they could not make their new high-performance processes work in their old organizations. This transition began slowly in the early 1990s with a handful of companies like Texas Instruments, Xerox, and Progressive Insurance. Since then, the stream has become a flood. Dozens of organizations are now making this change, and hundreds more soon will be. Companies like American Standard, Ford, GTE, Delco, Chrysler, Shell Chemical, Ingersoll-Rand, and Levi Strauss, to name just a few, are all concentrating on their processes.

The change to process centering is not primarily a structural one (although it has deep and lasting structural implications, [. . .]. It is not announced by issuing a new organizational chart and assigning a new set of managerial titles. Process centering is first and foremost a shift in perspective, an Escherian reversal of foreground and background, in which primary (tasks) and secondary (processes) exchange places. Process centering, more than anything else, means that people – all people – in the company recognize and focus on their processes. This apparently modest and simple shift has endless ramifications for the operation of businesses and for the lives of the people who work in them. Before we begin to examine these, let's examine why process is such a departure for Industrial Age corporations.

We can think of a process as a black box that effects a transformation, taking in certain inputs and turning them into outputs of greater value. Thus order fulfillment basically turns an order into delivered goods. It begins with an order from the customer that describes a need and ends with those goods in the customer's hands. In fact we might say that the order fulfillment process creates three outputs: the delivered goods, the satisfied customer, and the paid bill. The surest indication of a satisfied customer is the paid bill. This latter, seemingly obvious observation is revolutionary. It says that the operational work of order fulfillment goes beyond mere inventory handling and shipping to include billing, receivables, and collections – the activities needed to actually get cash in hand. These latter activities have traditionally been the sanctified province of the finance department. To suggest that they should be linked with operational activities in a common process and that the line between operations and finance should consequently disappear defies one hundred years of corporate theology.

Product development is another process encountered in many organizations. It takes as input an idea, a concept, or a need and ends with a design or a functioning prototype for a new product. Many kinds of people participate in the product development process. Research and development (R&D) people contribute technical expertise, marketing people offer their knowledge of customer needs, manufacturing experts say what can be produced efficiently and economically, and finance people assess whether a product can be made and sold at a profit. The difference between product development on the one hand and R&D on the other is central: The former is a process whereas the latter is an organizational unit, a department comprised of technical and scientific personnel.

People from R&D are needed in processes other than product development. In many industries, from electronics to chemicals, R&D people participate in the customer service process. When customers call with complex questions about sophisticated technologies, the technical people are the only ones who can respond. In other words, processes transcend organizational boundaries. Xerox executives discovered this when they constructed a simple matrix diagram. Across the top they wrote the names of their processes, down the side went the names of their departments, and in the squares of the matrix an X went to any department involved in the performance of the corresponding process. When the diagram was complete, they were astounded to discover that nearly all the squares were Xs. Virtually every department was involved in virtually every process. This is the moral equivalent of saying that no one had any responsibility for anything. Or to put it another way, everyone was involved, but with a narrow focus on the activities of their own department, and so no one had end-to-end responsibility.

It is important to realize that companies moving to process entering do not create or invent their processes. The processes have been there all along, producing the company's outputs. It is just that heretofore the people in the company were unaware of their processes. People on the front line and their direct supervisors were so focused on their specific tasks and work groups that they could not see the processes to which they contributed; most senior managers were too removed from the fray to appreciate processes. So the processes have always existed, but in a fragmented, invisible, unnamed, and unmanaged state. Process centering gives them the attention and respect they deserve.

Most managers are blind to the performance of their processes. I like to ask them such simple questions as: How long does it take your company to conduct such and such a process? What is its accuracy rate? What is the degree of customer satisfaction with it? What is its cost? The answers are almost always hopeless shrugs of the shoulders. Managers can offer huge amounts of performance data on tasks and departments, but not on processes, which are the very heart of the entire enterprise. Everyone is watching out for task performance, but no one has been watching to see if all the tasks together produce the results they're supposed to for the customer. At the end of the day, the question has always been, "Did you do your job?" So the warehouse maximizes inventory turns, shipping focuses on shipping costs, the credit department assures that credit standards are met. But no one asks, "Did the customer get what was ordered, where it was wanted, and when we promised it?" So long as workers did their jobs, the result for the customer, it was assumed, would take care of itself. Nothing, of course, could have been more wrong.

Process centering changes all this by altering the perspective of an organization. As always, language is key in shaping how people view the world. We have said that a process is a group of tasks that together create a result of value to a customer. The key words in this definition are "group," "together," "result," and "customer."

A process perspective sees not individual tasks in isolation, but the entire collection of tasks that contribute to a desired outcome. Narrow points of view are useless in a process context. It just won't do for each person to be concerned exclusively with his or her own limited responsibility, no matter how well these responsibilities are met. When that occurs, the inevitable result is working at cross-purposes, misunderstandings, and the optimization of the part at the expense of the whole. Process work requires that everyone involved be directed toward a common goal; otherwise, conflicting objectives and parochial agendas impair the effort.

Processes are concerned with results, not with what it takes to produce them. The essence of a process is its inputs and its outputs, what it starts with and what it ends with. Everything else is detail.

Another commonly encountered process reinforces this point: order acquisition. At first blush, "order acquisition" sounds like consultant mumbo jumbo. There ought to be, one would think, a clear, monosyllabic, red-blooded, American word for this process – namely, "sales." In fact, "sales" does not do at all. "Sales" is, first of all, a word that most organizations use for a department full of sales representatives; it denotes an organizational unit, a department. But even more seriously, it identifies only one of the many activities involved in the process of acquiring an order from the customer. "Order acquisition," in contrast, indicates the desired outcome, the purpose of the process – namely, getting an order in hand. The difference between the two terms is the difference between mechanism and outcome, between means and end.

The single most important word in the definition of process is "customer." A process perspective on a business is the customer's perspective. To a customer, processes are the essence of a company. The customer does not see or care about the company's organizational structure or its management philosophies. The customer sees only the company's products and services, all of which are produced by its processes. Customers are an afterthought in the traditional organization: We do what we do and then try to sell the results to customers. But a process perspective requires that we start with customers and what they want from us, and work backward from there.

A process approach to business is particularly appropriate today, for we are living in the age of the customer. For most of industrial history there were more buyers than things available to be bought. Companies were limited by production capacity, not by market demand. Though not technically monopolies, many industries behaved as though they were and took their customers for granted. This is no longer the case. Today, customers have ever more choices and they are very aware of them. A company that does not resolutely focus on its customers and on the processes that produce value for its customers is not long for this world.

The time of process has come. No longer can processes be the orphans of business, toiling away without recognition, attention, and respect. They now must occupy center stage in our organizations. Processes must be at the heart, rather than the periphery, of companies' organization and management. They must influence structure and systems. They must shape how people think and the attitudes they have.

Some companies convert to a process focus in dramatic fashion. For instance, on January 1, 1995, American Standard, the $5 billion manufacturer of plumbing products, heating and air conditioning systems, and truck brakes, totally converted itself to a process-centered philosophy. It abolished old titles, realigned management roles, instituted new measurement and reward systems, and implemented a host of other changes consistent with a process view of the company.

This approach is relatively rare. To begin to focus on its processes and become "process centered," an organization need not make official pronouncements, need not issue a new organizational chart, need not employ the term "process centered," need not go through any formal procedures whatsoever. It merely has to start behaving in a different manner. Most companies join the process revolution in a decidedly low-key and evolutionary fashion. Managers and workers alike simply start paying attention to their processes, and eventually all aspects of the company are realigned with this new perspective.

To be serious about its processes, to start down the road to process centering, a company must do four things. First, the company must recognize and name its processes. Every company has its own unique set of business processes. Earlier we mentioned order fulfillment, product development, and order acquisition as representative processes found in many different companies. But these are not universal, nor are they the only processes that companies have. Most enterprises discover that they have a relatively small set of key processes – typically between five and fifteen – but their identity depends on the company's industry and the key results it produces for its customers. "Market selection," "provide after-sales support," and "develop manufacturing capabilities" are examples of other processes I have encountered. Obviously, no small number of such processes will suffice to completely describe the work of a business. Often companies divide primary processes into a small number of subprocesses, which are then describable in terms of basic tasks or activities.

The identification and naming of a company's processes is a critical first step, and not one to be taken casually. It requires rigorous care to ensure that real processes are being identified. This is difficult because processes cross existing organizational boundaries. A rule of thumb is that if it doesn't make three people angry, it isn't a process. Many organizations fool themselves by simply relabeling their existing functional units as processes. Process identification requires a new cognitive style, an ability to look horizontally across the whole organization, as if from the outside, rather than from the top down.

The second key step is to ensure that everyone in the company is aware of these processes and their importance to the company. The key word is "everyone." From the executive suite to the shop floor, from headquarters to the most distant sales office, everyone must recognize the company's processes, be able to name them, and be clear about their inputs, outputs, and relationships. Moving to a process focus does not immediately change the tasks that people perform, but it does change people's mind-sets. Process work is big-picture work.

One company where everyone appreciates its processes is Hill's Pet Nutrition, the division of Colgate-Palmolive Company that manufactures and sells animal nutrition products under such brand names as Science Diet. In the old days, if someone approached a worker on the Hill's manufacturing floor and asked what he did, the worker would have said that he was operating a machine. If the machine was running and he was meeting his daily quota, then he felt he was doing his job. If the output of his machine piled up, that wasn't his problem. If the product didn't get shipped, that wasn't his problem either.

If you ask the same question today, the worker will say that he works in the production subprocess of the order fulfillment process. Is this just new corporate jargon? Not at all. It represents a refocusing of the individual and his activities from the small to the large.

Now the worker realizes that he is not there merely to do his own thing, to run his machine. He's there to contribute to the overall effort, namely to perform the process that leads to the result of shipped goods. Now, if his output piles up, he will take it upon himself to see what's happening further down the line. He will do this not out of company loyalty, but because his sense of who he is and what he does has been reshaped by the shift from a task to a process orientation.

We have already remarked on the importance of language in any fundamental change in perspective. The Industrial Revolution not only turned peasants and artisans into factory workers, it practically created the term "workers" to describe them. Today this term, with its narrow task connotation, is dead language; it doesn't fit as we move to a process focus. Instead of (task) workers, we must speak of (process) performers, people who understand that in doing their work they are contributing to the performance of a process.

The third step to process centering is process measurement. If we are to be serious about our processes, we must know how well they are performing, and that means having a yardstick. Companies must identify the key measures by which each of their processes will be assessed. Some of these measures must be based on what is important to the customer. By studying customers and their requirements of the output of the process, a company can decide whether to measure cycle time, accuracy, or other aspects of process performance. Another set of measures must reflect the company's own needs: process cost, asset utilization, and other such typically financial matters. Measures are essential not only for knowing how the process is performing but for directing efforts to improve it. The converse of the old saw "that which is measured improves" is "that which is not measured is assuredly in the tank."

Whatever measures are employed, they must reflect the process as a whole and must be communicated to and used by everyone working on the process. Measures are an enormously important tool for shaping people's attitudes and behaviors; they play a central role in converting unruly groups into disciplined teams. "Team" is also an important word in process-centered organizations. Unfortunately, it has been much used and abused of late. A team is not a group of people who work together, or like each other, or share opinions. A team is a group of people with a common objective. The same measures for all performers of a process turn them, no matter where they are or how diverse they may be, into a coherent team. Some processes may be performed from beginning to end by individual performers, but, as a rule, processes are performed by teams.

The fourth step in becoming serious about processes is process management. We have already seen how the shift to a process focus began when companies applied process-focused improvement techniques to persistent performance problems. These efforts began the process-centering revolution; but process centering is a revolution that, like Trotsky's, must be permanent. A company must continue to focus on its processes so that they stay attuned to the needs of the changing business environment. One-shot improvements, even dramatic ones, are of little value. A process-centered organization must strive for ongoing process improvement. To accomplish this, the company must actively manage its processes. Indeed, we can now see that the heart of managing business is managing its processes: assuring that they are performing up to their potential, looking for opportunities to make them better, and translating these opportunities into realities. This is not a part-time or occasional responsibility. Attending to processes is management's primary ongoing responsibility. Process centering is not a project, it is a way of life.

These four steps start an organization on the road to process centering, but they are not the whole journey. Process centering is a fundamental reconceptualization of what organizations are all about. It permeates every aspect of the business: how people see themselves and their jobs, how they are assessed and paid, what managers do, the definition of the business, and, ultimately, the shape of the societies that depend on these organizations. [. . .]

NOTE

* This chapter has been adapted from, Hammer, M. (1996) *Beyond Reengineering*, ch. 1, London, HarperCollins Business.

14

STAPLE YOURSELF TO AN ORDER*

Benson P. Shapiro, V. Kasturi Rangan and John J. Sviokla

It's fashionable today to talk of becoming "customer oriented." Or to focus on that moment of truth when customers experience the actual transaction that determines whether or not they are completely satisfied. Or to empower frontline workers so they can delight the customer with their initiative and spunk.

None of this advice, however, focuses on the real way to harness the customer's interests in the operation of a company. The simple truth is that every customer's experience is determined by a company's *order management cycle* (OMC): the ten steps, from planning to postsales service, that define a company's business system. The order management cycle offers managers the opportunity to look at their company through a customer's eyes, to see and experience transactions the way customers do. Managers who track each step of the OMC work their way through the company from the customer's angle rather than their own.

In the course of the order management cycle, every time the order is handled, the customer is handled. Every time the order sits unattended, the customer sits unattended. Paradoxically, the best way to be customer-oriented is to go beyond customers and products to the order; the moment of truth occurs at every step of the OMC, and every employee in the company who affects the OMC is the equivalent of a frontline worker. Ultimately, it is the order that connects the customer to the company in a systematic and company-wide fashion.

Moreover, focusing on the OMC offers managers the greatest opportunity to improve overall operations and create new competitive advantages. Managers can establish and achieve aggressive goals – such as "improve customer fill rate from 80% to 98%," "reach 99% billing accuracy," or "cut order cycle time by 25%" and force otherwise parochial teams to look at the entire order management cycle to discover how various changes affect customers. When the OMC substitutes for narrow functional interests, customer responsiveness becomes the overriding goal of the entire organization, and conflicts give way to systemic solutions. The best way for managers to learn this lesson and pass it on to their whole work force is, in effect, to staple themselves to an order. They can then track an order as it moves through the OMC, always aware that the order is simply a surrogate for the customer.

A REALISTIC WALK THROUGH THE OMC

The typical OMC includes ten activities that sometimes overlap or interact [. . .]. While OMCs vary from industry to industry and are different for products and services, almost every business, from the corner ice cream stand to the global computer company, has these same steps. In the following discussion, a number of important lessons will emerge that explain both the customer's experience with a company and that company's ability to achieve ambitious cost and quality goals. For example, as we "walk" an order through the OMC, note the number of times that the order or information about it physically moves horizontally from one functional department to another. Since most companies are organized along vertical functional lines, every time an order moves horizontally from one department to another it runs the risk of falling between the cracks.

In addition to these horizontal gaps, a second lesson to be learned from tracking the OMC is the likelihood of vertical gaps in knowledge. In field visits to 18 different companies in vastly different industries, we invariably found a top marketing or administrative executive who would offer a simple, truncated – and inaccurate – description of the order flow. The people at the top couldn't see the details of their OMC; the people deep within the organization saw only their own individual details. And when an order moved across departmental boundaries, from one function to another, it faded from sight; no one was responsible for it or the customer.

A third lesson concerns the importance of order selection and prioritization. In fact, not all orders are created equal; some are simply better for the business than others. The best orders come from customers who are long-term, fit the company's capabilities, and offer healthy profits. These customers fall into the company's "sweet spot," a convergence of great customer need, high customer value, and good fit with what the company can offer. But in most companies, no one does order selection or prioritization. The sales force chooses the customers, and customer service representatives or production schedulers establish the priorities. In these cases, the OMC effectively goes unmanaged.

Finally, the fourth lesson we offer involves cost estimation and pricing. Pricing is the mediator between customer needs and company capabilities and a critical part of the OMC. But most companies don't understand the opportunity for or impact of order-based pricing. Pricing at the individual order level depends on: understanding the customer value generated by each order; evaluating the cost of filling each order; and instituting a system that enables the company to price each order based on its value and cost. While order-based pricing is difficult work that requires meticulous thinking and deliberate execution, the potential for greater profits is worth the effort. And by gaining control of their OMCs, managers can practice order-based pricing.

When we started our investigation of the order management cycle, we recognized first that the OMC, in fact, begins long before there is an order or a customer. What happens in the first step, *order planning*, already shows how and why bad customer service and fragmented operations can cripple a company: the people farthest from the customer make crucial decisions and open up deep disagreements between interdependent functions right from the start. The contention and internal gaming that saw in order planning is an effective early warning sign of the systemwide disagreements that plague most order management cycles.

For example, people close to the customer, either the sales force or a marketing group at company headquarters, develop a sales forecast. At the same time, a group in the operations or manufacturing function drafts a capacity plan that specifies how much money will be spent, how many people hired, and how much inventory created. And already these functional departments are at war. Lamented one production planner, "The salespeople and their forecasting 'experts' are so optimistic and so worried about late deliveries that they pad their forecasts. We have to recalculate their plans so we don't get sucked into their euphoria." From their side, marketing people counter distrust with equal distrust: "Production won't change anything, anyhow, anywhere." Ultimately, the people deepest in the organization and farthest from the customer – production planners – often develop the final forecast used to hire workers and build inventory.

The next step in the OMC is *order generation*, a stage that usually produces a gap between order generation, order planning, and later steps in the cycle. In our research, we saw orders generated in a number of ways. The sales force knocks on doors or makes cold calls. The company places advertisements that draw customers into distribution centers or retailers where they actually place an order. Or, increasingly, companies turn to direct marketing. But regardless of the specific marketing approach, the result is almost always the same: the sales and marketing functions worry about order generation, and the other functions get out of the way. Little coordination takes place across functional boundaries.

At the third step, *cost estimation and pricing*, battles erupt between engineers who do the estimating, accountants who calculate costs, a headquarters group that oversees pricing, and the field sales force that actually develops a price. Each group questions the judgment, competence, and goals of the others. Working through the organizational barriers takes time. Meanwhile, of course, the customer waits for the bid or quote, unattended.

Order receipt and entry comes next. It typically takes place in a neglected department called "customer service," "order entry," "the inside sales desk," or "customer liaison." Customer service representatives are usually either very experienced long-term employees or totally inexperienced trainees. But regardless of their experience, customer service reps are, in fact, in daily contact with customers. At the same time, these employees have little clout in the organization and no executive-level visibility in either direction. That means customer service representatives don't know what is going on at the top of the company, including its basic strategy. And top management doesn't know much about what its customer service department – the function closest to customers – is doing.

This unlinked group of customer service reps are also often responsible for the fifth step in the OMC: *order selection and prioritization*, the process of choosing which orders to accept and which to decline. Of course, the more carefully companies think through order selection and link it to their general business strategy, the more money they stand to make, regardless of physical production capacity. In addition, companies can make important gains by the way they handle order prioritization – that is, how they decide which orders receive faster, more complete attention. However, these decisions are usually made not by top executives who articulate corporate strategy but by customer service representatives who have no idea what the strategy is. While customer service reps decide which order gets filled when, they often determine which order gets lost in limbo.

At the sixth step, *scheduling*, when the order gets slotted into an actual production or operational sequence, some of the fiercest fights erupt. Here sales, marketing, or customer service usually face off with operations or production staff. The different functional departments have conflicting goals, compensation systems, and organizational imperatives: production people seek to minimize equipment changeovers, while marketing and customer service reps argue for special service for special customers.

And if the operations staff schedule orders unilaterally, both customers and their reps are completely excluded from the process. Communication between the functions is often strained at best, with customer service reporting to sales and physically separated from production scheduling, which reports to manufacturing or operations. Once again, the result is interdepartmental warfare.

Next comes *fulfillment* – the actual provision of the product or service. While the details vary from industry to industry, in almost every company this step has become increasingly complex. Sometimes, for example, order fulfillment involves multiple functions and locations: different parts of an order may be created in different manufacturing facilities and merged at yet another site, or orders may be manufactured in one location, inventoried in a second, and installed in a third. In some businesses, fulfillment includes third-party vendors. In service operations, it can mean sending individuals with different talents to the customer's site. The more complicated the assembly activity, the more coordination must take place across the organization. And the more coordination required across the organization, the greater the chance for a physical gap. The order is dropped and so is the customer. The order ends up on the floor, while different departments argue over whose fault it is and whose job it is to pick it up.

After the order has been delivered, *billing* is typically handled by people from finance who view their job as getting the bill out efficiently and making the collection quickly. In other words, the billing function is designed to serve the needs and interests of the company, not the customer. In our research, we often saw customers who could not understand a bill they had received or thought it was inaccurate. Usually the bill wasn't inaccurate, but it had been put together in a way more convenient for the billing department than for the customer. In one case, a customer acknowledged that the company provided superior service but found the billing operation a source of constant aggravation. The problem: billing insisted on sending an invoice with prices on it. But because these shipments went to subcontractors, the customer didn't want the actual prices to show. The finance function's response: how we do our invoices is none of the customer's business. Yet such a response is clearly self-serving and creates one more gap – and possibly a loss to the company – in the cycle.

In some businesses, *returns and claims* are an important part of the OMC because of their impact on administrative costs, scrap and transportation expenses, and customer relations. In the ongoing relationship with the customer, this ninth step can produce some of the most heated disagreements; every interaction becomes a zero-sum game that either the company or the customer wins. To compound the problem, most companies design their OMCs for one-way merchandise flow: outbound to the customer. That means returns and claims must flow upstream, against the current, creating logistical messes and transactional snarls – and extremely dissatisfied customers.

The last step, *postsales service*, now plays an increasingly important role in all elements of a company's profit equation: customer value, price, and cost. Depending on the specifics of the business, it can include such elements as physical installation of a product, repair and maintenance, customer training, equipment upgrading, and disposal. At this final step in the OMC, service representatives can truly get inside the customer's organization; because of the information conveyed and intimacy involved, postsales service can affect customer satisfaction and company profitability for years. But in most companies, the postsales service people are not linked to any marketing operation, internal product-development effort, or quality assurance team.

At company after company, we traced the progress of individual orders as they traveled the OMC, beginning at one end of the process where orders entered, concluding at the other end where postsales service followed up. What we witnessed was frustration, missed opportunities, dissatisfied customers, and underperforming companies. Ultimately, four problems emerged, which are tied to the four lessons discussed earlier.

• Most companies never view the OMC as a whole system. People in sales think that someone in production scheduling understands the entire system; people in production scheduling think customer service reps do. No one really does, and everyone can only give a partial description.

- Each step in the OMC requires a bewildering mix of overlapping functional responsibilities. Each step is considered the primary responsibility of a specific department, and no step is the sole responsibility of any department. But given the fact that responsibilities do overlap, many disasters occur.
- To top management, the details of the OMC are invisible. Senior executives at all but the smallest operating units simply don't understand the intricacy of the OMC. And people with the most crucial information, such as customer service reps, are at the bottom of the organization and can't communicate with the top.
- The customer remains as remote from the OMC as top management. During the process, the customer's primary activities are to negotiate price, place the order, wait, accept delivery, complain, and pay. In the middle of the OMC, they are out of the picture completely.

Of course, today top managers know that customer service and customer satisfaction are critical to a company's success. In one company after another, managers pursue the same solutions to problems that crop up with customers. They try to flatten the organization to bring themselves and nonmarketing people into direct contact with customers. But while flattening the organization is a fine idea, it's not going to solve the real problem. No matter how flat an organization gets, no matter how many different functions interact with customers face to face – or phone to phone – what the customer wants is something else. Customers want their orders handled quickly, accurately, and cost-effectively, not more people to talk to.

Here's what top managers *don't* do: they don't travel horizontally through their own vertical organization. They don't consider the order management cycle as the system that ties together the entire customer experience and that can provide true customer perspective. Yet all ten steps are closely tied to customer satisfaction. Because the OMC is an intricate network that almost guarantees problems, top management's job is to understand the system so thoroughly it can anticipate those problems before they occur. That means managers must walk up and down and from side to side, every step of the way.

[. . .]

Consider two brief case studies. One is taken from a specialty materials producer, the other from a custom capital equipment company, but both exemplify the three most common and debilitating problems that plague OMCs.

At the specialty materials company, when customers complained about order cycle time, top managers responded by increasing the work-in-process inventory. As a result, the company could meet customer specifications from semifinished goods rather than starting from scratch. At the custom capital equipment company, when customers complained about slow deliveries, this company increased its manufacturing capacity. As a result, the company always had enough capacity to expedite any order.

Both solutions pleased customers. In addition, the first solution pleased that company's marketers and the second solution pleased that company's operations department. But neither solution pleased top management because, even after several quarters, neither produced economic returns to justify the investments. In fact, both solutions only made matters worse. At the specialty materials company, marketing staff took advantage of the increased work-in-process inventory to take orders and make sales that used up that inventory but didn't generate profits. And at the capital equipment company, manufacturing staff relied on the increased capacity to meet marketing demands but allowed productivity to slide.

The next step both companies took was predictable. Top management, frustrated by the failure of its solution and concerned over continuing squabbles between departments, called on managers across the organization to rally around "making superior profits by providing top quality products and excellent service." Top management translated "top quality" and "excellent service" into catchy slogans and posters that decorated office cubicles and factory walls. It etched the "superior profit" objective into the operating budgets of higher level managers. And it formed interfunctional teams so managers could practice participative decision making in pursuit of the new, companywide goal.

At the specialty materials company, a star sales manager who had been promoted to general manager set up an interfunctional executive committee to assess quarterly revenue and profit goals. We attended one meeting of this new committee. As the general manager sat down at the head of the table to begin the meeting, he expressed concern that the division was about to miss its revenue and profit goals for the second consecutive quarter. Committee members responded by pointing at other departments or making excuses. The vice president of sales produced elaborate graphs to demonstrate that the problem was not caused by insufficient order generation. The vice president of operations produced detailed worksheets showing that many orders had come in too late in the quarter to be completed on time.

However, given their new joint responsibility for profits, both sides agreed to put aside such arguments and focus on "how to make the quarter." All agreed to ship some customer orders in advance of their due dates because those items could readily be finished from available work-in-process inventory. While this solution would delay some long cycle-time orders, the committee decided to sacrifice these orders for the moment and take them up early in the next quarter. And immediately after the meeting, committee members started executing the plan: salespeople called their customers and cajoled them to accept early delivery; manufacturing staff rescheduled the shop floor.

Because of its small size, the custom capital equipment producer didn't need such a formal mechanism for coordinating activities. The CEO simply inserted himself into the daily workings of all functional areas and insisted on hearing all customer complaints immediately. While visiting this company, we heard a customer service representative talking on the telephone to a customer who had just been told her order would be late. The customer objected and asked for an explanation. After much hemming and hawing, the rep explained that her order had been "reallocated" to another customer who needed the product more. The customer on the phone, who purchased products from the company in a relatively large volume, demanded to speak to the CEO and, under the new policy, was connected right away. When the CEO heard this important customer's complaint, he instantly plugged the order back in at the top of the priority list.

But, in spite of such heroic efforts at both companies, customer service continued to slump, and financial results did not improve. At the materials company, customers who expected later delivery of their orders received them unexpectedly early, while those who needed them early got them late. At the capital equipment company, small customers who didn't know the CEO personally or didn't understand the route to him found their orders continuously bumped. At both companies, there was no real progress toward genuine customer satisfaction, improved service, or enhanced profits. Neither company had come to terms with the three critical problems embedded in their order management cycles: horizontal and vertical gaps, poor prioritization of orders, and inaccurate cost estimation and pricing.

The specialty materials company suffered from a fundamental horizontal gap: the marketing and manufacturing departments didn't share the same priorities for customer value, order selection, and order urgency. The real solution to this problem was to encourage and reinforce an understanding between these two critical OMC elements; both the marketing and manufacturing departments needed to address how their order management cycle generated customer value and where they were dropping customer orders in the horizontal handoff. Instead the company introduced an expensive buffer to cover over the gap between the functions – a semifinished inventory – and, when that failed, it decided to sacrifice real customer service to serve its own short-term financial needs. The immediate solution, simply shipping orders based on the amount of time it would take to complete them, merely pushed the problem from one quarter to the next without addressing the system failure. When the next quarter rolls around, top management will still have to contend with horizontal gaps, a lack of order selection and prioritization, and the inability of their order flow to generate value for the customer.

The same underlying systemic problems existed at the custom capital equipment producer. However, because of the small size of the organization, this company took a simple, politically expedient solution – let the CEO decide – and superimposed it on an expensive financial solution – add manufacturing capacity. If the company suffered from vertical gaps before, where people down the trenches failed to understand the strategy developed up in the executive suite, the CEO's intervention in customer orders only made the gaps worse. The CEO's involvement didn't address the systemic problems; he merely substituted his judgment and knowledge for that of lower level employees. The detrimental effects on employee morale more than offset any immediate gains in customer appreciation. Had the CEO invested his energy in helping employees understand how each order creates customer value, has specific costs attached, and involves a certain amount of processing time – and communicated the importance of the whole OMC – he would have generated more customer satisfaction, greater employee morale, and higher profitability without adding expensive manufacturing capacity.

HOW CAN I FIX MY OMC?

It takes hard work to improve a company's order management cycle. Most successful efforts involve three basic elements: analysis, system focus, and political strategy. Each plays a different role in overall upgrading of the OMC and requires different implementation techniques, so let's look at each in turn.

1. Analysis: Draw your OMC – and chart the gaps

In the course of our research, we visited a number of companies that were actively engaged in reviewing their OMCs with an eye to improvement. But only two companies had made progress; significantly, both had begun by trying to understand the whole OMC from start to finish. And they hadn't created a diagram on a single sheet of paper or a standard report format. Rather, one of these companies had built "war rooms": two adjacent, bunker-like offices. The walls of both rooms were made of poster board coated with color-coded sheets of paper and knitting yarn that graphically charted the order flow from the first step to the last, highlighting problems, opportunities, and potential action steps. With its multiple and overlapping sheets of paper, the entire chart easily exceeded 200 feet in length.

This visual tool made it possible for different people from different functions and levels in the organization to accept the OMC as a tangible entity. Everyone could discuss the order flow with a clear and shared picture in front of them. And by representing the OMC as a visible, tangible system, the chart guaranteed that disagreements over problems would focus on facts rather than on opinions about how the OMC worked.

A second type of successful analysis requires companies to look at the OMC from the customer's point of view. For example, at one company, the inhouse measurement system found that 98% of all orders went out on time. But another detailed survey noted that only 50% of customers said they were satisfied with deliveries. The company was unable to reconcile the two reports until managers looked at the issue from the customer's angle and compared it with their own point of view. For instance, the customer survey measured the date when the customer actually received the order; but the company's internal system was based on the date when it shipped the order. If an order consisted of 100 items, and the company correctly shipped 99 of the items, the internal report recorded a 99% perfect shipment. But the customer, who needed all 100 items before work could begin, recorded the order as a complete failure. And if the order contained an incorrectly shipped item, the company did not register the mistake at all. Of course, the customer did because an incorrect item could easily interfere with his or her ability to get on with the job. Once this company recognized the difference between its perspective and the customer's, it switched to the customer's view as the basis for its tracking system.

Finally, successful companies have explicitly stated that their goals are satisfied customers, higher profits, and sustainable competitive advantage without compromising any of them. One company realized that, while it currently relied on extensive competitive bidding, it would have to start tracking its own win–loss percentages by type of customer, geography, type of order, and other relevant data to meet its larger goals. Managers could then use such data to analyze the relationship between the company's prices and its competitors as well as between volume and price. That, in turn, could translate into better price and market share and less effort wasted on unattractive or unattainable business.

System focus: put the pieces together, move across boundaries

Analyzing the order management cycle should underline this fundamental point: the OMC is a system, and executives must manage it as a system. The goal, of course, is to fit together the horizontal pieces into a unified, harmonious whole. To encourage such alignment, managers have a number of tools at their disposal. For example, through the company compensation system, managers can introduce joint reward plans that encourage employees to take a systemwide view of company performance. Or in designing performance measurements, managers can include numbers that reflect performance across boundaries or throughout the system.

Perhaps the most powerful tool managers can use is interfunctional or interdepartmental investments in projects. These expenditures not only bring different units closer together but can also result in substantial financial returns to the company. Of course in most companies, project champions drive the decisions in the capital budgeting process. Most project champions embrace projects in their own departments or functions. Projects that cross boundaries tend to be orphans because they lack champions; even with champions, such projects require difficult, time-consuming negotiations and are often deferred or fail outright. But precisely for this reason, projects that cross department boundaries can create an integrated atmosphere. When the CEO or chief operating officer personally back investments, the whole organization gets the message that these investments reflect a new perspective. Significantly, interdepartmental projects, usually underfunded for years, often deliver the greatest returns to the company in terms of real improvements and financial results.

A company's information technology system can also play an important role. Computer technology is a crucial tool for integrating many steps of the order management cycle. Direct computer links with customers and integrated internal computer systems, for example, typically result in lower costs and better analysis. And while order processing was one of the earliest activities to be computerized in many companies, it's now time to update and reengineer such systems. When managers walk through the entire OMC, they have the opportunity to ask whether each step can be improved with a computer or, perhaps, eliminated altogether given new technology and processes. With more reliable computer systems, for instance, is manual backup still required? Or can data be captured at the source to avoid repeat entry and inevitable clerical errors?

All of these human resource, management, and information technology tools reinforce the idea, represented by the OMC, that the basic work of the company takes place across boundaries. And because obsolete or unnecessary tasks hinder coordination, all pieces of the system must fit together to meet customer needs in a seamless fashion.

Political strategy: staple yourself to an order

Given that the order management cycle is critical to so many daily operating decisions, it is often at the center of all political maneuverings in a company. Realistically, OMC politics will never go away; working horizontally in a vertical organization is always difficult at best. In our research, we saw hardnosed CEOs and high-ranking divisional general managers forced to admit defeat when confronted with stonewalling functional staffs. We watched young, analytically focused managers with innovative ideas face disinterest, distrust, and selfishness – and fail miserably. The only people who can succeed at interdepartmental management are usually hardened veterans who understand company politics and can cash in favors. But even they won't succeed without visible support from the top.

One way to improve the situation in any company is to "close the loop" between the service providers and the strategy setters or, in other words, to tie the company closer together through the order management cycle. Managers should try what we did in our research: we "stapled" ourselves to an order and literally followed it through each step of the OMC. When managers do this, descending from the executive heights into the organization's lower depths, they come into contact with critical people like customer service reps and production schedulers. Reps, schedulers, order processors, shipping clerks, and many others are the ones who know fine-grained information about customer needs. For example, customers might want the product delivered in a drum rather than a bag or prefer plastic wrapping to styrofoam.

For most executives in most companies, there is simply no organizational setup for listening and responding to people at all levels. The McDonald's policy of having executives regularly work behind the counter is a worthwhile example of creating such an opportunity. Requiring top managers to work as cashiers and cooks sends a message about the company's values to all staff and enables executives to experience the OMC firsthand.

However, this idea can degenerate into an empty gesture or just another management fad. Take, for example, CEO visits to customers that become official state visits in which corporate heads discuss company relationships at a level of abstraction that has little to do with reality. In most businesses, managers can learn more from salespeople, customer service representatives, production schedulers, and shippers than from a customer's CEO.

All too often, managers who try to focus on internal conflicts directly without charting the OMC find themselves thwarted by politics and recalcitrant employees. But the wall charts and interdepartmental measurements engendered by focusing on the OMC can create an overall vision that transcends vertical politics. The customer is not involved in organizational infighting, and when a company takes on the customer's perspective, politics must take a different and more productive turn.

When companies improve their order management cycles, there are three important benefits. First and foremost, they will experience improved customer satisfaction. Companies will fill orders faster, become more accurate, and generally keep their promises to customers. A well-run OMC has a huge impact on customers: most OMCs perform worst when demand is greatest, which means that the largest number of customers experience service at its poorest quality. Fixing the OMC reverses that downward trend.

Second, interdepartmental problems will recede. When the OMC is not working well, it both reflects and causes monumental internal strife in a company. People in each department feel they are working hard to achieve their goals; they feel let down by other functions when customer service or financial performance fails to measure up. In the absence of unifying efforts and signs of improvement, the infighting can take on a life of its own and become even more divisive than the operating problems that started the battle. A systemic view helps everyone understand that all departments are interdependent.

Finally, companies will improve their financial performance. We saw companies lose sales, waste labor, and fumble investments because of poor order management cycles. Typically, companies throw money at their problems, building excess capacity, adding inventory, or increasing the body count, all of which are expensive and none of which solve the real problem. The simple fact is that when an OMC is poorly managed, greater sales, lower costs, higher prices, and smaller investments all seem impossible. But when the order management cycle works efficiently, a company can achieve these goals – and more.

NOTE

*   This chapter has been adapted from, Shapiro, B. P., Rangan, V. K. and Svikola, J. J. (1992) *Harvard Business Review*, July/August.

15

FRAMEWORKS FOR UNDERSTANDING BUSINESS PROCESS RE-ENGINEERING*

Steve Childe, Roger Maull and Jan Bennett

INTRODUCTION

The drive to improve manufacturing productivity has heightened international interest in the techniques associated with Business Process Re-engineering (BPR). Many large manufacturing companies are currently undertaking major BPR programmes throughout their international organizations.

[. . .]

While many different views of BPR and related approaches have been presented (and will be described later in this chapter), a unifying theme is the focus upon the sequence of activities which form various processes involved in doing business. This is quite different from existing improvement schemes which generally fail to go beyond the functional boundaries which exist in organizations structured along traditional lines. In BPR, a business process is seen as a horizontal flow of activities while most organizations are formed into vertical functional groupings sometimes referred to in the literature as "functional silos".

In some cases it appears that the initiative to move towards BPR originates in Information Systems (IS) departments which, because they have responsibility for the provision of information services to various business areas, already have a cross-functional perspective. Focusing the business activities around information flows represents one way of improving the process. Furthermore, IS departments may see BPR as a means of achieving the radical improvements in productivity expected, but not achieved, through the application of information systems developed using traditional analysis and design approaches. As Rhodes suggested in 1988[1] "integration is more fundamental than linking computers and unifying databases, it is a management philosophy".

The ideas underpinning the concepts of "time-based competition" and "lean production" are of considerable importance to BPR. Stalk[2] claims that time is the contemporary firm's most important competitive weapon. The exploitation of time in the manner suggested by

Stalk requires firms to slash the elapsed time involved in the performance of each of their key business processes. Time-based competition is, by its very nature, process-oriented in that it aims to reduce radically the time required for an entire process to be carried out. Concomitant benefits include increasing productivity, increasing price, reduced risks and increased market share.[3]

Lean production is defined in Womack et al.[4] as transferring:

> The maximum number of tasks and responsibilities to those workers actually adding value . . . and it has in place a system for detecting faults that quickly traces every problem, once discovered, to its ultimate cause.

The movement towards lean production cannot be made without understanding how processes operate. In the absence of such an understanding, no attempt can be made to identify added value.

BPR is also related to *Kaizen*, a process-oriented philosophy of continuous improvement from Japan. Imai[5] contrasts radical and innovative change, which is often associated with Western management, and *Kaizen* which focuses on managerial, group and individual continuous improvement. *Kaizen* does not replace or fundamentally change the status quo, however, and Imai asserts that firms should consider the radical change option as soon as *Kaizen*'s marginal value begins to decline. In turn, continuous improvement efforts should follow as soon as any programme for radical change has been initiated.

One consequence of the widespread interest in BPR and related approaches has been the emergence of a number of BPR "gurus", notably Hammer and Harrington[6]. Despite the existence of a growing body of work in the field, however, very little guidance is currently available outside the large consultancy organizations on how to carry out re-engineering programmes.

In this regard, Bartezzaghi et al.[7] have noted a general lack of conceptual models and operating tools to support any process re-engineering. Similarly, Heynes[8] cautions that, in the absence of any agreed, correct modelling techniques and languages for describing business processes, IS departments increasingly appear to be using their "mechanistic" systems development models to model business processes.

In the remainder of this article the authors will examine the nature of business processes and they will propose a means of identifying business processes in manufacturing. They will then discuss the concept of Business Process Re-engineering and present a framework for classifying types of BPR interventions.

WHAT IS A BUSINESS PROCESS?

Despite the current high profile of BPR in the UK business community, the proliferation of change programmes throughout UK commerce and industry, and a wide range of BPR consultancy offerings, companies are only now beginning to explore the central questions of "what is a business process?" and "how can I identify processes in my business?"

According to Davenport and Short,[9] a business process is:

> The logical organisation of people, materials, energy, equipment and procedures into work activities designed to produce a specified end result.

Davenport and Short also state that processes have two important characteristics. First, they have customers and second, they cross organizational boundaries and are generally independent of formal organizational structure.

Similarly Hickman[10] defines a business process as:

A logical series of dependent activities which use the resources of the organisation to create, or result in, an observable or measurable outcome, such as a product or service.

The authors would add that a business process must be initiated by and must provide results to a customer, who may be internal or external to the company.

A useful structure established by the CIM-OSA Standards Committee[11] sub-divides processes into three main areas: Manage, Operate and Support. The CIM-OSA framework regards *manage processes* as those which are concerned with strategy and direction setting as well as with business planning and control. *Operate processes* are viewed as those which are directly related to satisfying the requirements of the external customer, for example the logistics supply chain from order to delivery. These are sometimes referred to as core processes. *Support processes* typically act in support of the Manage and Operate processes. They include the financial, personnel, facilities management and information systems provision (IS) activities. This structure will be used in the next section.

The definitions are all extremely general. Furthermore they bring us no closer to establishing consensus with regard to the characteristics or identities of the key processes involved in manufacturing. There is a need for a framework upon which to identify the processes within a manufacturing company.

Definition of business processes

In the authors' view business process operates in a manner analogous to the operation of an industrial or chemical process in as much as it comprises "a series of continuous actions or operations . . . "[12] which are performed upon a commodity. It may also be regarded as a conduit along which a commodity flows. In this context, a commodity might be conceptual or material. Such commodities pass along their process conduits and are transformed, at different stages in their progress, as various operations are performed upon them. A process can therefore be identified by the type of commodity which flows through it. For example, if we regard the product development process as a conduit for a product concept, we can see from Table 15.1 that the initial concept is transformed into a completed concept as it progresses through the product development process.

In a concurrent engineering environment, the appropriate mixed-disciplinary team (which might include representatives from supplier and customer organizations) would initially agree a product specification. That specification would then be used to create a number of potential product solutions, the "best" of which would be selected for design. The product design operation would be followed by the development of an engineering prototype and so on until the finished concept emerges – a product design capable of being manufactured.

This idea of flow may be extended to other business processes. These are shown in Figure 15.1.

Table 15.1 The product development process

Input	Transformation	Output
Market/customer requirements; the initial concept for the product	Development of concept to completion	Completed concept describing the product in detail, including the design drawing and parts list and a specification of how it is to be made

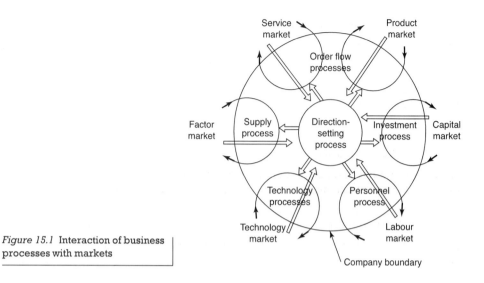

Figure 15.1 Interaction of business processes with markets

MANAGE PROCESSES

Direction setting

This process includes all high-level strategic-planning activities. It acts as an overall managing activity which takes ideas about direction based upon business and environmental information, including customer feedback, and transforms these into a set of strategies, operational goals and performance measures.

OPERATE PROCESSES

Order Flow (products)

The Order Flow process takes the customer order and transforms it into a finished product. The commodity which flows through this process is the customer's specific product requirement. This initially takes the form of an order and is transformed into a product which embodies the customer's requirement. As the order flows in one direction, money flows in the other: thus the process ends only when the product is accepted and paid for by the customer. Activities within this category may include raw material purchasing, product assembly, the production of the product, obtaining orders, delivery and installation of the product, invoicing and money receipt.

Service

This process takes the customer's requirement for a service and satisfies it by providing that service. For example the requirement could be the need to keep machines operating reliably, transformed by the service into an assurance of trouble-free performance. Activities include the management of customer enquiries and the provision and management of the necessary technical support to satisfy the customer.

SUPPORT PROCESSES

There are a considerable number of activities which are required to support the key business processes. These relate the company to its business environment, which can be thought of as a series of markets within which the company operates. These have been identified by Fine and Hax[13] as capital markets, labour markets, technology markets, factor markets and product markets. Each of these markets is addressed by the company through a business process.

Capital markets

The process attracts investment into the firm and provides benefits (typically shareholder dividends) thus maintaining the company's position in the capital market.

Labour markets

The process of recruiting, training, remunerating, motivating, appraising and retiring employees. By processing employees, the company maintains its human resources and its position with respect to the labour market.

Technology markets

The assessment and development of available technology, and the selection, installation and maintenance and disposal of plant and equipment.

Factor markets

The establishment and development of relationships with suppliers, supplier development and liaison, and the termination of relationships with suppliers no longer required. This process may also be concerned with the make-or-buy decision.

Product markets (and the market for services)

The company retains its competitive position in the market place by a process which maintains the awareness of its potential customers. This "marketing" activity may be seen as part of the operating process since it involves obtaining orders and providing service, and since the company's position in the product marketplace must ultimately depend on the way in which orders are satisfied.

WHAT IS BUSINESS PROCESS RE-ENGINEERING?

Various authors have described approaches known as Business Process Re-engineering; Business Process Redesign; Business Process Management; Business Process Improvement and Core Process Re-design. Their approaches have different characteristics in terms of the degree of change (radical or incremental), the scope of the exercise (internal or external), the potential risks and the potential benefits.

Hammer[14] states, for example, that firms can only hope to achieve radical performance improvements using Business Process Re-engineering methods which strive to "break away from the old rules about how we organise and conduct business". He states that:

Re-engineering cannot be accomplished in small or cautious steps but must be viewed as an all-or-nothing proposition.

Hammer's intervention strategy, which he has referred to as the "neutron bomb" approach to business improvement,[15] clearly exists at one extreme of a wide spectrum of opinion regarding the most appropriate BPR strategies for firms to adopt: "We'll leave the walls standing and we'll nuke everything on the inside". Indeed, an element of tension clearly exists between those who favour an incrementalist approach and those who prefer "root and branch" radicalism where business process improvement is concerned.

Aikins[16] adopts a much more IT-related position than Hammer, when he states that BPR is "the current popular term for examining an organisation's business processes and recommending automation or changes to achieve strategic goals". Similarly Gant sees BPR as simply "the redesign of processes to take advantage of the enormous potential of information technology.[17] On the other hand, Harrington's ideas on the subject[6] may be said to inhabit the more incrementalist and less IT-dominated end of the BPR opinion spectrum. He defines the concept of Business Process Improvement as:

> A systematic methodology developed to help an organisation make significant advances in the way in which its business processes operate.

A more complete representation of the spectrum of process improvement activities is presented in Figures 15.2 and 15.3. The axes on Figure 15.2 differentiate between the radical and incremental types of BPR, the potential benefits and risks to be gained from the change programme and the scope of the programme. Figure 15.3 depicts four of the functional "silos" which may be found in a typical business organization. For the purpose of this article we have not named them, but, for example, they could represent the marketing, design, manufacturing and assembly functions. The horizontal box represents a process which flows across each of the four functions. For example this could be the "Order Flow" process.

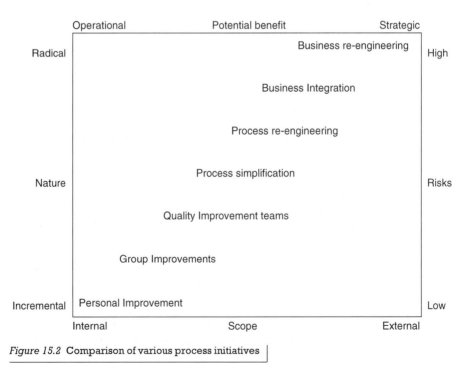

Figure 15.2 Comparison of various process initiatives

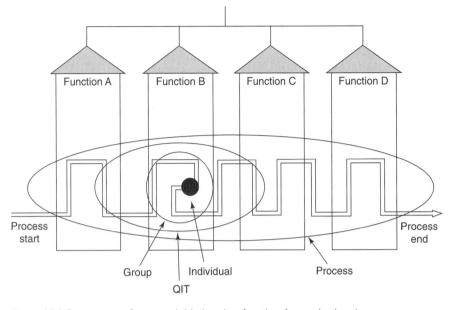

Function A   Function B   Function C   Function D

Process start   Process end

Group   Individual   Process

QIT

Figure 15.3 Processes and process initiatives in a functional organization

The scope of change in the bottom left hand corner of Figure 15.2 is restricted to personal improvement. This type of change, where an individual within a function seeks to improve his or her part of the process, is depicted on Figure 15.3 by the dark circle. Such improvements are essentially small in scale, internal in scope, low in risk and operational outlook.

Group improvement is represented on Figure 15.3 by the circle within the design function. Here a group of individuals may come together to improve the manufacturability of their PCB designs, for example. Such change tends to be wider in scope than individual improvement, however it is still essentially operational in nature, entails minimal risk to the organization and can be regarded as incremental.

The work undertaken by Quality Improvement Teams (QITs) is depicted in Figure 15.3 by the small ellipse that extends beyond the localized small group improvement activity and into other functional areas of the firm. QITs typically have the freedom to consider customer/supplier relationships as well as their own process. QITs are often able to bring about some radical changes, however they tend to be constrained by existing organizational boundaries and to be centred upon a particular business function.

Process Simplification (PS) may regarded as the first real type of process-based change. PS focuses on the whole process. Often a Process Improvement Team (PIT) will have been established whose job is to analyse the whole process for such non value-added activities as storage and inspection, and who will be seeking to remove these activities. The benefits of this type of change are related to Price of Non-Conformance (PONC) in the process and typically would be around 20 per cent of the cost of the process. However in most organizations the establishment of PITs is expensive and time-consuming often requiring external consultancy help.

Process Improvement (à la Harrington) and Business Process Re-engineering (à la Hammer) again focus on the whole process but have a wider scope than the removal of waste. Harrington takes an incremental view whilst Hammer's approach is more radical, and questions whether the *status quo* is relevant to the future system. A reduced number of activities, organizational and job redesign and new developments in information technology such as Document Image Processing (DIP) or expert systems may be used. This type of change seeks to reduce the number of activities by up to 90 per cent and addresses real strategic benefits.

Business integration focuses primarily on growth outside the organization through either vertical, or more probably, horizontal integration along the supply chain. Such change is strategic in nature and radical in orientation with the potential for substantial gain.

Business re-engineering (rather than Business Process Re-engineering) looks at the improvement of the (already process-focused) organization to exploit its capabilities in a way which leads to the growth of business in new and different areas. Stalk *et al.* define capabilities-based competition as the ability to capitalize upon "the organisational practices and business processes in which capabilities are rooted".[18] Such a capabilities focus identifies a set of strengths in core processes which enables companies to compete in entirely different ways in a competitive environment.

BENEFITS OF ADOPTING A BPR APPROACH

Kaplan and Murdock[19] have identified several benefits to thinking of an organization in terms of its core processes. They maintain that the adoption of such a viewpoint helps a firm to link its strategic goals to its key processes. These include the complete chain of organizational activities independent of departments, geography, cultures. They also embrace suppliers and customers.

The process-oriented viewpoint emphasizes cross-functional performance rather than encouraging departmental optimization and the consequent system-wide sub-optimization. It also encourages the firm to focus on business results, particularly where total lead times are concerned. Process focus also offers a company the opportunity to re-engineer the process or radically reduce the number of activities it takes to carry out a process, often through the application of IT. This in turn provides opportunities to reduce the cost base and/or improve service levels.

The process-focused approach concentrates first on identifying the business processes, then analysing and re-engineering each process. Thus BPR techniques should enable firms to:

- define business processes and their internal or external customers;
- model and analyse the processes that support these products and services;
- highlight opportunities for both radical and incremental business improvements through the identification and removal of waste and inefficiency;
- implement improvements through a combination of IT and good working practices;
- establish mechanisms to ensure continuous improvement of the redesigned processes.

MANAGING THE CHANGE TO A BUSINESS PROCESS ORIENTATION

Many companies have been seen to approach process-based analysis from a range of starting points. Pressure for a firm to re-engineer its business processes may surface in a variety of guises:

- *Well-known problem* A process may have reached breakage point when customers are lost through slow processing, for example of customer orders, or when the process ceases to function properly.
- *Convenient anchor* Many companies are currently adopting BPR as an add-on to existing TQM programmes that have "run out of steam".

- *Add-on* Some companies are using BPR to identify the potential for outsourcing, or as a prerequisite to activity-based costing programmes.
- *IT-driven* The authors are familiar with a number of BPR programmes which are being driven by IT departments seeking to identity a new banner under which to relaunch IT programmes. This often stems from substantial company-wide dissatisfaction with traditional IT approaches. Such programmes often begin by purchasing, for example comprehensive, parameter-driven software or Document Image Processing without a focus on first simplifying the process.

Once the firm has identified a need for process re-engineering, it may choose to introduce BPR using several different approaches. These include:

- *Top-down re-structuring* In this case the firm uses the process concept to superimpose horizontal work flows upon a functionally-orientated organization.
- *Green-field site* Here the firm creates a new process-oriented organization at a new site whilst gradually running down its existing functionally-oriented organization.
- *Bottom-up re-structuring* Here the firm might use Process Improvement Teams based around traditional quality programmes.

The type of change will also vary across BPR programmes. Smith[20] points out that there are two types of change:

- *Incremental* This has the features of being low risk, easy to manage, less disruptive in the short run, and is based on the belief that sustained effort leads to greater overall impact;
- *Radical* This is based on the belief that incremental change is non-change, particularly when the expected "half-life" of senior management is taken into account. Exponents of radical change believe that the only way to *really* change the status quo in any organization is by subjecting it to intense periods of disruption.

In business process re-engineering terms, the distinction between radical and incremental change presented above mirrors the tension between the more radical approaches advocated in BPR and the incremental view of business process improvement embodied in the Japanese continuous improvement philosophies.

Many authors allude to this distinction when specifying their approach to BPR. Gulden and Reck,[21] for example, distinguish between quality improvement techniques which are a "daily dosage for a chronic condition" and re-engineering which is a "strong medicine that should only be used for an acute condition".

Different approaches to business improvement tend to emphasize one or the other type of change. Davenport and Short[9] advocate radical change, for example, whilst Harrington[6] and many authors on the subject of quality recommend the adoption of an incremental approach.

While continuous improvement activities can be highly effective in improving products, skills and techniques within a company, Imai[5] notes that firms should consider the radical change option as soon as the marginal value of continuous improvement begins to decline. In turn, continuous improvement efforts should follow as soon as any programme for radical change has been initiated.

The major difficulty associated with attempting to implement a programme of radical change lies in the sheer scale of change being advocated. Such programmes usually require a heavy financial commitment on the part of the firm, but senior management, inhibited by the long payback periods involved, may be reluctant to proceed. Incremental change programmes require very little financial outlay and are thus highly attractive to firms seeking ways of improving their business performance.

DISCUSSION AND CONCLUSIONS

Despite the widespread interest in Business Process Re-engineering, there remains a significant lack of agreement, both among academics and industry practitioners, over the meaning of the term "process" and how to define processes in a manufacturing organization. The authors have addressed this issue by improving the definition of a business process and by presenting in outline some examples of business processes. The article has also described the principles of BPR and the benefits such an approach may offer. However there remain a substantial number of key issues facing researchers in the BPR field. For example, many companies are addressing BPR as an extension to Total Quality Management (TQM). In the authors' view TQM is an extremely useful technique for focusing attention on the internal and external customer, indeed focus on the process is a key TQM concept. However, TQM-led programmes are usually associated with continuous improvement efforts and not with the radical change brought about by re-engineering. TQM may thus represent a necessary but insufficient condition for a successful BPR programme.

Many companies also address BPR through IT and it is the authors' view that IT is an enabler to the re-engineered process – and indeed any re-engineering programme must take account of the tremendous advantages offered by such technologies as Document Image Processing, Expert Systems and 4GLs. However, the focus of attention should be on simplifying the process before determining IT requirements.

Finally, any company attempting to use BPR will find itself in a dilemma, either to train in-house staff or to buy in external expertise. For those buying consultancy time, there are a substantial number of vendors available. Those wishing to run the project internally will need to develop a method for delivering BPR that is robust and repeatable.

The authors believe that there is substantial commonality of processes across industry types. The strategic capability may vary. For example, engineer-to-order companies will have strengths in the product development process, make-to-stock companies will have to focus attention on the whole logistics supply chain. Many of the benefits could be enhanced through the development of a reference model of key processes, which could then be used to speed up the analysis stage of the BPR programme.

NOTE

* This chapter has been adapted from, Childe, S.J., Maull, R.S. and Bennett, J., "Frameworks for Understanding Business Process Re-engineering", *International Journal of Operations and Production Management*, Vol. 14 No. 12, pp. 22–34.

REFERENCES

1 Rhodes, D., "Integration Challenge for Medium and Small Companies", *Proceedings of the 23rd Annual Conference of British Production and Inventory Control Society*, BPICS, Birmingham, 2–4 November 1988, pp. 153–66.

2 Stalk, G. and Hout, T.M., *Competing against Time: How Time Based Competition is Reshaping Global Markets*, The Free Press, 1990.

3 Stalk, G., Presentation given at 8th World Productivity Congress, Stockholm, 26th May 1993.

4 Womack, J.P., Jones, D.T. and Roos, D., *The Machine that Changed the World*, Rawson Associates, New York, 1990.

5 Imai, M., *Kaizen: The Key to Japan's Competitive Success*, McGraw-Hill, 1986.

6 Harrington, H.J., *Business Process Improvement*, McGraw-Hill, 1992.

7 Bartezzaghi, E., Spina, G. and Verganti, R., "Modelling the Lead-Time of the Operations Processes", in Johnston, R. and Slack, N.D.C. (Eds), *Service Operations*, Operations Management Association UK, 1993, pp. 117–24.

8 Heynes, C., Presentation at British Computer Society BPR Conference, London, 29 June 1993.

9 Davenport, T.H. and Short, J.E., "The New Industrial Engineering: Information Technology and Business Process Redesign", *Sloane Management Review*, Summer 1990.

10 Hickman, L.J., "Technology and Business Process Re-engineering: Identifying Opportunities for Competitive Advantage", British Computer Society CASE Seminar on Business Process Engineering, London, 29 June 1993.

11 CIM-OSA Standards Committee, *CIM-OSA Reference Architecture*, AMICE ESPRIT, 1989.

12 Hawkins, J.M.H. (Compiler), *Oxford Paperback Dictionary*, Oxford University Press, Oxford, 1984.

13 Fine, C.H. and Hax, A.C., *Designing a Manufacturing Strategy*, WP No. 1593–84, Sloan School of Management, MIT, USA, 1984.

14 Hammer, M., "Reengineering Work: Don't Automate, Obliterate", *Harvard Business Review*, July–August 1990, pp. 104–12.

15 Hammer, M., in interview with Vogl, A.J., "appearing as "The age of Re-engineering", *Across the Board*, June 1993.

16 Aikins, J., "Business Process Reengineering: Where Do Knowledge-based Systems Fit?", *IEEE Expert*, Vol. 8 No. 1, February 1993, p. 2.

17 Gant, J.G., "Work Management: The Next Step in Imaging", *Chief Information Officer Journal*, Fall 1992, pp. 60–4.

18 Stalk, G., Evans, P. and Shulman, L.E., "Competing Capabilities: The New Rules of Corporate Strategy", *Harvard Business Review*, March-April 1992.

19 Kaplan, R.B. and Murdock, L., "Rethinking the Corporation: Core Process Redesign", *The McKinsey Quarterly*, No. 2, 1991.

20 Smith, K.K., *Philosophical Problems in Thinking about Organisational Change in Change in Organisations*, Jossey Bass, 1982.

21 Gulden, G.K. and Reck, R.H., "Combining Quality and Reengineering Efforts for Process Excellence", *Information Strategy: The Executives Journal*, Vol. 8 No. 3, Spring 1992, pp. 10–16.

16

BUSINESS PROCESS RE-ENGINEERING – CONTRASTING WHAT IT IS WITH WHAT IT IS NOT*

Clive Holtham

INTRODUCTION

It is argued here that BPR does have some core concepts that are valuable contributions to the evolution of management thought. However, these concepts are surrounded by subsidiary material that is either not novel, not necessary, or is even potentially antagonistic to the core concepts. BPR as evangelised may well be largely unremarkable or internally inconsistent. But this does not mean that all aspects of BPR should therefore be rejected. In looking to the future, there is in fact a need to correlate the core BPR concepts and other managerial concepts.

There are several recent articles that review BPR in some depth from theoretical perspectives (e.g. Grint, 1993; Earl and Khan, 1994). The aim here is to supplement these articles with a focus on some specific areas:

- The life-cycle of BPR as a managerial innovation
- BPR roots; the unrecognised debts
- BPR maps – needs, application and capability
- Process and task
- Process versus structure
- Definitely not BPR
- The key to BPR?
- A European perspective

The conventional definition of BPR

The text most widely used in business-oriented discussions of BPR is Hammer and Champy (1993) so this represents a well-known starting point. Their much-quoted definition of

BPR is the one that will be assumed here, although acceptance of the definition does not necessarily imply acceptance of any other aspect of their text:

> the fundamental rethinking and radical redesign of business processes to achieve dramatic improvements in critical, contemporary measures of performance, such as cost, quality, service and speed.

LIFE CYCLE OF MANAGEMENT INNOVATIONS – WHITHER BPR?

This paper assumes that BPR as an evangelical movement has a strictly limited life (Lawrence, 1994). The history of any management innovation can be divided into five phases; the actual or predicted dates for BPR are shown in Figure 16.1.

At the time of writing, Phase 3 is under way. Most of the major management consultancies and product vendors have already completed Phase 2 – rolling out either a *bona fide* product, or at least amending their sales and marketing material to refer to BPR. However, both consultancies and conference organisers already report a more discriminating audience for the BPR concept.

Explaining the success of BPR as concept – encapsulation

The great achievement of the evangelical advocates of BPR is not that they have invented something whose components are innovative. Not a single component of BPR is in any way innovative. Their first achievement is that they have coined a phrase which seems to strike a chord with managers across the world – what Grint (1993) describes as 'resonance'. The second achievement is that they have packaged and presented already existing concepts in a way that stimulates the interest of managers.

The great success of BPR is in creating a phrase, and related content, that encapsulates a number of important managerial themes. It is essentially a success of sales and marketing of existing managerial ideas, rather than contributing new ideas. There is an increasing trend to write-off BPR for this very reason, e.g.: 'We have known all this for 20 years' 'We should have been doing this anyway in the customer service process'.

	Stage	BPR
1	Initial research and conception.	to 1990
2	Conversion of academic concepts into consulting-oriented products for enthusiastic mass-market promotion and consumption.	1990–1993
3	Idea gains corporate momentum; negative experiences and conceptual problems begin to emerge.	1993–1995
4	Enthusiasts begin to run out of steam. Dramatic benefits fail to emerge consistently. New competitors emerge.	1995–1996
5	Falls into disrepute and disuse.	1996–1998

Figure 16.1 Five phases for BPR

LIBRARY
BISHOP BURTON COLLEGE
BEVERLEY HU17 8QG

Also, the fact that great management evangelists of the 1980s – Peters and Waterman – used as case studies some companies that subsequently performed extremely badly – creates in the current climate an in-built resistance by some managers who are now particularly sceptical of fads.

Because of these reservations and although the term BPR has only a strictly limited life, its valuable features will only be sustained or even remembered if they are clearly understood, and if these are considered independently from the sales and promotion for evangelistic BPR.

BPR ROOTS

To identify some of the enduring features of BPR it is necessary to return to its roots. Since it is not made up of original components, the valuable features are also present in its roots.

There are essentially two forms of roots. The first are the deep roots, the underlying and for all practical purposes invisible ancestors of BPR. The second one, the shallow roots, clear and visible but of much more recent vintage.

Perhaps surprisingly, given Hammer and Champy's persistent negative references to him, there is little doubt that Frederick Taylor was an active proponent of radical change. He is unfairly caricatured as preoccupied with task optimisation. He was naturally concerned with the pressing managerial priorities at the turn of the century. Nevertheless, he was regarded as highly revolutionary in his day, and believed as strongly as any BPR consultant in the importance of processes breaking down traditional organisational structures. Scientific management is actually one of the deep roots of BPR.

But for more direct lineage of BPR, reference can be made to the post-second world war management theorists. These can be divided into two separate groups. First, there was the quality movement, and in particular Duran. Second, there were the systems theorists, and a particularly relevant member of this group was Stafford Beer.

The unrecognised debt – breakthrough management

One of the major criticisms of the work of Hammer and Champy is their lack of apparent recognition of their historical antecedents. This criticism is much less valid of Davenport who includes a useful, if incomplete, review of antecedents. The basic concept of re-engineering was most visibly coined by Juran (1964). Although he used the term 'breakthrough' instead of 're-engineering', there is little doubt that his meaning is virtually the same. It is perhaps not surprising that an updated second edition of this neglected classic of management literature is reported to be imminent.

Juran summarises the task of management into two parts – control and breakthrough.

> Control means staying on course, adherence to standard, prevention of change. . . . We can become so pre-occupied with meeting targets that we fail to challenge the target itself.
>
> Breakthrough means change, a dynamic, decisive movement to new, higher levels of performance.

What is interesting about this is that Juran is concerned with the whole organisation, whether in the relatively steady state for which the control approach is valid, or whether radical change is needed via breakthrough management. One of the major weaknesses of BPR is its lack of a higher-level framework of relevance to most ongoing tasks. It is fascinating that the insights of Juran in this area have essentially been forgotten or ignored by later management writers.

It is also noteworthy that Juran's text did not make anywhere near the impact when it came out in the 1960s as might have been expected from its intrinsic worth. One of the reasons for this is that in the economic climate of that time, with full employment and the post-war economic growth still in train, there were not in general the same pre-occupations as found in the 1990s – of dealing with constraint and of survival. Juran's work on breakthrough was full of insight, but the potential audience did not see this as a central issue at that time.

The unrecognised debt – viable systems

At the same time as Juran was developing his breakthrough concept, there was a parallel set of work under way on systems thinking. It was initiated in pure science, particularly biology, but its commercial application arose out of some of the perceived pressures of managing major scientific projects, such as the US space programme, managing major infrastructure issues such as urban planning, and the conduct of war, most specifically by the USA in Vietnam.

In the words of the founder of general systems theory, Ludwig von Bertalanffy (1968):

While in the past science tried to explain observable phenomena by reducing them to an interplay of elementary units investigated independently of each other, conceptions appear in contemporary science that are concerned with what is somewhat vaguely termed with 'wholeness', i.e. problems of organization, phenomena not dissolvable into local events, dynamic interactions manifested in the difference of behavior of parts.

This belief in wholeness was implicitly very critical of naive management theory based on purely hierarchical management principles (Senge, 1990).

In the UK, cybernetician Stafford Beer was particularly critical of the classical managerial hierarchies – he dismissed them as 'mechanisms for apportioning blame' (Beer, 1981). Through his Viable System Model (VSM) he was searching for a vehicle that would enable an holistic perspective of the organisation in its environment, that would recognise the needs for autonomy in operating units, and which would reconcile the inevitable tensions between central and front-line units.

Why the roots were passed over

So some of the real roots of BPR were well established by the end of the 1960s. Why then did it take more than 20 years for these ideas to resurface in the mainstream perception of the practising manager? Several hypotheses can be put forward:

1 In the case of the systems approach, it never really became endorsed through widespread practical success. Indeed it became associated either with high profile perceived failures (see Lilienfeld, 1976) such as the application of systems thinking in the Department of Defense or urban management.
2 According to David Norton,[1] in the 1970s US businesses became increasingly function-alised, and in this climate there was simply no demand for systemic solutions that ran across functional boundaries.
3 The systems approaches were not presented in sufficiently simplistic terms. The packaging and presentation betrayed the underlying rigour of the approaches. Many managers perceived them as hard or demanding and preferred to search for more simplistic approaches such as those subsequently developed by Peters and Waterman (1982).

THE BPR MAPS – NEED, APPLICATION AND CAPABILITY

One of the weaknesses of BPR evangelists is that they are relatively silent on situations which are not BPR. In order to focus managerial thinking about BPR, we have found it useful to develop two grids or maps which set out some of the very basic considerations about the applicability of BPR to any given organisation and its processes. The first, Figure 16.2 contrasts the need for BPR with whether BPR is actually being applied or not. An early question to ask at this point is what proportion of organisations will, at any one time, fall into the 'Need BPR' category.

A starting point for the need for BPR is to ask how often does any organisation need to undertake 'radical redesign of business processes to achieve dramatic improvements'. The straightforward answer is 'Not very often'. In business, as in economic and social life, it is simply not viable to have revolutions on a regular or continuous basis. It can be expected that there will be periods of radical change interspersed with periods of greater stability. It may well be that this stability is accompanied by intense self-criticism and aggressive continuous improvement programmes, but this is not the same as continuous revolution, and approaches other than BPR are needed for these periods.

As a rule of thumb, it is difficult to see how any individual organisation can fundamentally and radically redesign itself more than about once every five years, give or take a year. This is not least because the process of radical transformation can itself take two to three years from conception to full implementation. One can develop from this the idea that at any given time about twenty per cent of organisations, or processes within a given organisation, might be candidates for radical redesign.

The converse is that eighty per cent are not. They may be candidates for process redesign or for continuous improvement, but they are not candidates for BPR. At any one time, the majority of organisations do not need BPR, and particular attention therefore needs to be directed to the Don't Need/Do Apply quadrant. It is much quoted that fifty to seventy per cent of re-engineering projects fail to achieve the dramatic results intended. It can be surmised that a good proportion of these failures are actually organisations for whom BPR was an inappropriate approach in the first place.

One of the problems for BPR consultants, is that there may be marketing and business pressures to configure an organisation's problems into a BPR perspective. It also has to be said that there are many executives who are frustrated by the accidental accretion of non-value added activities in the organisation. Such executives are emotionally highly attracted to the idea of radical change, and of business revolution, to enable radical and rapid pruning of unnecessary activities.

Even if an organisation needs BPR, it may not be currently undertaking it (Do Need/Don't Apply). These organisations need to address the barriers to BPR, and more particularly whether they have any reasonable chance of overcoming those barriers. One of the

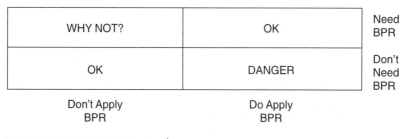

Figure 16.2 Need and application

HOW TO DEVELOP?	OK	Need BPR
OK	DANGER	Don't Need BPR
LOW	HIGH	

MANAGEMENT CAPABILITY FOR BPR

Figure 16.3 Need and managerial capability

most clear-cut and important barriers is the level of managerial capability, and this is the focus of the second map or grid. This contrasts the need for BPR with managerial capability.

Once again the Danger cell is present – carrying out BPR because the managerial capability exists rather than because it is appropriate.

The top left hand cell of Figure 16.3 highlights a key issue for many organisations – Need BPR/Low Capability. In these circumstances there may be a temptation to use external resources to lead the BPR effort. External resources can be invaluable to support a BPR effort but they can never lead it.

PROCESS AND TASK

There is great confusion over what a process is. Different BPR advocates have different definitions, for example. Hammer and Champy define a process as:

A collection of activities that takes one or more kinds of output and creates an input that is of value to the customer.

For Davenport (1993) it is:

A specific ordering of work activities across time and space, with a beginning, an end, and clearly identified inputs and outputs: a structure for action.

While these definitions quite legitimately include non-task or non-functional orientated processes, in fact they also cover task and functionally based processes as well. It seems that the definition of a process is defined at such an abstract level that the definition becomes almost meaningless, and hence the need to fall back on negative definitions – non-task or non-function activities – instead. Many of the publicised examples of business processes that have been re-engineered are not very far from conventional departmental or functional redesign – when the verbiage and hype are stripped away.

PROCESS VERSUS STRUCTURE

Process can be contrasted with structure or function. A focus on process places relatively little, or no, emphasis on current organisational and functional structure. But it needs to be recognised that one of the alternatives to BPR is extensive structural change, and this latter is actually a more attractive option to many managers.

Most managers in business have had careers in organisations dominated by structural considerations. Many managers in the UK have educational and career backgrounds rooted in a specific profession such as finance, marketing or production.

They may well be familiar with developing and changing processes that are specific to their own professional area. But they will be much less familiar with across-business processes.

In reality managers are much more familiar with changing structure than they are with changing process. There are many businesses where organisational structures are changed frequently; such organisations can seem to be in an almost constant state of structural change.

There are always valid reasons for changing structure: changes in the marketplace, in the components of a business, in the individuals available, and responses to budget cuts. However, it needs to be understood that often structures are changed for quite different underlying reasons (even where some of the valid reasons are overtly put forward to justify the change).

There are two hidden reasons for structural change.

1 Changing the organisational structure sends an explicit message to the organisation that something will be different from now on. This could be regarded as part of the unfreezing process in organisational change. This can be described as 'symbolic structural change'.
2 More worrying is the type of change that is often associated with crisis. The organisation is under-performing. Costs are not under control. Sales are falling. The owners or directors decide 'something has to be done'. They will expect something to be done and – more critically – they will expect something to be seen to be done. The executives running the business (old or new) are now under pressure. Something has to be done, and done fast. They need to tackle something that can be tackled.

   Hence the popularity of structural change. It can actually be done. It can be seen to be done. It can be justified by valid reasons. It carries an element of symbolic change. It can be done fairly quickly.

But in reality there could be immense problems with this type of structural change, which could be described as 'can-do structural change'. Its focus is short-term. There can rarely, if ever, be any clear demonstration of the business benefits of the change, with the exception of cost reductions. But the cost reductions could well be achieved without structural change.

Can-do structural change, especially when carried out repeatedly, consumes vast amounts of human time and effort. It increases the insecurity of people in the organisation (sometimes this is an explicit objective). It focuses the business on internal administration, not external customer service.

It needs to be appreciated that *process change is actually competing with structural change*. On the surface, process change is considerably less attractive to many managers than Can-do structural change.

- Process change takes some time to implement.
- Process change is often almost invisible externally during the planning stages.
- Whereas structural change can be directly associated with, and credited to, senior executives, process change is the result of many people's effort and can more rarely give personal credit.

Now although the outcome of process change can be very radical, including radical effects on the organisational structure, at the time the process change is initiated the form of such structural changes cannot be precisely predicted.

In the current business environment, senior executives may only be in a particular post for two to three years. So the idea of embarking on process change with unpredictable outcomes, a relatively long gestation period, and no immediate credit to that executive, is not necessarily a comfortable one.

Too often the reluctance of senior executives to sponsor process change is interpreted in terms of inertia, fears about their own job, or active resistance to change. All these have some truth, but the underlying reluctance may be far more to do with how much credit executives will get, and how quickly they will get it.

Structure can be seen; process is difficult to see

There are a variety of reasons why an organisation needs a formal structure. Examples are: accountability, external and internal comprehensibility, resource allocation and providing a basis for remuneration.

A formal structure gives a degree of security to individuals. They know where they fit in. Above all an organisational structure can be embedded in a chart – it is physically visible. Names can be attached to function. It does not matter that the chart is only one representation of organisational reality, and not necessarily the most important one. By contrast, processes are much more amorphous, even though they too can be charted. It is difficult or impossible to show exactly where any given individual fits into a process chart, especially with multi-functional teams.

For those who have grown up in organisations dominated by structure, it is a huge psychological leap to move to a process orientation. It is still necessary to examine how to provide a degree of security in a process-driven organisation comparable with that in a structure-driven one.

DEFINITELY NOT BPR

Many of those who have joined the BPR bandwagon are advocating solutions where the term BPR is used in association with their product or service. Much of this is at best peripherally associated with BPR, and at worst has no logical connection to BPR at all. This can be described as 'definitely not BPR'.

Software re-engineering led change

The term 're-engineering' is an older term than 'business process re-engineering'. In the 1980s it was used particularly to describe the replacement of long-standing computer systems with more up-to-date hardware or software technologies. The terms 're-engineering' and 'software re-engineering' were commonly used, which directly related to the long-standing phrase 'software engineering' (Spurr, 1993).

This earlier use of the term software re-engineering should not have caused any problems when the concept of BPR was promulgated, but unfortunately it has. There has been some tendency for academics and consultants, predominantly with a computer science background, to use the terms BPR and software re-engineering almost interchangeably. The apparent logic underpinning this interchangeability is:

1 Software re-engineering is an important part of re-engineering computer systems.
2 Re-engineered computer systems are often an important part of BPR.
3 Therefore software re-engineering is often an important part of BPR (or even identical to it).

The fallibility of this logic is fairly clear. There is no dispute that re-engineering of computer systems is one of the elements required to implement BPR, sometimes representing a very significant element. But the confusion between software re-engineering and BPR is now so great in the quarters identified above that it is most straightforward to describe software re-engineering as: 'definitely not BPR'.

Technology-initiated change

Very few of the successful case studies in BPR have ever been initiated out of the new opportunities offered by IT (or technologies generally). Once again, this is not to say that BPR implementation will not draw on these technologies. However, the development of technologies such as workflow, groupware or document image processing have no *a priori* connection to the need to re-engineer business processes. Therefore they also fall to the category of: 'definitely not BPR'.

Tools-led change

There has been an explosion in computer-based tools to support BPR, plus considerable re-badging or re-positioning of existing tools so that they can be perceived to support BPR. Many such tools are invaluable in BPR implementation. However, they can play no part in the initiation of BPR and so they are: 'definitely not BPR'.

This harsh categorisation of 'definitely not BPR' is a direct response to exaggerated claims made for software re-engineering for technology-initiated change and for tools-initiated change. Such exaggeration actually harms the genuine claims in support of specific aspects of BPR which can be made for all three approaches (Huckvale and Ould, 1993).

The relationship between IT and BPR

BPR does not absolutely require any use of IT at all. However, one of the distinctive features of BPR is the way that IT is almost invariably used to 'informate' in Zuboff's terminology – to reconstruct the nature of work. IT is a key feature of implementing BPR, but its revolutionary possibilities in reconstructing the nature of work has led to deep confusion amongst some IT practitioners and consultants.

Misconception – business process versus process in computer science

One of the greater misfortunes in the analysis of BPR is that the term 'process' has already been used to some degree in the fields of computer science and software engineering. There are, once again, academics and consultants in these fields who have, for example, developed methodologies and computer-based tools for 'analysing business processes'.

There are people in these fields who have latched on to the phrase BPR, with its clear link to strategic business success, and have re-positioned their methodologies to appear directly related to BPR.

This misconception may not always be deliberate, but it is unfortunate. It is certainly the case that such methodologies and tools can be useful in the process of implementing BPR. So too are interviews and meetings. It is as ridiculous to equate computer science-oriented methodologies and tools with BPR, as it is to suggest that interviews and meetings are also its equivalents.

The difficult and dominant issues of BPR are the strategic business issues, the need for revolution, people issues, business processes, and the capability of the organisation to go through a revolution. Methodologies and tools can be very important, but they are not of primary importance in the way some of the above issues tend to be. So it is particularly facile to suggest that they can by themselves be drivers of BPR.

Misconception – Business Process Redesign

In Venkatraman's model (1991), Business Process Redesign is one level of the revolutionary approach. It is a level that focuses more on the internal than network redesign or business reorientation. Again unfortunately, some IT-based advocates have used this term for the mere upgrading or replacing of existing computer systems.

Re-engineering the re-engineering process

Second-grade management consultants see BPR as a wonderful marketing opportunity – and some of them have been proved only too correct. The problem is not, of course, the second-grade consultant. It is the business unit managers who hire these consultants. It needs to be made crystal clear that business process re-engineering – if it is genuinely innovative – requires radical change to the consultancy process. If BPR on a business can lead to eighty per cent cost reductions, a reasonable suggestion must be that effective BPR consultancy should lead to eighty per cent reductions in consultancy costs (or four-hundred per cent better value from the same consultancy costs).

THE KEY TO BPR?

In having presented on the theme of BPR to many hundreds of practising managers in several countries, one is struck by the desire of at least a significant minority of these managers to discover the central core of BPR, the big idea, the specific key to unlock the process of business transformation in their organisation.

If it was possible to identify such a key, it would undoubtedly be the combination of:

- A weak or disastrous level of current performance.
- A charismatic, hard driving newly appointed chief executive, who can articulate the new vision, and then successfully set in train the whole range of practical implementation steps necessary.

The problem with this key is that relatively few organisations can either manoeuvre or accidentally develop this combination.

The majority of organisations are not actually sufferers from weak or disastrous performance levels. It may be, as external advisers like to emphasise in marketing their services, that weakness and disaster are only just around the corner. But it seems to be far more persuasive in most organisations if it has already happened, than if it is a future theoretical possibility.

There is then the question of the appointment of the new chief executive. The weak performance may well have precipitated the demise of the previous chief executive. But there is no guarantee that appointment of the new leader, with the personality characteristics listed above, will itself lead to the necessary changes being successfully implemented.

The new chief executive may well be able, over time, to force through a number of top-level changes in personnel to create a new or revamped top team that has the will and competence to secure the new vision. But equally, they may not be able to create quite the team needed, and overt or covert internal resistance can then thwart the radical changes necessary.

There is also an issue related to the style and personalities of the workforce generally. It is one thing to create a vision of a new, process-led, flexible and empowered workforce, but many of the existing workforce may be unhappy with such a vision. They may well prefer functionally-based, hierarchical, stable environments. Even organisations that have moved entirely to the process-led approach, will be the first to admit that:

1 They lost a number of staff at once who had no desire to be part of such an approach.
2 There is a significant minority, perhaps twenty to forty per cent of the workforce, who would strongly prefer to return to the traditional ways.

It is therefore ironic that some of the classic BPR case studies relate not to the re-engineering of existing businesses, but rather the creation of startup organisations that embody a process approach. An early example was the Batterymarch fund management organisation; another was the Midland Bank subsidiary First Direct.

CONCLUSION – A EUROPEAN PERSPECTIVE

The concepts of business process design or business process re-engineering are essentially North American concepts. They may, or may not, be capable of being transplanted to European business. But it is advisable to begin from a perspective of scepticism and caution. It should not be automatically and (it has to be said) somewhat naively assumed that American management thought is relevant outside America; indeed there are even doubts about the extent to which the principles are valid within America itself.

One is often struck, when listening to American management speakers in Europe, how insensitive they are to the different history, culture and style found in Europe. As in the media and other areas, it is simply assumed that Europe is like America except most of the people speak different languages.

For example, in a German language article on BPR (Behrens and Groothuis, 1994), the head of Siemens, Heinrich von Pierer, commented:

> I don't feel completely comfortable with the radical theses of Mr. Hammer. Our employees are not neutrons, but people. That's why dialogue is important.
>
> [my translation]

There is not the space here to introduce the detailed content of a European approach to BPR. But on a preliminary view, it needs to be rooted in distinctive European managerial features:

1 Acceptance of the humanistic and holistic stream in European thought, in contrast to the more mechanistic and fragmented US approach.
2 Promotion of the concept of collaboration, between levels in the organisation, across organisations, between supplier and customer, and also across national boundaries.

The core elements of BPR have value beyond the evangelical North American approach, and BPR has value for Europe if it is set in a European context. However, it is essential that the subject is approached with a much greater awareness both of what BPR is, and is not.

NOTE

* This chapter has been adapted from, Holtham, C. (1994), Business process reengineering – contrasting what it is with what it is not. In C. Coulson-Thomas (Ed.) *Business Process Reengineering: myth and reality*. London: Kogan Page.

1 Conversation with author, June 1994.

BIBLIOGRAPHY

Beer, S. (1981), *The brain of the firm.* (2nd ed.). Chichester: Wiley.

Behrens, B. and Groothuis, U. (1994), *Vergeudung ist Sünde. WirtschaftsWoche,* 18th February, No 8, pp. 68–73.

Davenport, T. (1993), *Process Innovation: Reengineering work through information technology.* Boston: Harvard Business School Press.

Earl, M. and Khan, B. (1994), How new is business process redesign? *European Management Journal,* Vol 12 No. 1, March, pp.20–30.

Grint, K. (1993), *Reengineering history: An analysis of business process reengineering.* Templeton College, The Oxford Centre for Management Studies, Management Research Paper 93/20.

Hammer, M. and Champy, J. (1993), *Reengineering the corporation: A manifesto for business revolution.* London: Nicholas Brealey.

Huckvale, T. and Ould, M. (1993), Process modelling – Why, what and how. In K. Spurr *et al.* (Eds). *Software assistance for business re-engineering.* Chapter 6. Chichester: Wiley.

Juran, J.M. (1964), *Breakthrough management.* London: Macmillan.

Lawrence, A. (1994), BPR – Tool of controversy. *Computer Business Review,* March, pp.11–14.

Lilienfeld, R. (1976), *The rise of systems theory – An ideological analysis.* New York: Wiley-Interscience.

Peters, T. and Waterman, R. (1982), *In search of excellence.* Harper and Row.

Senge, P. (1990), *The fifth discipline.* New York: Doubleday.

Spurr, K. *et al.* (Eds). (1993), *Software assistance for business re-engineering.* Chichester: Wiley.

Venkatraman, N. (1991), IT-induced business reconfiguration. In M. Scott Morton, (Ed). *The corporation of the 1990s.* New York: Oxford University Press. pp.122–58.

Von Bertalanffy, L. (1968), *General systems theory.* New York: George Braziller.

INDEX